$\mathcal{W}$HAT EVERY WOMAN SHOULD KNOW ABOUT DIVORCE AND CUSTODY

$\mathcal{W}$HAT EVERY WOMAN SHOULD KNOW ABOUT DIVORCE AND CUSTODY

JUDGES, LAWYERS, AND THERAPISTS SHARE WINNING STRATEGIES ON HOW TO
KEEP THE KIDS, THE CASH, AND YOUR SANITY

GAYLE ROSENWALD SMITH, J.D., AND SALLY ABRAHMS

A PERIGEE BOOK

Before using the advice and information in this book, consult with legal counsel to be sure they are appropriate for you. The information in this book is not intended to take the place of legal advice. It reflects the authors' experiences, studies, research, and opinions regarding divorce and custody issues. All material included in this publication is believed to be accurate. Custody laws vary from state to state, so be sure to consult with a legal professional for your particular situation or needs. The publisher assumes no responsibility for any health, welfare, or subsequent damage that might be incurred from these materials.

A Perigee Book
Published by The Berkley Publishing Group
A division of Penguin Putnam Inc.
375 Hudson Street
New York, New York 10014

First edition: November 1998

Published simultaneously in Canada

The Penguin Putnam Inc. World Wide Web site address is
http://www.penguinputnam.com

Library of Congress Cataloging-in-Publication Data
Smith, Gayle Rosenwald.
    What every woman should know about divorce and custody : judges, lawyers, and therapists share winning strategies on how to keep the kids, the cash, and your sanity / Gayle Rosenwald Smith and Sally Abrahms. — 1st ed.
        p.   cm.
    "A Perigee book."
    Includes bibliographical references and index.
    ISBN 0-399-52447-9 (pbk.)
    1. Divorce—Law and legislation—United States—Popular works.   2. Custody of children—United States—Popular works.   3. Women—Legal status, laws, etc.—United States—Popular works.
I. Abrahms, Sally.   II. Title.
KF535.Z9S62   1998
346.7301'66—DC21   97-52177
                                                                                            CIP

Printed in the United States of America

10 9

To my father, Judge Edward Rosenwald (1910–1998) who passed on his passion for law and psychology.

To Stephen Burger (1951–1996), who inspired me to write.

To David, Rachel, and Aaron. All my love. Thanks for sharing.
—G. R. S.

To David, a great lawyer, editor, husband, and friend, and to my children Anna, Nick, and Julia, whom I cherish.
—S. A.

We also dedicate this book to all women who have struggled or are struggling with divorce and custody in their lives.

Contents

Foreword

"If I sleep with my boyfriend, could I lose the kids? Is it okay for him to stay over when the children are asleep?"

"I need my family to help me take care of the kids when I go back to school, but they live in another state. Will I have a problem with the courts if I move and take the children with me?"

"I don't have enough money to live, but if I go back to work, will I lose my kids?"

"Whenever my ex-husband wants to change weekends with me and I don't agree, he threatens to take the children away from me or bad-mouths me to them. What can I do to stop this harassment?"

"I don't want to lose my son, so should I make a deal with my ex-husband and just accept less child support from him?"

"I want to go on a trip and leave the kids with my husband, but I've been told the judge might consider it abandonment. Is that true?"

"I want to work, but my ex-husband's new wife stays home to care for their baby. Do I stand to lose the children to her?"

"I'm involved in a lesbian relationship. Will this make it more difficult for me to convince the court that I will make a good custodial parent?"

"My ex-husband takes my daughter for two weeks during Christmas and six weeks in the summer. Does he have to give me the full amount of child support then or can he reduce it since she's not with me?"

"I smelled liquor on my ex-husband's breath the last two times he drove our sons home. I feel that I have to protect the boys, but if I refuse to let him take them next time, could the court see that as with-holding them and violating our custody agreement?"

"My ex-husband is trying to indoctrinate the children every chance he gets. We have joint custody, so he's with them a lot. His is not the only religion they're being raised in. I can't get him to stop proselytizing. What are my options?"

"Why is it okay for my ex-husband to have his girlfriend around all the time and not have it impact *his* custody?"

These are the kinds of questions many divorcing mothers have, but they often can't find satisfactory answers. Sometimes they are uncomfortable broaching these subjects with their lawyer. Sometimes they are not sure what or how to ask. With many of these questions, there are no simple, predictable answers because judges' attitudes vary from courtroom to courtroom and state to state and the outcome is determined by facts specific to each family's situation.

Unless you have been through a custody contest before, you will be faced with a constellation of formidable emotional, economic, and legal decisions for the first time. The judicial process is probably foreign to you. You have to rely on your lawyer and other experts to help you make the vital decisions that will affect your life and the lives of your children for years to come. The goal of our book is to strip the system of its mystery. We tell you what the issues are and what strategies have been successful in the past so that when your lawyer asks, "What do you want to do?" you will be able to answer the question confidently in the context of a well-considered plan.

Our book will explore the critical questions and the circumstances that affect the answers so you can make smart decisions. This is truly an insider's guide. We have interviewed judges across the country to find out what influences their decisions and makes them rule for one parent over another. They share what impresses them about parents and their lawyers and what they find objectionable. As far as we know, our approach is a first. What better way to find out about the court system than by going to the source? By understanding what appeals to judges and what turns them off, we hope to place mothers in the strongest legal position possible.

We concentrate on issues specific to women because the issues and the process *are* different for women. At one time, mothers were automatic custodians, but this presumption has shifted in favor of a more level playing field for men and women. More fathers are bringing claims for custody, some with the backing of fathers' rights groups that know how to fight the court system. The legal landscape has changed, and so have the tactics women must adopt to win a custody contest. These tactics are a major focus of our book.

Our advice is designed for women at every stage of divorce: those merely contemplating it, mothers in the throes of it, and the already divorced. All of these groups should find our book helpful because it addresses the latest legal trends and, at the same time, dispenses solid, proven advice for parents and their children. Today, more than one-quarter of all U.S. children live with only one parent, and that figure jumps to one-half by the time they reach adulthood.

Besides speaking with judges from different geographical regions, we have also interviewed matrimonial attorneys, custody evaluators, guardians ad litem, mental health professionals, custodial and noncustodial mothers, and fathers. These groups are the other players in a custody conflict. They have shared their personal and professional experiences. We have reported for you what has worked and what has not in seeking custody. This book contains advice from all of the participants—the decision-makers, the advocates, and the parents—so that you will have the best possible information and guidance on how to succeed in a custody contest from all perspectives.

Our book seeks to empower women. It gives readers the tools to ask intelligent questions of their lawyers and to make decisions about their conduct so they can win in court. After reading this book, you will not be at the mercy of others. You can take charge of your life and your case and not be a victim of what can be a complicated and mysterious court system. You *will* get through this and we will help you. But you have to stay focused on your goal—your children—and try to deal with the anger and pain separately.

You will have to take charge of your case, because, children aside, your financial future depends on it. Women typically become poorer after divorce; men make out better. According to a U.S. Department of Commerce survey, the standard of living for recently divorced women has dropped as low as 37 percent, while their ex-husbands' has risen 10 to 15 percent. A Brandeis University study found that divorced women over sixty-five years old had the highest poverty rate of any unmarried group, including those who had never married and widows. One 1997 government study found that only one out of five women eligible for child support payments actually receives them.

We will cover all the financial bases. Our book will tell you about monies to which you are entitled, how to do a budget and establish your own credit, ways to cut costs, how to decide whether to stay in your house, move, rent, or buy, and how to make sure your ex-husband is not hiding assets.

Your husband may do the right thing by you and your children, and he may behave honorably. You may never need the clever tactics we offer to give you the upper hand in resolving custody disputes, but you should still be aware of them and know how to use them because divorce and custody can be volatile. What may seem reasonable today may not be in the future. If you are lucky, you won't end up in court; there are other, less contentious alternatives, like mediation, and we will explore them, too. But there are thousands of custody battles every year because, in the emotional maelstrom of divorce, you can't count on your ex-husband to be reasonable or fair. In fact, you should count on just the opposite. As in any struggle, you have to plan your strategy if you hope to come out victorious.

For any mother trying to gain or regain custody, divorce is a two-part process. Not only is there the legal piece to master, but the psychological aspect as well, which is equally critical in a custody contest. It is a wrenching process that produces a variety of emotions, including anger, shock, and helplessness—but then, you already know that. The legal and the psychological are integrally related in custody. It's important to understand what you are feeling so that you don't allow your emotions to lead you into making strategic blunders. For instance, while it is understandable for you to be angry with your ex-husband and not want to be cooperative with him in arranging visits with the kids, that uncooperative behavior is harmful for your children and will be used against you by your ex-spouse and his lawyer if the custody issue goes to court. On the other hand, a cooperative attitude will show a judge that you are a competent, caring parent who places the welfare of your child ahead of your own self-interest. In a custody fight, you have to consider what works and what doesn't in the court system. Judges look for certain behavior in the contestants, and they make their decisions in part based on those observations. You have to scrutinize your actions so that, from a legal and psychological standpoint, you are helping yourself win your case. This entails knowing what to do and say, both at home and in the courtroom. It also means knowing what not to do. You have to think and act "legally" if you want to win; our book tells you how.

The best way to use this book is to read it in its entirety and then go back and study individual chapters when you are having a specific problem or issue. Our book is meant to be an ongoing resource guide.

We may be coaching women, but we do not feel that in every case they are necessarily the better custodial parent nor that children should be in their exclusive custody. Even though custody battles seem otherwise, the lines are not drawn between bad guys and good gals. This is not a male-bashing book nor is it intended to incite mothers. We have stated repeatedly throughout the book that children need the love and participation of both their mother and father, and that parents need to try to get along for their children's sake, if not their own.

If getting custody is your primary goal, you need to think through all of the issues, fully understanding their implications and outcomes. In fact, not choosing custody could be the best choice for you. After reading this book, you should be in a stronger position to know and get what you want.

We use the metaphor of a chess game throughout the book. Custody in many ways is strategy: analyzing your moves, identifying your objectives, anticipating your opponent's replies and positions, and making sure you prevail in the end.

Acknowledgments

I would like to thank the following attorneys who helped in this endeavor. Norman Levine Trusch of Texas tirelessly steered me toward key people I interviewed and graciously provided me with information on a variety of important topics. David H. Kelsey of New Mexico, Joy Feinberg and Judy Smith of Illinois, Amy Goldstein of New Jersey, Albert Momjian and Lynne Z. Gold-Bikin of Philadelphia, Nancy Palmer of Florida, and George Stern of Georgia helped with contacts and information about differences in state law.

I wish to thank the many family judges throughout the country who spoke with me and offered their opinions on divorce and custody issues as it applies to women. They also enlightened me about regional differences in resolving these issues. I am especially grateful to Judge Myrna Field, who, through her enthusiasm and support, was instrumental in helping to get the project launched. She also helped in other ways, including reviewing parts of the manuscript.

Thanks, too, go to Francis McCloskey, who continues to make sure all relevant information and new legislation makes its way across my desk. Dr. Dennis Barouch provided me with an insightful psychological perspective. My in-laws Bernard and Evelyn Lieberman were always there for me. My mother Ruth Rosenwald understood when I couldn't be present during my father's lingering illness. And to my father, who did not live to see the book in its final form but has always been an inspiration and will continue to be.
—G. R. S.

I am especially indebted to Dr. Carolyn Newberger of Harvard Medical School, who, even in her busiest professional moment, was generous with her ideas and her time. Susan Hackley of the Program on Negotiation at Harvard Law School was terrific, too, reading the manuscript and offering comments and endless encouragement. Attorney David Cherny was astute and willing to share his knowledge. Maryanne Witkin continuously offered her financial acumen and helped streamline some complicated business concepts. I also want to thank author Karen Tucker for her publishing strategies, Dr. Rochelle Robbins for her psychological insights, Mel Schwartz who taught me what makes a first-rate mediator, Dr. Michael Mendelsohn, Dr. Joseph Klawsnik, Dr. Laura Benkov, Marc Abrahms, Emily Tufeld, Beth Abrahms, Lorraine Greenfield, Jane Pliner, Merrill Diamond, Barbara Chintz, Professor Frederick Lawrence, Ann Koufman, Jamie McCourt, John Lauerman, and Catherine Lawrence. I also want to acknowledge Georgia Hilgeman of Vanished Children's Alliance for sharing her story. She was as helpful with this book as she was with my last.

I am especially grateful to my mother Phyllis Abrahms, who taught me to love words, and my father John Abrahms, the most loving parent imaginable. My husband David has been a helpmate in the true sense.
—S. A.

Our literary agent Jane Dystel has been wonderful and backed this project enthusiastically, as did our editor Sheila Curry. Even though she was swamped with manuscripts, she never made us feel rushed and offered incisive answers to our questions. Her suggestions were always on target.
—G. R. S. and S. A.

Why Women? Why Now? Why You Need to Take Charge

SUZANNE

Suzanne is chief of psychiatry at a teaching hospital in the South. During her grueling medical residency she still managed to breast-feed her son and daughter. These days, she leaves for work before dawn so she can be home soon after the children, now eight and ten, get back from their after-school activities. Suzanne's estranged husband has contested custody. He claims his wife's career is less conducive to raising the children than his more flexible work schedule as a salesman.

NANCY

Nancy and Dan, both forty-six, have been married for twelve years. When Dan lost his engineering job because the firm downsized, the couple decided to move from Wisconsin to Michigan. They thought new surroundings might also revive their marriage. Nancy found a job first, a great position in public relations, and rented an apartment, expecting to put their house on the market.

The couple decided to let Nancy move ahead of Dan and the children and start work. He would follow with Jessie, ten, and Lauren, fourteen, when the school year was over. Dan used that time to start his own engineering consulting company. After reflecting, he decided the marriage wasn't going to work and he would not move. Nancy, in Michigan, had come to the same conclusion. She began making summer plans for the girls when Dan announced they were staying with him.

When the couple went to court to determine whether she would be allowed to relocate with her children in September, some of the issues that arose were the quality of the girls' new schools, the neighborhood (whether it was residential, accessible to public transportation, a library, their church, and soccer fields) and the number of children their daughters' ages who lived in the new area versus the old. Dan came prepared for these questions. He had researched both school systems and told the judge that the students at the school the girls currently attended scored much higher on standardized tests and were accepted to top colleges in greater numbers than in Nancy's new hometown. *By asking questions before the case went to court*, Dan found out there were more children his daughters' ages in their old neighborhood. He reminded the judge it can traumatic for a teenager of Lauren's age to be uprooted from friends and provided research from mental health experts who said the same. He said both girls had important friendships in Wisconsin and reeled off the children's after-school activities. Dan told the judge he was able to work around the girls' schedules and had a steady, loving baby-sitter from their area who stayed with them when he had appointments. The baby-sitter testified that the girls seemed happy. Dan also agreed to share the driving so the children could see their mother on weekends and vacations. Nancy, on the other hand, did not think relocation would be a problem and did not know to do her homework.

KATE

Ten years into their marriage, Kate, a homemaker, took their identical twin sons and left her husband Paul, a government worker. She moved in with her mother, a receptionist at an insurance company, who lived a mile away. Paul didn't want a divorce, but Kate insisted. The judge awarded them joint physical custody, with the eight-year-old twins spending one week with their mother and the other with Paul. Kate enrolled in accounting classes so she could earn a degree and then get a job.

Six months after the marriage was legally dissolved, Paul married Laurel, a stay-at-home mother with a seven-year-old daughter. Paul's work kept him out of the house some of the day, but since he had an early shift working as a physical therapist and was home by 4 P.M., he also had plenty of time for the children.

Paul became increasingly unhappy with his custody arrangement. He felt that shuttling the kids back and forth was disorienting to the children and was having a negative effect on one of his sons in particular. Kate was constantly putting Paul down in front of the boys. He was sure it was because she was jealous of his new life. He went to court to gain custody of the twins, arguing that he had more time to devote to the children than Kate and that her constant criticism had begun to upset the children. They began acting rudely toward Paul, he told the judge, and they put up a fight when it was his turn to take them. A minister testified that Paul was a caring and responsible father.

Suzanne, Nancy, and Kate each lost the custody battle for her children. It wasn't because they were neglectful, inept, or irresponsible mothers. They happened to be both warm and loving. But so were their ex-husbands. More importantly, their ex-husbands (and their lawyers) were properly prepared to win a custody contest. They knew that today is a good time for a father to wage a custody fight and win.

While women still gain custody 85 percent of the time, you can no longer assume you are going to prevail in court. Fathers are contesting custody in increasing numbers. Only 15 percent of custody cases end up in court, yet *a father who goes to trial has a 60 to 70 percent chance of winning*. In the family court of today, a woman may be scrutinized and penalized for the exact things her husband does, such as working and dating. These normal, everyday activities can be used against you unless you are prepared and know how to respond.

WHY NOW?

The custody landscape looks different today than even a decade ago. As a mother, you need to know how to look at this new scene so you can read it correctly. You have to assume you no longer have the edge in custody and, in fact, approach the issue as if your husband does. You must be willing to do the preparatory work necessary to convince the court that you are a good, if not better, choice for custodian. Judges today want the primary custodian to be the more nurturing, hands-on parent who puts his or her child's needs above his or her own. You will need to show that you are.

Since the tables have turned in this custody climate, you must have a plan. You will need to view custody as a mind game and position yourself to win. (Judges and mental health professionals may abhor the concept of winning and losing, but mothers and fathers who desperately want to retain custody of their children see these cases as life-and-death contests in which winning is what matters most.)

Think of custody as a chess game where every move is carefully analyzed because it has a direct impact on future moves for you and your opponent, and of course, the outcome of the contest. You will need to understand both the legal steps and the psychological ramifications of those steps: not only what you want, but what your ex-partner wants and how that will affect your strategies and actions. How will your ex-husband react to your requests? Is there a move you can make that will impact on him positively rather than negatively but will still put you in the position you want to be? Ultimately, if your husband is satisfied with the arrangement, he will probably be less hostile and interfere less in your life. If you can capture his support, you may not only get what you want, but you may retain a cooperative rather than an obstructive parenting partner. Will you make a move that may get you in trouble because it is not well thought out and may cause you to lose because of it? In chess, your goal is to reach checkmate by making intelligent choices. In a custody battle, the goal is to keep your kids.

In the past, mothers would never have had to think in terms of moves and countermoves. But they were not in the precarious position that they are today. English Common Law automatically awarded young children to fathers, but that changed in the early twentieth century when mothers were believed to be more nurturing for children, particularly those under the age of seven. Unless a woman were mentally ill or clearly incompetent, she would automatically get custody. In the 1970s, the preference for mothers began to be viewed as discriminatory. Today, this tender years doctrine has been eroded and just a handful of Southern states award custody to the mother when all other factors are equal. In all other states, custody decisions are gender neutral. In most states, rather than the sex of the parent, the determining factor is the best interests of the child. That term is open to interpretation depending on the jurisdiction, and sometimes the judge, but it refers to which parent will do the better job of nurturing the child and allowing him or her to maintain contact with the other parent.

In years past, more women stayed home. Today's workplace is strikingly different. Between 1970 and 1992, there was a 79 percent increase in working mothers. According to the U.S. Department of Commerce, Bureau of Labor Statistics, in 1994, 68 percent of married mothers and 70 percent of all mothers were in the labor force full time, twenty-four million of whom had children under the age of eighteen. What a family is and means in 1998 has changed from even a decade ago, and this change has had a significant impact on mothers. Now, only 14 percent of all families in the United States fit the traditional mold, with the father at work and a mother at home. Just twenty years ago, nine out of ten parents grappling with custody were married. Now, many of the cases in front of judges involve unwed couples. During a twenty-year span, from 1970 to 1990, for example, the births to un-married parents increased 300 percent and currently three out of ten, or 1.2 million children, are born out of wedlock annually. The ages of the children also have dropped dramatically. It used to be that most parents divorced when children were around nine or ten; today, it is not unusual to see judges trying to figure out which parent should have custody of a nine- or ten-month-old.

In a society where so many parents are divorced and so many women are working, there are myriad custodial arrangements from which a judge can choose. Parents who have been divorced two or three times may find themselves with more than one custody battle at a time. There are gay custodial parents, stepparents with custody of their own children, parents who are legally in charge of their stepchildren but not their own biological children, and grandparents with custody of their grandchildren. Even murderers can get in on the act. A Florida court decided in 1996 that a father who had killed his first wife and spent eight years in prison was a better potential parent than the twelve-year-old girl's lesbian mother. The judge ruled that the girl, who had been living with her mother for three years, should be turned over to her father. (The mother appealed the case, but died of a heart attack before it was heard.)

"Courts are being asked to decide things that only God should decide," said one Florida family court judge when queried whether or not lesbians should be granted custody. Another judge in Pennsylvania was equally bewildered: "If you give custody rights to a partner of a lesbian and that partner has a relationship with another woman who has a child, do I need to grant visitation rights to the second partner for the first kid? Where does it end?"

Twenty years ago, either a mother, father, foster parent, or in certain circumstances, another third party could ask for custody or visitation. Today, the number of people who have that right has grown. Yet not just anyone can ask for custody or visitation. It is an issue of standing, or who has the right to sue and request custody. The person filing the request must have a special relationship with the child. A caregiver, for instance, may want custody, but may not have the legal right or the proper relationship to allow her to go to court. The "right" relationship would either be a blood tie, such as a parent or grandparent, or a legal connection, such as a foster parent or guardian. Who gets custody, however, is ultimately determined by what is in the best interests of the child. A person may have a positive influence on that child but still may not be legally entitled to obtain custody. As more plaintiffs test the notion of the "right" relationship, the possibilities for custodians increase.

In the latest high-tech custody battle, divorcing husbands and wives are fighting over frozen embryos fertilized in a petri dish. Cases in Tennessee, New York, and Massachusetts have produced different custody outcomes. In the 1992 Tennessee case and the 1996 Massachusetts case, the courts ruled that the mother should not be allowed to use the embryos to become pregnant. In New York, a judge sided with the woman. Case law allows a mother to decide what happens to a fertilized egg inside her body, but there is no established law for eggs fertilized outside the body. Justice Anthony Nesi of the Suffolk Probate and Family Court in Boston wrote in his decision that although a man cannot force a woman to become pregnant or have an abortion, both had equal decision-making authority over the embryo. The case was further complicated because the husband had signed an agreement while they were married saying that if they did decide to separate, his wife would get the frozen embryos. The case is on appeal.

All of these scenarios, among others, expand the possibilities for judges in deciding who the custodians can be, how family is defined, and who is a suitable parent. These new family structures only make it easier for people other than the mother to be considered the only ones who should fulfill the role of the primary caretaker, which was a radical notion just twenty years ago. In fact, judges may decide that neither parent would make a competent custodian and give the child to a grand-parent or another relative.

As families are being redefined, it is not surprising that it has become more socially acceptable for a father to gain custody and be a full-time nurturer. Men are no longer ostracized or considered weird for wanting to take care of their children. Today, when people hear a father is the custodian, they are likely to think, "Oh, how interesting!" or "What a great dad!" Imagine anyone thinking that about a mother!

There are 2.9 million single fathers; 44 percent of the children they care for are below school age, 30 percent are age three or younger, and 42 to 43 percent are girls. So much for the assumption that single fathers usually take care of older children or just their boys.

In the last few years, courts have been more receptive to fathers' custody claims, and more claims are being made. Judges are more willing to listen to a father's plea for sole custody or primary physical custody (the children live primarily with that parent and "visit" with the other parent). Young fathers who have been active partners and have shifted their jobs and other commitments to be available for their kids are en-raged to think they may be deprived of their custodial rights simply because of their gender. Their role as involved fathers before the divorce makes for a strong—and often winning—case for joint custody at the least, if not sole custody, should they decide to ask for it. Since parents are more egalitarian in their relationships than ever before, the custody dilemma only mirrors what is going on in today's marriages.

The father's rights movement, and the men's groups it has spawned, have also bolstered Dad's fight for custody. A well-organized network of disgruntled fathers, weary of playing zoo daddy, has emerged, sharing winning custody strategies and know-how with other men who want custody. Some of these groups circulate lists of attorneys, mental health professionals, and guardians ad litem (experts who represent the child) who are sympathetic to fathers seeking custody. The availability of such resources underscores the need for a mother to be well-prepared before contesting custody.

Society views noncustodial mothers less charitably. Some women in this growing group do not opt for joint custody and then lose the battle for sole custody; other mothers decide selflessly that their children are better off with their ex-spouse for financial or psychological reasons. Whatever the reason, noncustodial mothers almost always suffer from this arrangement. It may be the enlightened nineties, but society still expects mothers to take care of the children. Women who do not have their children commonly think that if they do not have custody, they have flunked motherhood. Not getting the children feels unnatural, and many women are ashamed. As one prominent Mid-Atlantic family law attorney opines, "When a mother does not get her children, she feels she has failed in the role she was put on earth for." Custody can be a double whammy for these mothers: First, they feel like a failure because their marriage did not work out, then because they cannot fulfill the role that society has told them is theirs.

It is not just societal attitudes that make custody unpredictable and, therefore, extremely frustrating. The custody laws vary from state to state, as do the guidelines used to award custody (although thirty-one states and Washington, D.C., have introduced statutes for custody guidelines). This inconsistency, the subjective interpretation of these guidelines, the personal bias of a judge, and the lack of accountability—judges don't necessarily have to provide reasons for their decisions—make it difficult to predict the outcome of a custody dispute. "Five different judges sit in Cambridge. I can present the same set of facts to all of them and get five different outcomes," said one Boston matrimonial lawyer. Judges want to do the right thing, but they may not understand the implications of their decisions.

The caliber of the jurists also varies and is not always impressive. According to Judge Robert Robles of Las Cruces, New Mexico, who was vice-chair of the U.S. Commission on Child and Family Welfare, "Family-related courts have historically been given lower legal status, fewer resources, and in some instances, less experienced judges."

WHY WOMEN?

Up until now, women have assumed that they will prevail in court, so they have not thought sufficiently about the strategy needed to come out on top. Many believe they will receive custody because they are the mother, and they have not considered any other outcome. This overconfidence and resulting lack of preparation is tripping them up. They may feel confident about other parts of their lives, from getting the jobs they want to obtaining the promotions they seek, but, although the women's movement has helped mothers gain equality in many areas, it has created a backlash in custody disputes. "You want equality?" fathers ask. "Well, guess what, you've got it. But that means we are just as equal and just as able to be parents. Why shouldn't we have at least equal access to our children?"

The laws may mandate equality on paper, but in practice, judges who apply those laws hold mothers to a higher standard, whether it involves sex and dating, moving out of state, going back to school, working, or not working. Not only have women lost their advantage in the courtroom, but the rules of the custody game are often applied against them in favor of fathers. In thirty states, task forces have found judicial discrimination in the courtroom against divorcing mothers.

Dating is one area where a double standard in favor of men exists. The courts don't blush if men fool around or have more than one girlfriend, but you had better not try it if you are a mother. A woman who has more than one relationship after a divorce may be accused of promiscuity. Even a mother in a serious relationship can be viewed by the courts as selfish and lacking in sensitivity to the children. As one renowned appellate court judge in Pennsylvania puts it, "Men can have girlfriends and it's all right. With women, we find it highly objectionable, and if she wants to lose her kids, that's how to do it!"

Women's work is also treated differently by jurists. A working mother who wants custody has to prove to the courts that her job will not affect her ability to be a good parent. Fathers, on the other hand, do not have the same burden of proof. They may have demanding jobs, but there is far less scrutiny of how those demands will affect their ability to fulfill parenting responsibilities. They are applauded for being involved even minimally in their children's lives, but mothers are simply expected to be there.

Unless you are independently wealthy or your husband has money, it is difficult without two incomes to survive after a divorce. It is usually mothers who take the biggest economic hit—an average 30 percent decline in a woman's standard of living after divorce, especially if they do not remarry. Yet mothers may lose custody because they must work. Some judges still harbor prejudices toward working women, believing good mothers stay home. A 1990 survey of Massachusetts probate judges, in fact, found that half felt women should be home when their children returned from school and that preschoolers are likely to suffer if their mother works. The question of whether fathers should be home when their children got out of school never came up.

Research from the New York–based National Center on Women and Family Law found that when both parents work, courts judge a mother more severely than a father for having a job outside the home.

Just a few years ago, Sharon Prost, the deputy chief counsel for Utah Senator Orrin Hatch, was ordered to surrender her two young sons to her ex-husband, a labor union administrator. "A woman is entitled as defendant . . . to put her work and career ahead of the other demands in her life. Having consciously made that decision, however, plaintiff [Prost] must live with its consequences." The judge was Harriet R. Taylor, a working woman. The point is that men and women, on the bench and off, still view mothers differently.

Many women who have become professionally successful find that their success is often used against them in custody cases. These mothers have earned law degrees, M.B.A.'s, or gained promotions to office managers or assembly line fore(wo)men. For such working women who have achieved a semblance of equality in the workplace, the playing field may not be as level in custody contests. Since courts are expected to be fair, promote the concept of equality between parents, and show that a child is entitled to share a warm and loving relationship with both parents, the courts have tried to even the score by giving more time and more custody awards to fathers. But on this so-called level playing field, mothers are really the weaker player in custody battles because the legal system has not yet evolved to the point of accepting that women can achieve professional success outside the house and be good mothers.

Consider the case of Jennifer Ireland. She is the University of Michigan student who put her young daughter in day care so she could attend classes, get a college education, and support herself. Even though the three-year-old's father (the couple never married) also worked and the little girl was used to living with her mother, the judge ruled that the father's mother, who was at home all day, would make a better day parent than a day care center and took the child away from Ireland. (Ireland appealed the case and ultimately settled for a shared arrangement with her daughter's father after intense media coverage and public criticism of the judge's initial custody ruling.)

Mothers who work long hours are definitely at risk, particularly when their husbands have greater job flexibility. The recession and downsizing of many corporations have also worked against women. They are finding their divorcing husbands have home offices and flexible hours that judges like to see in awarding custody. Home offices and telecommuting are no longer the domain of the privileged. Close to forty-three million people work at home (or in small offices), a 77 percent increase from 1988, claims the Small Office/Home Office Association.

Fathers with more flexible work schedules, whose ex-wives have rigid work hours, are increasingly gaining custody with the argument they are better able to nurture and tend to the needs of the children. *Remember: The parent with the more established position usually has the upper hand in court, and that is often not the mother,* who may be entering the workforce for the first time. A custody contest could not have come at a worse time, when a mother needs to be available to her children (and show that to the courts), and also be available to her new boss. Someone starting a new job usually does not have the leverage to ask for flexible hours, and many mothers have jobs that will never allow them that leverage.

In a sense, the women's movement has freed mothers to do two jobs: produce economically and care for the family. A mother may lose her children if her job prevents her from proving she is the "better" parent. Or she may lose for a variety of other reasons relating to work.

Mothers are also being impacted by changing views of joint custody. While joint legal custody (where both parents make major decisions in a child's life but do not necessarily split time equally) is still a serious option and the preferred choice, at least by many courts, there are judges and parents who are now steering away from joint physical custody (the child lives half time with each parent). The concept of joint custody was considered a parent's panacea in the 1970s and 1980s—a way to give both mothers and fathers time with their children and a sense of empowerment.

Many of those living with joint physical custody have not been satisfied with the day-to-day realities of the arrangement. It is the same with the courts, which have begun to see joint custody couples returning to ask for sole custody for one parent or to renegotiate and clarify their joint custody status. "The bloodiest cases I have are modification cases, because the couple didn't rid themselves of anger the first time and are not psychologically divorced," said one divorce lawyer, who estimates that 30 to 40 percent of his case load is change-of-custody cases. Ten years ago, he said it was closer to 10 percent.

Today, virtually every state permits joint custody, and eleven states have declared a preference for joint custody. That means joint custody will be awarded if a parent asks for it. Some jurists do not think this arrangement works well over time, especially in contentious divorces.

Women can lose out from this changing view. What it means is that if only one parent gets custody and both parents want it, mothers and fathers will probably wind up in court. Today, when parents do not request joint custody or decide it is just not practical, a judge will seriously consider awarding the father sole custody, and when it's a draw, a judge may do so to equalize a custody situation previously tipped toward mothers.

When women have joint custody and both parents have equal legal status, any misstep by the mother could be grounds for taking the children away (for example, if she denies her ex-husband access to the children or poisons them against him). Mothers, therefore, are not necessarily home free with this kind of arrangement. Joint custody makes both parents appear equal, but mothers really are not, since they are often judged more harshly than their husbands by the judicial system. Fathers who want equal rights but may not think they have a chance of winning sole custody may ask for joint custody. Later disenchanted, they may go back to court and fight for sole custody.

The very nature of custody—that it can change at any time—makes mothers insecure. And they should be. Women who win custody should not assume they will always have it. Custody is never really over until the children are grown or are able to choose where they want to live. Fathers may decide they no longer want to be the noncustodial parent or may feel joint custody is not working for them. State laws stipulate that any losing litigant may return to court to seek a modification of custody based on proving a substantial change of circumstances. O. J. Simpson prosecutor Marcia Clark illuminated the problem of the perpetual custody battle when, during the Simpson trial, her estranged husband hauled her back to court to try to gain custody of their two young sons who had been temporarily awarded to her. Her changed circumstances—working around the clock during the Simpson trial—was the basis for his position and her peril.

It is not always a parent who asks for a change in custody. As children grow up, what might have worked for a toddler does not necessarily work for a teenager. Boys who have lived with their mothers often decide they want to be with their fathers full time, so it's back to court.

WHY IT'S UP TO YOU

Much of how custody is resolved depends upon how you act. Of course, it is possible that you are not in a position to win custody. You have good reason to worry if you are severely depressed, mentally ill, have a drug, alcohol, or gambling addiction, are sexually promiscuous at the expense of your children, refuse to allow your husband to see the kids, or work around the clock (when your husband doesn't). In that case, your best strategy is to focus on changing these circumstances so you can win or maintain custody.

You can have the best lawyer in town, but unless you behave in a way that demonstrates to the court that you are the parent to whom the judge can feel comfortable giving the children, you may not get them. Therefore, you need to know what judges view as good and bad behavior. You will have to accept the fact that you may want the children to be with you all the time and it will not be that way, that you have to share with your ex-husband and still *talk* to the guy, that he will not do things with the children the way you want him to or think they should be done.

You know how wrenching divorce can be. When there is an issue of who gets the children, the stress and pain can drive even the sanest, most civilized parent to become irrational and punitive. You may feel a wide range of terrible emotions when your marriage ends. The last thing you need is a legal battle over custody. How can you be expected to make the wisest strategic judgments for yourself and your children in this state? The assistance of good friends, a therapist, a support group, or an experienced attorney will help. Ultimately, it is up to you. It is your life, and you have to make intelligent decisions. Understanding the various custody options will help you regain a measure of control. Knowing the advantages and disadvantages of each arrangement can help you figure out what you want so that when it comes time to discuss your choices and strategies with your attorney, you are prepared to make decisions that will work for all of you.

Dealing with Your Emotions

At the very least, you are feeling disillusioned and deep sadness that your marriage is not what you wanted it to be or thought it was. If you were the one to end the relationship (two-thirds of all divorces are initiated by women) and are relieved to be free of your husband, you may still be angry that you picked such a jerk and will have to continue to deal with him regularly because of the children. You may also experience guilt for making this move and subjecting your husband and children to the inevitable pain the divorce will cause. Even if you cannot live with your husband, it is likely your children think he is the greatest thing in the world, particularly if they are young. Remember, he is still their father; the courts won't forget it.

When your husband has an affair or decides he wants to end the marriage for other reasons, you may feel stunned, undesirable, depressed, suicidal, embarrassed, untrusting, scared, full of self-pity, worthless, and enraged about having to start over again. If he has a new girlfriend, you may worry that she is going to take your place with the children. It may make you angry that your children will see or know that he is sharing a bed with her. The pain can be so intense it feels as though you have died, or it may make you want to die. You may be so hurt that you want to make your husband hurt, too. You might even hope he dies (painfully would be better); some women fantasize about killing their ex-partners.

Mental health experts have long described the phenomenon that ordinarily gentle, law-abiding people may experience during this time.

Essentially, it is temporary insanity or psychosis. That raging state can cause you to act out of character and become irrational. Beware.

A lot of mothers do punish their spouses for breaking up the family and causing intense pain to them and their children. They do it by being hostile, bad-mouthing their ex-husbands, denying or making up excuses to avoid the father's visitation, or by intentionally bringing the children late to those visits. However, remember that you want your child's other parent to be as good to your child as he can be. If you are nasty and uncooperative, it can affect your child and backfire. Don't do it! For one thing, it is a short-term high and ultimately counterproductive. *It can also cause you to lose your child.*

Note: Chess is a thinking game, not a feeling game. Nevertheless, you need to understand and acknowledge your feelings so that you can move on. Like work and dating, women are often held to a higher psychological standard than men. That is, if they are not emotional, the court may view them as cold, and if they are, they could be labeled "unstable." You will need to maintain your psychological equilibrium during the divorce process, so getting counseling may be critical. You will be judged on your emotional appearance, no matter how much stress or abuse you have experienced.

One way to cope is to stop fighting your feelings and acknowledge them. There is no shame in being divorced and experiencing sadness and heartache. As one Massachusetts psychologist put it, "If divorce were viewed as a disease, it would be a medical crisis." If you approach divorce as a terrible but inevitable process you (and others) will experience, it is easier to believe there is an end point. There *will* be a time when you will be able to resolve many of the heated issues of the moment and gain a sense of control. You *will* survive this period.

Even if you were the one to initiate the divorce, you will still feel loss: loss of your sense of trust, security, and shared goals. If you are not behaving as well as you would like during the divorce, it may be because you have not come to grips with your feelings. When you do, it should be easier to cope with the situation in more effective ways. Do not panic if you are civilized and magnanimous one moment and petty and mean-spirited the next. There is no straight emotional path in the divorce process.

If you hold on to your anger, it will be hard to move to the next stage in the healing process. You also run the risk of displacing your anger onto your children or others with whom you interact. Not letting go of the anger can cause you to fight over the "wrong" issues with your husband. "I represented a mother who was leaving her husband," said one New England attorney. "They had amicably agreed the children would live with her and how most of their marital assets would be disposed of. It was an easy exchange until the husband started screaming that he should get the stereo because the children would want to listen to music when they visited him. My client said she should get the stereo because that way the children could listen to music more of the time. But the husband had a fit. It was obvious the outburst wasn't about the stereo."

Anger is a natural emotion. Most people think of it as an explosive, out-of-control outburst, but it does not have to be that way. If you can acknowledge your anger, you may feel less helpless and more in control so that you can make good choices and cope more effectively. Once you understand your emotions, you may be able to discuss them with your ex-husband. Instead of blowing up at him, you might be able to say, "I'm angry because I feel that I do most of the driving to the extracurricular activities." Done in a calm and rational way, it can lead to a constructive interchange. Of course, being civilized and candid with someone who has hurt you badly or whom you do not respect may not be realistic.

Part of women's anger is not feeling in control of the situation. The reality is that there will be areas of your life that you will not be able to control. These include how your husband behaves toward you and the children, whom he dates, and how he handles his own life. You may not be able to change him, but you can make some good choices of your own. When you do that, it will help you feel better about yourself, if not the situation. Like everything else about divorce, how *you* behave will affect your children. Research has shown that if divorce is not handled well, with as little acrimony as possible, it can have a devastating effect on children.

The legal system may also contribute to feelings of anger. In a contested custody case, you become open to judgment by third parties who do not really know you or your history and have to weigh your word against your husband's (or your lawyer's against his). Part of the anger for women is when judges and other professionals don't get it right, when they see the situation differently than you or rule in a way that you believe is not best for your children. You not only have to struggle with all the feelings generated by the marriage but also those generated by mental health professionals, lawyers, and a judge who makes assumptions about your competence and veracity.

There is no better time to seek support. A good therapist or support group can help the healing process. Getting professional help, however, can be considered a liability to the court if it is for such reasons as severe psychological problems, suicidal tendencies, child abuse, or alcoholism. If, however, a mother goes to a therapist to work through stress and sadness occuring after a breakup or another traumatic event, or simply because she wants to be a better mother or partner, it should not affect custody.

WHY DO PARENTS CONTINUE TO FIGHT?

There are many reasons the marital battle continues after the relationship is over. One of the partners or both may have unresolved anger about the marriage: how it ended, that your ex-spouse could not meet your needs, or that you simultaneously must deal with unresolved problems from your past. Other couples play out their anger through unrelated issues. Acting intentionally difficult may be a way to torture the parent who inflicted the problem and caused the pain.

Relationships that were violent during the marriage also tend to be confrontational after it has dissolved. In some cases, there is conflict because one of the parents, typically the mother, fears her children may be unsafe when they are with their father. This is particularly true if visitation is unsupervised. Still other parents will fight just to stay emotionally involved with their ex-spouses, even if it means continued strife.

Anger can mask deeper feelings. It is often easier to feel anger than sadness, failure, or abandonment. It is also a way to deal with the demise of the relationship. Resentment of your husband can also make you angry. You may be raging that you are economically less well off than he or that you have to start the dating process over after all these years. Dating may be logistically more difficult for you than for him, particularly if you have been at home with the children and he is in the workplace, where there are more opportunities to meet new prospects. If you have the children more, it may be harder to find the time, not to mention the man, to date. Your children may also object to your being with anyone but their father, so you may have to wrestle with their feelings about this difficult issue, too.

MANAGING YOUR ANGER

It is critical to get your anger under control as soon as you can. Serious decisions like custody and terms of settlement require self-control, levelheadedness, objectivity, and strategic planning. Impulsive decisions based on revenge or hurt can cause you to make concessions that are not good for your family. Anger is such a huge part of conflict that there are conflict resolution workshops across the country that teach strategies to control anger.

Know when to compromise. If giving in to your ex-partner's anger is not abusive or does not adversely affect your overall game plan, it might be a smart move. Remember: Focus on what is really important to you. If your husband is angry about something that is not meaningful to you, let him feel he has "won." A small victory may lead to a big victory later on for you.

Experts say it is best not to overreact when your ex-husband explodes. Rather than fire back, which can push the conflict even further, you should temporarily disengage. When you are verbally attacked, try using some relaxation techniques, which include taking deep breaths, counting backward, giving yourself a time-out, such as running, gardening, soaking in a bath—anything that works for you. Having a phrase you could say to yourself can help control your anger, too. You could also practice what William Ury, cofounder of the Program on Negotiation at Harvard Law School, calls going to the balcony. This tactic entails detaching yourself mentally and assessing the situation objectively as you might if you were watching a scene below from a balcony. Or you could walk away and suggest you talk later.

It is important to recognize your and your husband's "anger cues." They might be physical signs that tell you that the situation is escalating. It might be your pulse racing, or you or your spouse may have a red or contorted face, or clenched fists. If you are aware of these cues, they will give you advance warning to disengage before you lose your temper or see your husband lose his. You want to take advantage of the window of opportunity that exists before you lose your temper and act in inappropriate ways that will make the conflict worse.

The strategies below should guide you during this horrific period.

· **Every time you want to punish your husband, chant this like a mantra.** *My kids, my kids, my kids.* Or you could try other simple phrases such as *Don't lose it, Take it easy,* or *I'm doing the best I can.* Do not do anything that will jeopardize your chances of getting the children and keeping them emotionally healthy. If you are unable to separate from the anger, you are likely to make terrible mistakes. The stakes are so high you don't have a choice but to cooperate as a parent. Judges don't like uncooperative parents, and if they have to make a choice between a mother who is uncooperative and a father who is, guess who is likely to win?

· **Ask yourself how your child will feel if you behave poorly.** Put yourself in your child's place. Separate out how you feel about the divorce, custody issue, and their father from how *they* feel. Your needs and feelings will be different from theirs.

· **Think about how you want to be remembered.** Do you want your children to think of you as short-tempered, depressed, or petty? Behave, when it is possible, in the way you want to be remembered: making time for your children, being a positive thinker, and not acting vengeful. You do not have to change your personality, but just conduct yourself in a way that makes you proud of yourself.

· **It's okay to be angry about your situation, but don't be vindictive.** Anger can actually motivate you to take positive action and move on with your life. Your relationship can be dealt with in therapy, where you will be free to rail at your child's father, cry, and figure out what went wrong so you do not repeat mistakes in your next relationship.

· **Realize that your children will probably have a relationship with their father, so don't fight it.** Regardless of what you think of him, it is important for your child to have a good relationship with both parents. You may not want him around and feel your husband is not as good a parent as you want him to be, but remember, making their relationship easy and free of strain will help your child be emotionally healthy. Also realize that today, the courts are reluctant to deny access to a parent, so the reality is, except in a case of child abuse or other specific circumstances, your son or daughter will have a relationship with his father. Children of absent fathers can have serious problems, from severe psychiatric difficulties to poor school performance to lower self-esteem, teen pregnancy, and even criminal behavior.

Besides doing the right thing for your kids, it is to your advantage to allow them to develop an excellent rapport with their father. Men who feel satisfied with their relationship with their children are more likely to treat you and them better, both emotionally and financially.

· **Be sensitive to your children's feelings**. Your stress level is likely to triple during divorce because of the children. Just when you are emotionally strung out and less able to cope with adversity, expect your children to present you with more adversity as well as being more needful of parenting. Be careful: If you are overwrought about the divorce, you may be less sensitive to your child's needs. You may feel anger and resentment toward your husband, which makes you incapable of being there for your child. If he's very young, he won't understand the concepts of marriage, divorce, and custody, but he will know something important is missing. Depressed parents may depend on their children to keep them going, to boost their self-esteem, and be their companion. This is not healthy for your child, but it is an easy trap to fall into as a way to stave off your own sense of abandonment. Who wouldn't want to spend time with an adoring five-year-old who tells an emotionally fragile adult, "Mommy, you are the most beautiful woman I know. I want to marry you when I grow up"? No matter how traumatized and angry you are, you will have to address your feelings so you can get back to being a high-functioning parent whose child's needs come first.

During this period, you may resent the demands your child makes on you, and, at the same time, feel guilty for feeling this way. (If you are impatient with your children, apologize. Tell them you are sorry for being so irritable and that it is not their fault.) While you may be overwhelmed by your emotions, they will be stressed and needy, too. Expect your children to suffer. They will also be angry that this has happened to them, and particularly with the parent who has left the marriage. They may feel abandoned, responsible, rejected, embarrassed, and different from their friends in intact families. Depending on their age and personality, they may whine more, act out, withdraw, regress, reject you, be overly solicitous, or possibly attempt to hurt themselves. Studies of how divorce affects children show they usually suffer from many of the same symptoms adults do: depression, anger, denial, low self-esteem, shock, shame, and guilt.

Children react differently to divorce. Some become ultraobedient, hoping their good behavior will reunite their parents. At the other extreme, youngsters may behave monstrously, also hoping it will force their parents back together to deal with them. Other children act as if the divorce does not bother them and have a delayed reaction called "the sleeper effect." Their pain and unresolved emotions may not surface until adolescence or adulthood. Girls, in particular, sometimes act out sexually or have a difficult time with commitment later in life. Young boys may become more aggressive and also be afraid of getting involved in a serious relationship when they are older. There is a higher percentage of divorce among children of divorce.

It is important to encourage children to talk about their feelings so they don't become overburdened. It is confusing and difficult for an adult to grapple with myriad feelings; imagine the problems it poses for a child who may not have the sophisticated vocabulary or emotional resources to discuss and process it.

Just as you feel angry at your husband (and yourself) for a failed marriage, your children are also likely to be angry at you for separating them from their father. You need to acknowledge that anger, which is hard to do when you are also hurt. Rather than telling them they shouldn't feel angry, it isn't your fault, you're doing the best you can, or their father left you, tell them, "I understand why you feel that way, and I'm sorry. Things will never be the same and I understand you are angry about that."

Even in an abusive situation, if it was your decision to leave the marriage, young children will not understand and probably think it is your fault. While adolescents cognitively understand the situation, they are dealing with their own issues, so the issue of separation is more complex. They may be angry with you for making them see their father if they don't want to, even if it is the court's order. Children look to mothers to heal their hurts, to take care of them, and to fix the problem. They may be angry at your inability to change the situation.

What further complicates the issue is that your needs at this time are very different from your child's. There is a great disparity between an adult's view of divorce and a child's. Grown-ups may regard divorce as a solution, but for children, it is the source of problems. You might think, *I'm better off without this person,* and distance yourself psychologically so you can move on with your life. It may be healthy for you to separate from your ex-husband, but your child needs to connect with both of you. Therefore, what you do to separate psychologically can hurt your son or daughter. You need to understand this tension.

Typically, it takes children at least one year to accept the situation, but that does not mean that after that, they shed all their feelings of sadness or anger.

There are ways you can help your children.

Treat your husband like their father, not as a stranger or someone you detest. The better you treat him, the easier it will be for them to recover. Keep the lines of communication open. Try to parent consistently and discuss areas of mutual concern and joy.

Make individual time for each child. Realize that youngsters who feel a lack of attention will do anything, including act terribly, to get it.

Notify your children's teachers, after-school coaches, day care providers, and other adults they see regularly. Tell these people about the situation so they will be empathetic and extra understanding.

Make changes slowly. Having both parents no longer living in the house is an enormous change, so try to keep constant other areas of their life, such as school, friends, and activities. If you must move, try to encourage your children to enroll in the same activities in the new location.

Stay calm and in control. If you fall apart, the children will feel compelled to worry about you. Having to take care of a parent is a huge psychological burden for a child.

Consider therapy for your child. It can be beneficial, even if she does not seem to be suffering. Remember, you can't always tell. Don't panic if the children are having a rough time. It is normal. Some signs of significant trouble, however, include plummeting grades for several months, aggressive behavior, intense mood swings, cheating, lying, stealing, alcohol or drug abuse, or excessive grieving.

You might want to consult a child therapist to get an idea of how you can help your children and to find out if their behavior is developmentally appropriate or truly problematic. If your husband will consent, a couple of joint sessions with a therapist on what you can expect of and from your children during this period could be invaluable. Your local bookstore or library should also have good resources for helping yourself and your children through this process under parenting, child development, or relationships.

One East Coast lawyer remembers a female client who seemed sensitive to her children's needs and was trying to have a peaceful divorce. Her husband wanted to reconcile and sent her a huge bouquet of roses. The client did not want to rekindle the marriage and never took the flowers out of the box. She left them on the dining room table and only disposed of them after they had shriveled up and died. "I wondered, what were her children thinking?" recalls the attorney. "It must have been hard on them and I don't think that ever occurred to my client. It's obvious she had a lot of unresolved issues."

Many family therapists now provide divorce counseling where couples receive therapy to help them split amicably and behave civilly. These can be private practitioners or services through a marriage counseling center. There are also support groups for the children of divorce.

Look into parenting courses. They are increasingly available across the country. In some counties of some states, and in all courts in Connecticut, Arizona, and Utah, a formal class with a mental health professional is mandated before a judge will grant a divorce when a couple has children; spouses do not have to attend together. There are also private centers that offer classes and counseling. Parenting courses teach mothers and fathers about the impact of separation and divorce on children, how to deal with children at various developmental ages and stages, the kinds of behavior that benefit and hurt them, and anger management techniques. The sessions usually include role playing. For instance, a mother might learn how to react if her daughter says she does not want to go visit her father. (Instead of the mother saying, "Cut it out. You know you have to go," a mother should say, "Tell me why you don't want to go." She can talk with her daughter and determine her concerns. It could be that the father has a new girlfriend the daughter does not like. While the mother should still encourage her child to be with her father, she might be able to broach the child's concerns with her ex-spouse.) The universal question posed in these parenting courses is: "Do you hate your spouse more than you love your children?" That question often prompts parents to rethink their behavior.

· **Find cooler heads at this time.** You will definitely need them. The person who will be most objective is a therapist, which is a good reason to go to one. You have to get the emotional support you need in order to maintain the proper equilibrium through the divorce and custody process. That is because you will be judged on your behavior irrespective of what has happened to you.

· **Figure out a contingency plan for when you cannot take it anymore.** Make a mental list of whom you can trust and count on. Because you are so consumed with intense feelings, your judgment may be flawed. These friends should be able to keep you on track when you are not yourself. (Not many people are, during divorce.) You will want friends with whom you can share ideas and perceptions. Keep in mind that friends have their own biases. They may hate your husband and only see your viewpoint, for example. That is good for empathy, but not necessarily for a reality check. Therefore, seek out the advice of people who are objective, who won't agree with you because they know it's what you want to hear.

· **Develop ways to keep yourself under control.** Because you are in so much pain, you will probably find yourself more emotionally fragile and unpredictable. It's important to be aware of this. Learn relaxation techniques such as taking a deep breath and counting to ten when you feel you are losing your temper, or call a friend and vent to her. An organized support group for divorcing mothers or parents, often run by a trained leader, will allow you to commiserate constructively, offers professional guidance, gives you a chance to make new friends, and if there are fathers in your group, provides insight into a man's perspective.

· **Try to control yourself and not scream at or threaten your husband.** He could use your outburst against you in court. Telling him off may make you feel better in the short run, but what you are interested in is the long run. The more you lose control, the worse it may be for you. Shrieking at him in front of the children will be added ammunition for him and his attorney. Some fathers antagonize their ex-wives in subtle ways: being way too early or late for visitation, changing visitation schedules arbitrarily or not giving enough notice about a different schedule, or bringing home the children dirty or without their clothes.

Don't give in to the harassment. Your husband could claim you are unstable; judges do not want to place a child with an unstable parent. This issue is significant. A strategy attorneys and their male clients sometimes use is to goad a mother until she explodes. Then they can tell the court they are dealing with a "hysterical female." You have to be strategic yourself: Realize the other side may try to make you lose your temper, and do not play that game. Again, lean on family and therapists here. Be the queen, not the pawn. She is the most valuable player on the chess board.

If your husband loses control and screams at you, disengage. Don't scream back. Use relaxation techniques, walk out of the room or house, and wait until you are in your car alone to scream. Also, children can become terrified when their parents shriek at each other. Do you want that for your children?

· **Do not bad-mouth your husband to your children.** Judges do not like to hear that one parent disparages another to the children, and they usually come down hard on the indiscreet party in a custody ruling. If all other factors are equal, the parent who speaks poorly of the other to the children can lose custody. It is your job not to undermine your child's relationship with his father. At the same time, it is natural to want to let your children know that it is not your fault for some of their hardship. If your husband refuses to pay child support, for example, and you have a shortage of cash because of it, you will probably resent your husband. But as much as it might feel good to vent at the moment, you do not want your child to know that his father is not living up to his agreement.

If you bad-mouth him to them, they may be confused about whom to believe and trust. Mudslinging can also mean problems for your children later in life with adult relationships. If you have a daughter, she may have a hard time with men, and your son may have trouble with commitment.

If your child is the one to criticize your spouse, you have to be careful. If you tell him you agree, he may begin manipulating both parents, allying himself with you against his father and with his father against you. While this may give your child a sense of power, it places him in a destructive and potentially damaging position. This dynamic will definitely not get you and your husband closer and can create even more bad feelings. It will not be great for your relationship with your child, either.

What do you do if you agree with your child's assessment of his father? One divorced New York therapist, who is the father of two sons, ages eleven and eight, recently had that dilemma. His older son was confiding to his father about how selfish and inconsiderate his mother was. "I couldn't deny what he said and say, 'No, she isn't,' because it would be a blatant lie. I happened to agree completely. I came back with, 'She's under a lot of pressure, and that may affect her ability to be considerate.' I wanted to validate his feelings but at the same time excuse her for her behavior." Save the bad-mouthing for your friends and therapist.

· **View divorce as a chance for personal growth.** You might be thinking, *Cut the Pollyanna stuff. Get real!* You might believe that everyone who advises you to "look at the positive" has never been through a divorce and certainly never with children. Attitude, however, is important. It will affect your relationship with your ex-husband, your children, and your future relationships and friendships. Even though the situation may be unbearable, it will change.

According to a five-year study of divorced couples conducted by social workers Judith Wallerstein and Joan Kelly and chronicled in *Surviving the Breakup*, many parents improved their lives after the breakup by learning more about themselves. For you, that could mean taking responsibility for your part in the marriage that did not work, accepting your husband's deficiencies, or acknowledging that you were just wrong for each other. At any rate, it doesn't matter anymore who did what to whom or who caused the marriage to fail. It won't change the situation. Only you can do that, by focusing on yourself and your children.

· **Acknowledge the loneliness.** A big issue for most newly separated parents is adapting to being without the children some of the time. As one mother of two boys explains it, "I used to be a couple and don't know what the hell to do with all this time. What now? What do I do with myself to fill the hours? Not having them makes me ache." This is where developing interests outside the children, immersing yourself in a job, friends, hobbies, feel-good adventures (a trip to the museum, a lecture series, a workout at the local gym, piano lessons), and keeping active and involved will help you acclimate yourself to sharing your children and filling potentially painful stretches of time.

· **Assume you will not reconcile with your husband.** You may, but it is best not to convince yourself of this if there is no factual basis. If it works out and that's what you want, great, but try to get on with your life. Otherwise, you may feel even angrier if it doesn't happen. Be discreet while you are separated. Should you get back together with your husband, you will not want the world to know the details of your relationship.

· **Exercise regularly to reduce anger and stress.** As little as twenty to thirty minutes of aerobic exercise three times a week (brisk walking, running, swimming, cycling, cross-country skiing, in-line skating, or dancing) will get your lungs to produce more oxygen, making your heart stronger. Exercise produces a physiological response that will make you feel good emotionally. Being less angry and stressed should have an effect on your children. Other ways to relax, such as drinking, smoking, or gambling, can harm you in a custody contest. Consider joining a health club, where, besides getting or staying fit, you will also meet other people. Or you could think about hiring a personal trainer who will work with you either in your home or at a health club. They charge $25 to $80 an hour; you can find one through a health club, a YMCA or YWCA, or your local high school or college.

· **Be aware of your diet.** You may turn to liquor, caffeine, cigarettes, or junk foods to reduce stress, but they can actually increase it. Foods supposed to have a calming effect are fruits, vegetables, legumes, whole grains, seeds, fish, nuts, and starches.

· **Keep a diary.** Write down your feelings; get them out. Throw it out if you decide it has served its purpose.

WHAT YOUR BEHAVIOR SAYS TO YOUR CHILD

There is another reason why you should try not to lose control. As a parent, you are a role model. Your children will learn that even though one relationship may end, they will be able to form new, healthy relationships because they have seen you do it. Your behavior may free your children to have a loving relationship with both their father *and* mother. This takes enormous self-control and maturity, especially when you can't stand your spouse, but it will pay off.

If you remember that your child's best interests come first, you may be able to deal more sanely with your ex-husband. It will not only help your child cope as well as he can, but behaving will let you keep your dignity and should help boost your self-esteem at a time when it has plunged off the charts.

If your ex-husband is committed to parenting, try to isolate that area from the rest of the ruined relationship. Think about acting as devoted and dedicated parents, even if it cannot be as loving husband

and wife. It is an imperfect situation, but if you view each other this way, you might be able to create an island of civil coparenting amid the uncivil war raging between you. You may need a professional to keep you focused on what is best for the children.

WATCH WHAT YOU TELL YOUR CHILD

It is natural to turn to your children for comfort, particularly if it is your husband who ended the relationship. That doesn't mean you want to stonewall your son if he asks a question, but don't try to get him on your side. Don't look to your child for empathy and discuss how badly you feel treated by their father or the courts. This is not appropriate. A more appropriate forum is to address any problems you have directly with your husband, a therapist, friend, or support group.

If you have other important people in your life, you are more likely not to depend on your child for emotional support. Your job is to let your children know you will take care of them. It is not healthy for them to think they must take care of you. Remember, their world has fallen apart, too. In the midst of change, let them see that their parents are capable of meeting *their* needs. When parents cannot, it becomes a double blow for children. They are frightened to see a parent out of control, and it can lead to long-term psychological problems for them.

If your husband ended the marriage, part of your anger may be that you have had to watch your children suffer from the fallout. If they have trouble separating from you during this time to be with their father, you need to address this. You should tell them you are sorry you can't be with them more and be honest that it makes you sad, but let them know you want them to have a good relationship with their father. They may have torn loyalties, so assurances that you encourage their relationship with him may allow them to enjoy their time with him. This approach will also acknowledge both their feelings and your own.

When your husband doesn't choose to spend time with the children, it creates a different set of issues and problems. From your perspective, it intensifies the anger. How could he not see his own children or realize the pain he is inflicting? On the practical side, the children are with you all the time and you do not get a break. You are justifiably resentful. Here he has created this mess and left it for you. You will need to deal with that anger so you can cope well with your children. Acknowledging your sadness about the situation for them is important. (See chapter 11.) You will have to work through this issue. You do not want to convey anger and bitterness to your children about their father; sadness is different. You also do not want your anger at him to become directed at them. When you are dealing with your kids full time due to an absentee ex-husband, be sure to take time for yourself. Get a sitter or friend to watch the children and go to a movie or museum. A small break from the kids can be beneficial to you all.

WHAT MEN THINK ABOUT CUSTODY AND WHY YOU NEED TO CARE

WHAT FATHERS SAY IS HARDEST FOR THEM

1. Not being permitted to be with their children more.
2. Fighting over little changes in their custody schedules, which makes them feel angry and resentful.
3. Not being consulted about parenting decisions.
4. Having their ex-wives assume that they know best and don't care what the fathers know or are feeling.

Divorce can transform the sweetest people into bitter, vindictive aliens. Fathers, in particular, tend to get very defensive and offended about custody—and for legitimate reasons. Many times, they are ordered to leave the marital home and their children. They feel as if they have lost everything: their wife; their house; and now, their sons and daughters. Visitation can be artificial and awkward. On top of this, their ex-wives may make it difficult for them to see the children but eagerly accept child support checks and maintenance money.

How would you feel? You need to realize that your husband may be hurting as badly as you over the breakup and is probably just as terrified by the new living arrangements and the uncertainty of the custody outcome. Why should his feelings matter to you, especially if he has hurt you? Understanding his perspective (and he yours) will, at least theoretically, make you nicer to each other and behave better as coparents. And that is the point. Think about what kind of father you want him to be.

Men have a laundry list of complaints about their wives around the issue of custody. You may not have considered how he sees the situation or that there is more than one way to see it: yours. That is because you are in pain.

What *do* men have to say about women and custody?

- **She doesn't communicate with me.** Many fathers feel their ex-wives do not share enough information about the children with them when they are at the other house. (Mothers, by the way, often have the same complaint.) "It's not that I disagree with my ex-wife on most things. The problem is that she makes assumptions without talking to me," said one Southern father. "Generally, she has good reasons for doing what she does, like taking our first grader out of school for a day to do something special. But she shows no respect for me when she fails to discuss it with me beforehand."

    Another father from Connecticut had this to say: "I don't get all the information and I am playing divorce war. My son hit another child accidentally in the face with a football, and the other boy had to go to the hospital. My wife never told me about the incident. I wish she had so I could have talked to our son about it and called the boy's parents and told them how sorry we were. Why didn't I know? It's because my wife is crippled by anger and it is her way of sticking it to me."

- **I'm not the father she thinks I am.** "You should never make assumptions about your ex-husband," said one newly separated father of boys ages nine and six, who has joint legal custody and almost equal physical custody. "Just because I might not have been home very much during the marriage doesn't mean I can't be a very good parent. You've got to ask me why I wasn't home much. It wasn't because of the kids but because I felt there was no place for me in the house. My wife and I got into a pattern. She would be the one doing all the things with the kids and I felt I was being pressed out. I didn't feel welcome in the process of parenting. Now I can do all of these things with my sons when they're with me."

Some fathers say that because of the strains in their marriage, they could not always be the kind of father they wanted to be, and their performance as a parent was affected. They might have been distant or physically absent to escape the tension of the marriage, or impatient with their child because of their own problems. Now that the conflict has diminished, many fathers say they are free to establish a new relationship with their child for the first time away from the presence of their ex-wife.

· **My wife doesn't own the children just because she gave birth to them.** "Neither one of us has greater rights to the children than the other," said a separated father of four. "I'm not going to be content with, 'They are really *my* kids and you can see them every other week.' She doesn't own the kids any more than I own them. I don't think a female is superior or inferior. I think healthy children require both parents. I don't think it would be any healthier for me to have my children 90 percent of the time than for my ex-wife."

Another father from Missouri remarked, "Some fathers don't want to be involved more than for ceremonial occasions like PTO meetings and other public displays of parenting. But I don't want a superficial relationship with my children. I want a real relationship, a *parental* relationship."

· **I'm a much better father now that I'm no longer married to her.** Many fathers claim there is an upside to divorce: They get to know their children in a way they might not have, had they stayed married. "I wouldn't have had the same intimacy and bonding with my kids, and they wouldn't have gotten to know me if I had not gotten a divorce," one father mused. "My children now have a deeper relationship with their father."

Said another father who has joint legal custody of his three children, ages four to thirteen, "If I were still with my wife, I would not have had this amount of uninterrupted time with my kids. I have no choice but to spend time with them when they are with me, and that's a good thing."

· **My sons have a right to a male role model, and that happens to be me.** Gender is a giant issue. If you have a son, you want him to be emotionally well-adjusted. Boys look for role models of what it is to be a man. When a father is absent, a boy will often go outside the family to look for them. (The research shows they may find bad role models. There is a greater prevalence of criminal behavior among boys with absentee fathers.) You should encourage your child to spend time with his father because he needs him so he can grow up and have a healthy image of men. If, however, your ex-spouse is mentally unbalanced, truly abusive, or unfit, find alternative father figures or role models.

· **The legal system skewers fathers.** Men feel the system is weighted toward mothers. "The mother still gets a better shake," said the West Virginia father of an eight-year-old girl and ten-year-old boy from his second marriage and two teenagers from his first wife. "To say that the kids should be with the women—to just assume this—is inappropriate in this day and age."

· **She's holding the kids hostage by threatening that if she doesn't get the financial settlement she wants then I won't get to see my kids.** "I'll never forget my ex-wife's line to me: no money, no kids," said one joint-custody father. "You want to know why some fathers seek custody even if they don't really want it? They think it's the only way they will get to see their kids." A divorced father who is also a social worker and mediator in New York believes "often it is just posturing. Having custody may be ridiculous and impractical and will only exacerbate the problem. Children should never be part of the divorce conflict. Women should separate the financial settlement from custody issues. Treat them as separate issues or else your children will become pawns."

Remember, how you act is as important as what you say. Use all means necessary to make sure that your emotional state remains healthy and balanced during this process. In order to provide support and guidance for your children, you have to take care of yourself. The best way to lose custody is to lose control of your emotions and to prevent your children from having a good relationship with their father.

Getting a Grip on Custody Arrangements

Deciding on a custody arrangement is likely to be the biggest and most emotional struggle you have with your spouse. Regardless of who asked for the divorce, both you and your husband will probably feel you have lost something important with a new custody arrangement. You will be going from living in one household with total access to the children to getting used to chunks of time without them. If you want any arrangement to work, you must be sensitive to your children's and husband's needs but also protect your own. And you will have to compromise.

Understanding the legal concepts involved in custody will empower you so you will be in a position to make smart choices. This knowledge should also give you the upper hand.

COMING TO TERMS WITH CUSTODY

There are two basic components to custody: who will make major decisions in the children's lives and take legal responsibility for them, called *legal custody*, and where they will live, or *physical custody*. Both natural parents have equal rights to custody. Parents who legally separate or divorce may go to court to seek a custody determination. They either decide together what that determination will be, or, if they can't reach an agreement, they ask the court to make the decision. When parents are able to come up with a custody plan, the court will review it and approve it, provided it is reasonable. The parent who doesn't receive custody will have visitation, unless it isn't in the best interests of the child. That could mean the parent had a drinking or drug problem or a history of child abuse, for example. If the court decides that the child would still benefit from seeing that parent, it might order supervised visitation. This arrangement can include visits in a court-supervised center or other neutral locations, or with a third party (family or friend) at your house.

There are a variety of custody configurations. These include sole custody, joint legal custody, joint physical custody, and split custody. Before you decide which situation you want, you need to do some soul-searching.

In determining the best custody arrangement for your family, ask yourself four questions:

1. What are my needs?
2. What kind of husband do I have?
3. What is my child like?
4. What arrangement would best serve the needs of my child/children?

Consider Your Needs

What do you really want? Is it to make all the major decisions regarding the kids by yourself and have them live most of the time with you? Or do you think it would work better to share the decision making with your ex-husband but still have the children with you? Would you be more comfortable having both of you make the major decisions and splitting the time so the children live with both of you pretty much the same amount? Or do you think they would be better off staying with your ex-husband and seeing you on weekends?

In order to answer these questions, you have to carefully consider your situation. If you work, what are your hours? Do you or your ex-husband travel? With the demands of household chores and child-related activities (car pooling, monitoring homework, after-school activities, doctors' appointments) and time for yourself, how often would you like to be with your children? Do you want time without them to pursue a career, resolve personal problems, or explore outside interests, or do you prefer to be with them every spare minute? If your ex-husband has a girlfriend or new wife, what kind of caretaker is she and would she be the primary "parent" at his house? How do you feel about that?

Decide what *you* can live with. Can you stand living near your ex-husband, which will probably be better for the kids if he is a decent guy? Think about the areas in which you are willing to bend (an extra night with their father? ballet? ice hockey?) and which ones are not negotiable (school? religion? braces?). Can you tolerate flexibility or do you feel more comfortable with a defined custody schedule? If you have the children for the weekend, for example, and they want to bike over to your ex-husband's house, is that okay with you, or do you want to keep the visits separate?

The biggest question: Can you negotiate well with your ex-husband? The custody arrangement you work out will be greatly defined by this question.

What Kind of Husband Do I Have?

You have to figure out your husband's level of commitment to the children and his competence in parenting them. Do you think he *really* wants custody or are there other motives here? As one experienced family law attorney who represents both men and women observed, "Only a small percentage of custody fights are really about custody— most of the custody claims by men are strategically and tactically oriented." Is your ex-husband a loving, responsible dad who will pay attention to the children's needs and take good care of them? Remember, he doesn't have to do things your way in order to parent well.

Put yourself in his position. If you were the father, what would you want? Is it reasonable and will it benefit your child? Can you help him get what he wants without sacrificing your needs? Was he a hands-on parent? If not, do you believe he can learn to care for them? If you are comfortable in these areas, you may be more willing to work out a custody arrangement where he has generous time with the children. If you are convinced he wants the kids for reasons that are not altruistic— so he can pay less child support or for spite, let's say—then you may decide to fight harder.

Be totally honest. If you don't want to share the children, is it because you think your ex-husband is a lousy parent or because you really want to hurt him or are engaging in one-upmanship? Acting out of anger or basing a custody decision on your desire to get your husband will not only adversely affect your legal outcome, it could also hurt your children and your relationship with them.

What Is My Child Like?

Your job is to make sure your son or daughter has the best situation possible. In order to determine that, you need to figure out where your children are developmentally and what arrangement is best at a particular stage or age. What is good for a three-year-old might not work for a ten-year-old. You have to try to come up with a plan to meet their needs. Obviously, if you have children of different ages, you have to decide what will work best for the family as a whole. It may be that your infant would have day visits with her father, but not overnights right away. Or there could be a different schedule for children of different ages, so the older ones would spend the weekend. Typically, younger children prefer frequent visits with the noncustodial parent, even if the visits are brief, while older children like longer visits at the expense of less frequent stays.

What kind of child do you have? Does he have a hard time with change, or is he the flexible type who could adapt well to both households? Does he have an easygoing disposition or is he difficult? Remember, even the calmest kid can have a tough time when there are many transitions. If your child doesn't deal well with change, you wouldn't want a schedule where you switch homes every few days. If you have other children, how do you think they would fare?

Unless your ex-husband is abusive or emotionally unfit, the best situation means having access to both parents. Putting your own needs aside, you must try to discern what your child will want, even if you can't necessarily give it to her. For instance, if she is like other children, she will want you and your husband to reconcile. You may not be able to grant that wish, but hopefully, you can help her with what children claim is their other desire: that their parents just get along.

The literature reports that children are affected by the kind of divorce their parents have. Research shows that active, hostile parental conflict often leads to detrimental results in children, ranging from low self-esteem to depression, substance abuse problems, and even to crime. The "ideal" divorce for the child, maintain experts, is one in which the parents might disagree but are respectful of each other and are on good terms. How you devise your agreement will depend, in part, on what kind of divorce you have. If it is amicable, you can probably have a plan that allows the children to have a substantial amount of flexibility and contact. If you two have a contentious relationship, consider a more structured and formal plan.

Your child should spend time with both parents, but the arrangement has to work for him first and foremost. A young boy or girl, age four or under, may have a difficult, even traumatic, time spending overnights with her father if he hasn't been active in child rearing. Very young children would most likely have no trouble with overnight stays, however, if both parents have always been involved with them. In determining overnights for a young child, it's important to evaluate the kind of involvement your child has had with each parent. If you have been the one to care for your child exclusively, think about day visits only for a while for your child with your husband. (That assumes you and your husband live close enough for this arrangement and he consents to it.) Some judges grant overnights even for very young children, and you must comply unless you have a compelling reason to withhold your child. In that case, you must file a petition with the court to modify the judge's order.

Babies tend to be insecure and need extensive contact with their primary caretaker. Children eighteen months to three years typically have separation anxiety, even in intact families. That feeling is likely to be exacerbated when parents break up. Your child may cry more than he ordinarily would or regress to more infantile behaviors. You will want to provide consistency in the routine and contain conflict between you and your husband when the kids are around. Preschoolers are egocentric. They usually blame themselves for the divorce and fear they will be abandoned. *If one parent can leave me, why can't both parents leave me?* they may wonder. A five-year-old may be angry at you or your ex-husband for getting a divorce, and she may think her anger will make you abandon her.

Children from four to five years old can tolerate separation better from the primary caretaker. They have more sophisticated cognitive understanding that they will see their other parent again, and that separation is temporary.

Your ex-husband might not have been an active parent when the children were infants, but he may want more of a relationship with them as they get older. Try to understand the situation. Not relating to infants doesn't mean he won't make an excellent father for a toddler, preteen, or adolescent. Rather than keep a score card (because you would definitely win), think about how important it is for your five-year-old to get to know his father.

THE REAL ISSUES

Divorce has two major components. The first is psychological. Before you consider any custody arrangement, you need to understand this part well. Then you can approach the next area: the legal. This part will help you get what you want.

On the psychological side, take comfort from the fact that experts believe the actual hours you spend with your child don't matter. This knowledge may free you up a bit when you are negotiating your custody agreement. Mental health professionals say that whether your husband gets two or twenty-four hours on a Wednesday or four hours on a Thursday is inconsequential in terms of your child's postdivorce adjustment. According to experts, what matters most for children is not what legal custody arrangement they have but what type of relationship they continue to have with both parents after the breakup.

Social worker and author Judith Wallerstein, the founder and executive director of the Center for the Family in Transition in Corte Madera, California, has studied the effects of divorce on children over a twenty-five-year period. She maintains that what ultimately counts for children is the quality of the relationship they have with their mother and father in the hours that they spend with them, the psychological health of both parents, being mutually supportive of their child, and their willingness to work cooperatively around the children. If you add to that a commitment to reevaluate the arrangement as their needs (and yours and your ex-husband's) change, whatever setup you have can work.

Don't get hung up on custody labels. Parents sometimes waste enormous energy fighting over whether they will have sole legal custody, let's say, or joint legal custody. It's possible that your ex-husband could be the noncustodial parent but see the kids the same amount of time, or even more, than if he were a joint legal custodian. So before you become convinced that you must have a certain custody arrangement, know what you are asking for. Make sure you understand the legal terms. Know what you want—how many hours or days you can logistically spend with your kids and when you need to work or be outside the house. Try to get your legal arrangement to dovetail with your daily needs.

Also realize that if you have a teenager, your child may call the shots. You can have any custody order on the books, but if your adolescent won't abide by it, there's little you or your husband can do. In that case, you might as well go along with the child's plan. If it's to live with your husband, you have to hope that this arrangement works well for your child or that after a while, she will miss you enough to move back or spend significant time with you.

Before you decide on a specific arrangement, you have to understand your legal options. Either through negotiation or court decree, and usually with lawyers on both sides, you will draw up a custody agreement. Courts ask parents to work out as many issues as possible before going to court. In more enlightened jurisdictions, the court may have professionals in-house who work with parents to draft the custody agreement. The staff helps parents grapple with issues around child care, values, and goals for their children. The courts have found it can reduce parental hostility and lawyers' fees as well as increase compliance with court orders.

A CUSTODY SAMPLER

Check your state statute to find out what custody arrangements it permits or favors. In general, a court will award either sole or joint custody.

- The courts of South Carolina and Tennessee are allowed to award sole custody to the mother when the children are young, typically age seven or less. But Alaska, California, the District of Columbia, Florida, Kansas, Missouri, Utah, Delaware, and Hawaii bar judges from awarding sole custody to the mother just because the children are of tender years.

- Only Arkansas, North Dakota, Rhode Island, and Virginia don't have laws on the books about joint custody but permit it by court order. Twelve state statutes establish joint custody as a preference, meaning courts must consider joint custody, or address why it is not awarded. Other states have a presumption that joint custody is in the best interests of the child unless there is evidence to refute this. Twenty-one states allow the courts to award joint custody even if one parent objects to this arrangement and doesn't want to participate in joint custody.

SOLE CUSTODY

One parent makes all serious decisions concerning the child's life, including what religion he will be brought up in, medical care, and schooling. That parent is also responsible for day-to-day decisions, such as which after school activities the child will participate in, which dentist to use, the musical instrument he will play, and which baby-sitter to hire.

The arrangement varies, depending on your situation, but typically, the noncustodial parent has every other weekend with the child, beginning Friday afternoon and ending Sunday night, plus a few hours or one sleep-over during the week or off week. Parents alternate holidays. The judge may split the Thanksgiving weekend, for example, or award Christmas Eve to one parent and Christmas Day to the other when it is feasible. The noncustodial parent typically has the children for four to eight weeks in the summer. Today, judges who award sole custody to one parent give liberal visitation to the other.

Advantages of Sole Custody

- It allows you to make major decisions relating to the children without consulting your ex-husband except about the time your child will be with him. It lets you be in control.

· It minimizes hassling with your ex-husband, so if you don't get along, you won't have to communicate with him around issues that could be contentious.

Disadvantages of Sole Custody

· Unless you allow your child substantial time with your ex-husband, she may feel cheated out of a full relationship with her father and suffer psychologically. The noncustodial father may feel so left out that he may choose not to see the kids, or he may even leave the picture entirely. Noncustodial fathers tend to drop out more than those in joint custody arrangements. A National Survey of Children study showed that 49 percent of children who lived with only one parent had not visited with their noncustodial parent in the last year, and only one in six saw that parent once a week or more. Having an absent father in a sole custody arrangement has been linked to cognitive, conduct, and learning problems, as well as gender identification issues.

· All the responsibility is on you. It can be lonely and exhausting. If you work, you probably have a full-time job at the office, and another when you get home. You may get no emotional or financial support.

· Full-time single parenting leaves you little time for yourself. If you want to move on with your life, get a rewarding job, or have a new relationship, it may be logistically challenging with children underfoot.

· You may feel a money pinch or economic instability. If your ex-husband doesn't see your children as much as he would like and has little say in their life, he's unlikely to chip in any extra money to raise your kids other than what is court ordered. A 1996 U.S. Commission on Child and Family Welfare report to the President and Congress states that to expect a father to continue to provide for a child's well-being through child support payments to an ex-spouse but to exclude him from his child's life may promote anger, resentment, and a sense of "taxation without representation."

JOINT CUSTODY

This arrangement is also called alternating custody, divided custody, shared custody, shared decision-making authority, and shared residential parenting. The term varies from state to state, but typically, both parents have equal legal rights and responsibilities, and the children live some of the time with each parent. If you have joint custody, your children don't necessarily spend an equal amount of time with you and your ex-husband.

Joint custody evolved in the late seventies from the belief that a father, who was usually the noncustodial parent, would feel better about the divorce if he could be on an equal footing with his ex-wife and stay involved in his child's life. The concept was also designed to mitigate the loss felt by children, who said they didn't get enough time with their noncustodial parent. Children could have two deeply involved, loving parents, if not a single, intact, loving household. This arrangement appealed to mothers, who now found time to pursue their own work and still remain hands-on parents.

Social scientists hailed the arrangement, arguing visitation was a major factor in how well children adjusted to divorce. Experts found that, in general, children in joint custody arrangements had increased self-esteem and more of a sense of overall competence than their sole-custody counterparts.

There are two kinds of joint custody: joint legal and joint physical. The legal side concerns responsibility, control, and power. You no longer have a marital partnership, but you have an ongoing child-rearing partnership. You have to convince your former spouse to agree on every item that you believe is important for your children: tutoring, orthodontia, religion, counseling, and elective surgery. At the same time, your ex-husband must convince you to go along with what he wants for your child. Everything becomes a negotiation and, at least theoretically, a power struggle.

The most important factor to ask yourself when you consider joint custody is, "Can I communicate civilly with my ex-husband to work out the issues in my children's life?" You will have to act like a team. If you can't or don't get along, this arrangement is not for you and is likely to be a disaster for your child. When one Mid-Atlantic–state judge ponders a joint custody decision, he looks at the relationship between the parents closely. "The burden will be on the parent to show that she or he can communicate in order for him to give shared or joint custody. You have to behave in a manner that will be interpreted as cooperating."

Joint Legal Custody

Both you and your ex-husband have the legal right to make major decisions (school, religion, medical issues) involving your child. You don't have to discuss every single issue with your ex-partner. The two of you could divide the major child-related areas. For instance, you could have the final say on religious upbringing, if that's more important to you, and your ex-husband could decide on whether your son should go to private or public school, or whether he plays one sport or another for an after-school activity (if he is too young to decide himself). You and your ex-husband are legal partners or coparents around major matters, but the day-to-day decisions belong to the parent who has physical custody.

Joint legal custody does not address where and with whom your child will live. It's possible that one parent would have legal custody and both would have physical custody, or that both would have legal custody and only one would have physical custody. The latter is the more common of the two arrangements.

Advantages of Joint Legal Custody

- Parents are legal equals. Your husband is less likely to feel like a second-class citizen or a money machine. The playing field is level, and theoretically there is less cause for resentment and hostility. Having your ex-husband feel positive about the arrangement should make it easier for you and your child.

- Both parents feel good about themselves (or as good as they can after a divorce) because they know they are working together for the sake of their child.

Disadvantages of Joint Legal Custody

· Regardless of what the custody decree says, one parent may try to control all of the decision making.

· When parents don't get along, it's hard to make effective decisions jointly for the child. The arrangement can highlight parental conflicts and problems and can be extremely stressful for the child.

· Mothers may believe joint custody is not in their child's best interest but feel pressure to agree to it. Some states follow a "friendly parent" provision that says the courts will favor the parent who allows the other parent the most contact with the child. A mother may not want to be perceived as obstructive, and thus will consent so she doesn't risk losing custody.

· If the court orders joint custody but one parent is opposed, it has little chance of working well. The hostility and lack of cooperation between parents doesn't necessarily decrease over time.

· In cases where there is real or threatened physical abuse, contact between the abuser and the victim can be dangerous.

Joint Physical Custody

The child has two residences and alternates living with each parent. The division of time can be equal or not, but is usually no less than one-third in one of the homes. Arrangements vary; children commonly spend four days with one parent and three days with the other, or one week at each house. Some youngsters alternate days; others switch once a year. An unusual, but not unheard of, setup called bird nesting is when children stay in the house and the parents take turns moving in and out.

Parents must live near each other in order for joint physical custody to work smoothly. Although the arrangement lets your child keep in close contact with both parents, some kids feel they are shuttled back and forth with no place to call home. The constant transitions can be emotionally wearing and confusing, particularly for small children. The logistical issues can be daunting: a homework assignment, beloved blanket, or soccer uniform left at the "wrong" house. Older children may want no part of this arrangement, finding it time-consuming (eating into their time away from friends and the telephone), inconvenient, and embarrassing.

Before You Seriously Consider Joint Physical Custody, Answer This

· Putting aside my own issues with my ex-husband, do I think he is the kind of parent with whom my child would do well? Does he have a history of drug or alcohol addiction, mental illness, child neglect or abuse, or family violence? Is he caring and responsible? (You don't have to agree on every parenting issue.) Will he want to be involved on a constant basis with the kids?

· Do my husband and I fight a lot? If we disagree on parenting issues, are we able to resolve them? Can we keep our anger out of our parenting?

· Can we both put our child's needs above our own and work our schedules and lifestyle around her?

· Are we mature enough to handle regular communication and decision making? (With very young children, you will have to talk about teething, sleep problems, and emotional issues; for older children, there are long-term homework assignments, school tests, telephone rules, and dating.)

· Can we discuss common rules we would like to see in both houses? (The rules don't have to be identical, but there should be mutual respect and a willingness to cooperate.)

· How will my children's ages impact my decision? (Research shows that joint custody may work better for elementary school children than the preschool or adolescent group. Preschool and younger children normally fear being abandoned and may have this feeling reinforced by moving back and forth between households; when it's time to move to the other parent's, they may believe they are being sent away because they have been bad. Changes tend to be easier for elementary school children, whose cognitive skills allow them to master the good-byes and understand they are wanted and loved in both households. One study of twenty-five joint custody families with children under the age of five conducted at the Center for the Family in Transition in Corte Madera, California, found children ages three and younger handled transitions better than three- to five-year olds. Teenagers usually prefer sole custody to joint custody because of their already packed social lives and their desire to be with friends as much as possible, rather than with their parents.

· Is our work schedule conducive to shared parenting? Do either one of us or both of us have any flexibility in our work? Do we travel too often to make the situation feasible? If so, who will stay with our kids if one of us is away? Will we use day care, baby-sitters, relatives, girlfriends/boyfriends?

· Do I see myself or my husband moving in the near future? Will we wind up back in court to change the arrangement to sole custody if one of us leaves the area?

· Do I live close enough to my ex-husband to make the situation workable? Can the children bike back and forth or be driven a short distance? If we live far apart, who will do the driving, and is it reasonable to ask the children to go the distance? How far is each of our places from our children's school? From after-school activities and religious school? From their friends?

· Are we capable of changing the custody arrangement or fine-tuning it if it's harming our child? How would either one of us handle joint custody if our child suddenly had a new stepfather, stepmother, or stepsiblings? Are we both able to recognize that things may change? Are we willing to talk about how to handle these changes? Are we flexible if we need to change schedules or if our child's schedule merits it?

• If I have a boyfriend or my ex-husband has a girlfriend, are they good to my children?

• What are our motives? Do we want joint custody for the right reasons? Because we love our child and want to stay an integral part of his life rather than because we are seeking to reduce child support, or want to stay inappropriately attached to each other, for example.

• Does my ex-husband have empathy for our child and me? (If not, you're probably not going to get much understanding, cooperation, or flexibility.) Do I have empathy for my ex-husband and our children?

Advantages of Joint Physical Custody

• Ongoing contact between your child and his father.

• Less chance of having to go back to court to change custody arrangements. Joint custody parents relitigate less than those in sole custody arrangements.

• You have increased cooperation and trust with your ex-husband and respect for your ex-husband as a good father. Joint custody dads are usually committed to parenting.

• Fathers are less likely to seek sole custody if they feel they have ample access to their children.

• Men may be willing to let their ex-wives make more decisions because they know they have the authority and the power to make them should they choose.

• It can lead to financial and emotional independence. In their time without the children, mothers can work or pursue personal goals, gain promotions that would have been more difficult had they had sole custody, and their work may qualify them for insurance and retirement benefits. The downside is that women still do most of the caretaking and typically earn less than men, often forgoing higher paying jobs because of their custody schedule.

· It may stop the rejected parent from stealing the kids, neglecting them, or failing to live up to financial obligations.

· There is no feeling of being a visitor or a custodian, so your child can have a more natural relationship with each of you. Theoretically, there should be less hostility since neither of you is the noncustodial parent. You don't come across as the Wicked Witch, the full-time parent who is the disciplinarian, while your ex-husband is Mr. Weekend Fun.

· There is a better chance of getting your child support payments than with sole custody. Fathers who see their children regularly through joint custody also tend to chip in extra money other than child support (camps, music lessons, allowances, car payments and repairs, extra medical), which can only help your child. According to the California-based Joint Custody Association, 60 percent of joint custody parents voluntarily contribute extra support, compared with 20 percent in sole custody situations. Another study on child support showed that the parents who paid the most support were secure in their jobs and had a decent relationship with their ex-spouses.

Disadvantages of Joint Physical Custody

· *Really* close contact with your ex-spouse. Regular contact means you get to know a lot about each other's lives. That can make for jealousy, resentment, and hostility, especially when one of you seems to be rebounding, dating, and thriving, and the other is not.

· More opportunities for the kids to play one parent against the other.

· If your husband is uncooperative, you're in for a bad time.

- It is potentially confusing for children to go back and forth between houses where there are different expectations, rules, and lifestyles.

- It is a potential logistical nightmare: a teddy bear, ballet shoes, or computer disk left at the "wrong" house.

- It is a more expensive option than sole custody. It costs more to support two households than one, particularly since there is often a duplication of major expenses (beds, computers, books, clothing, toys). Typically, at least half the money parents spend on children goes for housing and transportation. Even though children may live with only one parent part of the time, they still need a room all of the time. The costs increase as the number of children increase. One study conducted by the Child Custody and Child Support Project to determine the relationship between custody, visitation, and child support, involving 426 mothers and fathers in California, Minnesota, Connecticut, and Colorado, found that housing and child care costs were an extra $12,354 per child for ages eight to thirteen and $15,617 for preschool youngsters in joint physical custody situations.

- If you want to relocate, you may have a custody problem.

- There are more chances for loneliness, more separations from your children for longer periods than with sole custody. That is why it's important to have an independent life.

- If your ex-husband did not spend much time with the children during the marriage, you may worry that they are not being cared for well.

- If you and your ex-husband fight constantly, your children will be continually exposed to it. Animosity between parents has been linked to a poor long-term prognosis for children of divorce.

SPLIT CUSTODY

One parent has custody of one or more of the children, and the other parent has custody of the other child or children. This arrangement is uncommon and not favored by the courts or therapists. It may be ordered when there has been a history of fighting between one parent and a child, a breakdown in communications if the siblings can't get along and the parents ask to divide them, the parents live far apart, one of the older children insists on living with a specific parent, or the age difference between the siblings is so great that the children aren't close to each other. However, the courts usually keep children together, believing they provide one another with needed emotional support during this stressful time.

In some jurisdictions, split custody refers to the situation where children spend months at a time with one parent and months with the other, or alternate one year with each instead of having weekend visits.

Advantages of Split Custody

· You can concentrate on a child's individual needs, which is hard to do when there is more than one child.

· The children get to stay in one place for a long time and don't have to constantly move back and forth between parents.

· It can be good for family dynamics and the emotional well-being of the family. You can isolate problems so you can build on the positives.

Disadvantages of Split Custody

· The six- or twelve-month split may be disorienting and confusing for children: different schools, sets of friends, and neighborhoods. It can increase the sense of insecurity many children of divorce already experience.

· There is little time for your children to bond as siblings. This arrangement may make them feel even less like a family. As one mother put it whose teenage daughter lives with her in Massachusetts and whose teenage son lives in Indiana with his father: "It's a struggle to find time when my children can be together so they can fight!"

TAKE YOUR TIME

It's important to have a legal document describing your custody situation. When you first separate, you may not know what arrangement you will ultimately want. It may make more sense to enter into a temporary custody agreement until you have a better sense of what will work for your family.

Temporary custody is an interim custody arrangement after separation and before a permanent custody determination is made. A temporary order is enforceable, which means you can go to court and ask that the terms of the order be carried out. The temporary aspect of it means you will need to reach a more permanent custody arrangement or petition the court for a determination. (Keep in mind that custody is always subject to change.) Some parents go straight for permanent custody if they know what they want, but many obtain a temporary order. The goal of temporary custody is to try to avoid disrupting a child's life during the divorce. It can also buy you time to build your case.

If you suspect that your ex-husband may try to steal your kids— sometimes done as a way to get you to give in to his demands on other issues, such as child support or divisions of property or merely for spite— a temporary order is critical because it is enforceable. Without a custody decree, the police won't get involved to help you retrieve your children. Your first step should be to seek a temporary order as quickly as possible with an injunction against removing the child from the state.

Keep this in mind with a temporary order: If the arrangement is successful, you may be stuck with it, so make sure it's what you really want. Courts are reluctant to disturb the status quo. The longer the temporary agreement is in effect, the easier it is for a court to make it permanent. If it's an arrangement you find intolerable but your husband likes, he has a powerful incentive to delay reaching a permanent decree or negotiating a revision. The temporary decree gives him leverage that he can exploit to gain other concessions or just to torment you. That means you have to be very careful about how the temporary order is written and not sign anything that you couldn't live with for a long period of time. Of course, if you have never been through the custody process before, you may not know what you can or cannot live with.

Remember, it's usually easier to increase the time a child will have with his father than to take it away. Some mothers decide to give their ex-husbands more time with the kids than they might ordinarily want. Why? If they were the one to end the marriage, they may feel guilty and want to try to minimize the trauma for their husband and child. Or the men may agree to give them more money temporarily in exchange for extra hours with the children. Or they may not understand that temporary arrangements can last a long time. Don't cut this deal unless you are comfortable with the arrangement because it is unlikely your husband will want you to have the children more or give up some of his own time. Also, if you agreed to a particular set of terms, you may have a more difficult time explaining to a judge why your original agreement should not be continued.

Permanent custody is the final custody agreement. It is usually granted when the marriage is legally over, after a hearing in which a judge listens to the complete custody case or after you and your ex-husband agree that your arrangement is working and should be entered as a permanent order.

WHAT DO KIDS THINK?

Young children should never have the responsibility of choosing where to live. However, listening to your child's wishes can be helpful in coming to terms with your custody situation. Here are some insights from children about their arrangements:

Sole Custody

Nancy, age eight, lives with her mother and spends every other weekend from Thursday to Monday with her father. Both parents are remarried.

"I like having four parents. There are four people who love me instead of just two. I don't like that I don't get to be with my parents every day. I'd like to be at my dad's more. My sister and I miss him. It's really confusing. On Sunday nights, it's difficult to make the change. I miss everybody in my dad's house, especially my baby brother and sister [stepsiblings]. My parents say about each other: 'I don't like them anymore.' If I could change anything about the arrangement, I would like to get my parents to be friends at least."

Molly, age sixteen, used to live one week with each parent but now stays exclusively with her father.

"At age eleven and twelve, I didn't have strong feelings about the custody arrangement. But as I got older, I had more problems around school. I wasn't as organized. I had to carry everything back and forth between the houses and I'd forget my books. I didn't have a computer in one house and did in the other. It became hard to keep track of where I was. I carried a pager because it was confusing for my friends to figure out where I was when. This past year, I decided I didn't like the arrangement anymore and wanted to live with my father. My mother contested custody, and my lawyer listened to me and helped me to be with my dad.

"I have a lot of guilt feelings about not living with my mother. A friend of mine who lives in Maryland has a mother in Missouri. They fought and my friend moved to Maryland to live with her father. She's not as upset as I am because I live close by to my mother. It's different when your mom is in the same state and you don't see her.

"How my parents deal with each other has made a difference. They play games with each other and it ends up affecting my siblings and me. My parents put me in the middle, but they don't see it. They fight in front of me and say negative things about the other to us. What I need to know is that there is a person there for *me*."

Joint Custody

Dave, age nine, and his twin brother Pete spend one week with their mother and one week with their father. His father remarried and has two stepchildren.

"Sometimes when I want my dad and I'm at my mom's house, he's not there. When I want my mom and I'm at my dad's house, I don't have my mom. I don't like it when I change houses all the time. I change beds and have to pack. When I'm at my mom's house, my friends are too far away and can't come to play or vice versa at my dad's. I have two different sets of clothing and different toys, although I bring a lot of them back and forth. My mom is not remarried. It's quieter there."

Pete has the identical setup as his twin but a different view of the situation.

"I like that I get to see my mom and dad. This is fair because I get to spend equal amounts of time with them. There is a set schedule and I know exactly what's going on. I like to play and talk to the other kids [stepsiblings] when I'm at my dad's. When I'm at my mom's, I get a break from talking so much because it's only me and my brother."

What Two Siblings Have to Say about Split Custody

Diana, age thirteen, lives with her mother in Rhode Island. Her brother Mark, fifteen, lives with his father in Wisconsin. Both used to live with their mother, but when Mark was a freshman in high school, he decided he wanted to be with his father.

This is Diana's view of how split custody has affected her relationship with her brother. "This arrangement has been bad for our relationship and made us farther apart. I don't know as much about my brother as I used to, and that makes it hard to relate to him. We used to listen to the same music, but now we don't share anything in common.

"I hardly ever see him in the summer, because we'll switch. I'll go to my dad's and he'll come to my mom's. Some vacations overlap and some don't, depending on our school schedules. But this Christmas we didn't even spend together. My brother decided he wanted to stay with my dad and I wanted to be with my mom.

"We don't even fight as much as we used to which isn't even a good sign and is really sad. I actually miss the fighting! That's basically proof that we're drifting farther apart. Now if we disagree, he'll just say, 'Whatever.' "

Mark's perspective: "The arrangement has brought us closer because I can't argue with my sister that often and will forget about what we argued about more easily. I already know her, so it's not like I need to get to know her again. I do get to see her often enough.

"Naturally, I wish my parents wouldn't have divorced, but the situation has worked out pretty well. I had the option to go to Illinois.

I felt like Dad expected me to, and I didn't want to disappoint him and he had lived alone for so many years. It was only fair, and I didn't mind. I also get to see my grandparents a couple of times a week and I wouldn't have gotten to know them if I had stayed with my mom. I wouldn't say one place is better or worse. I get to see Mom enough. I'm used to living with one parent instead of two, just this time it's a different parent.

"It's a little bit weird, like having two separate worlds, but it's worked out and given me more variety."

Once you understand the different types of custody, the pros and cons of specific arrangements, and the impact they may have on your children, you will be better able to decide what you want.

Better Watch It! Risk Factors for Women

Work, sex, meetings, baby-sitters, and moving because of a job offer all sound like normal parts of a normal family life and career. They are, except when you are separated or divorced. That's because many of these everyday activities can be viewed negatively by the courts, especially if you are a mother.

If you wanted to play it really safe, you would never get involved in another relationship, take a vow of celibacy, turn down work that interfered with your children's lives, dismiss the idea of retraining or reeducating yourself, and not move out of state, even if it meant bettering your life and your child's.

When you fight for custody, these choices are serious. *They can make the difference between winning and losing your children.* Divorce doesn't have to mean that you stop living. You can get involved in a new relationship, move out of the neighborhood or state with your children, and have a good job. But you better know what to do, and when to do it, if you want to win custody and keep it.

Being on your best behavior is essential. Even if you win, you will still have to be on guard. Why? Fathers can and do haul mothers back to court and demand a change of custody. You are never safe from that threat, so you will need to conduct yourself defensively—that is, as though any action you take could cause your former spouse to bring his own custody action. It may sound paranoid, but in today's divorce climate, it's just playing it safe. It bears repeating: Custody arrangements can be, and are, challenged.

The unfair truth is that women have to be more careful than men, behave impeccably, and expect to be studied in a way that their ex-husbands and nondivorced female friends are not. Men and women are theoretically treated equally by the courts, but there is often a bias against females when it comes to sexual conduct and the pursuit of a demanding career.

Think twice before you do anything that could be twisted or turned around in court. As one appellate judge confided, "Judges have a moral code that exists only in heaven." Something that may be appropriate when you are not in a custody contest may get distorted so that even the most innocent of actions or relationships may be fodder for your ex-husband and his attorney. Going out with friends could be labeled "ignoring the children," volunteering to help a coworker on a project could be misconstrued as "staying at work for romantic reasons," and helping a friend move rather than taking your child to baseball practice could be termed derelict in your duties as a mother.

Divorced mothers have choices they have to make on a daily basis. Whether it's deciding to let their new boyfriend sleep over, leaving the children home alone briefly, or taking a new job that might lead to longer hours, *your main concern must be how it will look to a conservative judge*. If you have any doubts, don't do it! Think about what constitutes a "fit" parent, and don't do anything that could prove you unfit.

During or after divorce, if you have to ask, "Should I or shouldn't I?" err on the safe side. The judge who hears your case might be old-fashioned. So you may need to give up some things in your life, or low-key them, if you want to prevail in court.

What kind of things? Today, the largest risk factors for women are new partners, heterosexual or lesbian; relocating to another area of the state or part of the country; a job that requires long hours; and allegations by an ex-husband of physical, sexual, or emotional abuse of the children at the hands of you or your lover.

Some judges believe mothers belong at home or disapprove of extramarital sex and will rule for the father regardless. You may get stuck with one of these jurists. You have to take control of the things *you* can—your behavior and actions, your boyfriend's or new husband's—to get the best outcome possible.

To fight against these biases, you must have a lawyer who will be a fierce advocate. Regardless of what charges are flung at you—you are an unfit custodian because you have a boyfriend, you are selfish because you want to move, you are neglecting your children because you work—he or she must go to bat for you and convince a court of what you were *really* doing, and that it's in the best interests of your child to live with you.

What do judges want? Some of the factors that are typically weighed in a custody decision include: the parents' ability to provide stability and continuity for their child; what arrangements the parents have requested; the child's preference, provided he is at least age twelve; the parents' lifestyle; their mental and physical fitness; and their history or potential for domestic violence. Other considerations by the courts may be their willingness to share their child with their former spouse, the quality of the school near each parent's house, the availability of medical care, the child's ability to adjust to a blended family, the emotional bond between the parent and child, and the age and gender of the child.

Courts want to know which parent has been the mainstay in the house: who the child calls in the middle of the night, who listens to her problems, who shuttles her to appointments, after-school activities, and religious training, who helps with homework, attends school functions, and cheers or coaches at sports and social events. The parent who fits this bill and encourages the child's development and well-being will likely be the one the court determines serves the child's best interests. "When deciding custody, I look at the motives," said one Midwest judge. "Why does the dad want to contest custody? Is he trying to get something back from his ex-wife or use the children as weapons, or are his purposes altruistic?"

You Should Worry About Losing Custody If . . .

1. You suffer from severe depression or mental illness.
2. You have a drug, alcohol, or gambling problem.
3. You work long hours and your ex-husband has a more flexible schedule.
4. You refuse to share the children.
5. You bad-mouth your husband to your kids.

6. Your boyfriend or new husband has a terrible or inappropriate relationship with your children.
7. Your adolescent child expresses an interest in living with Dad.

KAREN'S CUSTODY STORY

Karen and Mike are divorced and have joint custody of their daughters, Maggie, nine, and Vicky, six. The children are with Karen during the week and stay with their father, the owner of a real estate firm, every other weekend and one night during the week. Karen works full time as a nurse on different shifts each week. When they're not in school, the girls are cared for by a live-out baby-sitter. Karen has been living with her boyfriend Tom for eight months; they plan to get married. Tom has a loving relationship with the girls and takes them to the movies, attends their ballet recitals, and goes to many of their soccer games.

At first, Mike was pleased that Tom took an interest in his daughters, but now he feels his role in the family is being usurped. Of course he wants Tom to be good to his daughters, but he's also jealous.

Tom would occasionally massage Maggie's shoulders at her soccer games. At one game she pulled a leg muscle, and Tom rubbed her upper thigh. Mike attended the game and was angered by Tom's behavior. He believed this type of touching was inappropriate.

Mike became dissatisfied with his custody arrangement and went to court to obtain physical custody of the girls during the week. He could not argue that Tom was too nice because that wouldn't work. He said Karen was openly displaying affection in front of the girls, even being provocative, by engaging in prolonged kisses with Tom, thereby providing an unhealthy role model. Karen didn't see it that way and thought she was showing the girls they could have healthy, affectionate relationships with men even if the relationship with their father had failed.

Mike charged he was better able to provide a nurturing and stable environment for his daughters. He claimed owning his own business allowed him more flexible hours for child rearing than Karen. He said her job as a nurse with different shifts had locked her into full-time, inflexible hours. To better his position, Mike said that Tom had touched

Maggie inappropriately. This allegation put Karen on the defensive and placed the burden on her to disprove the charge.

The judge ruled that the children should live with their father during the week and spend alternate weekends with Karen. He felt that her job left her with no flexible hours. On the other hand, Mike's offer to tailor his schedule around the children's needs impressed the judge. Although Karen's new boyfriend could help out, she lost that advantage by being too "physical" with Tom. On top of that, Tom's conduct led to an allegation of inappropriate touching. Even though jealousy might have been the motivating factor to seek primary physical custody, it shows how easily the facts can be slanted to one side's favor. The judge thought that Karen's cohabiting was a bad influence and showed she was not putting her children first. Tom did help pay the rent and was home for the children sometimes when Karen was not, both points in her favor. But these points did not outweigh the living together, open affection, and inappropriate touching issues.

Your job is to make sure only the positive stands out in a courtroom. Karen needed to be more conscious of what the courts view as factors that make a "good" mother and those that can lead to losing custody. If she had known the courts would hold her unpredictable work schedule against her, she would have considered another job or at least a regular shift that would have provided her with more time every day at home when the children were there. She would have had a talk with Tom about the court's take on being affectionate with her and her children.

If you want to win primary custody, keep these risk factors described below in mind.

POTENTIAL RISK FACTOR: WORKING WOMEN

The message from the courts to working mothers is clear: You are entitled to your own career as long as it doesn't affect your ability to care for your children. If a father can convince the court that he is more available to the children than the mother, then he stands to win.

The good news is that every custody case is supposed to be determined by "the best interests of the child," which means the courts can't deny custody just because a mother works. In fact, most states have laws that are "gender-neutral." Legally, the parents enter a custody dispute with equal chances. In reality, however, courts will scrutinize a woman's work schedule to make sure she can still meet her child's needs or to see if her husband's schedule can meet them better. Your husband may urge you to get a job, but once you do, he can then argue he can pick up the children at day care just as easily as you. So how do you get the court to consider you the more satisfactory parent if you work?

Strategies

You have to persuade the judge that your work will not adversely impact your child so that your job will not be held against you. You must show that your work situation provides you with the flexibility every hands-on parent must have. That means getting home to help the children with their homework, providing meals, taking them to the doctor, getting them up in the morning, putting them to bed, disciplining them, and caring for them when they are sick. Maintains one family court judge, "It's not the hours of your life, but it's the life in your hours."

If your child has serious medical problems that require constant attention, whether it is allergies or eating disorders, ask your employer for a note or an affidavit stating you can take off time when necessary. One family court judge remembers a custody case where the father was a city employee who had medical benefits at a clinic. The mother didn't take the children to the clinic because she said the trip was too far. The judge ruled for the father because she felt the children's needs were not being met. As the judge who decided the case observes, "Medical care is definitely an essential issue to me. A child with a medical problem, with a speech defect or poor teeth that are not being remedied, is a negative factor. If Dad will be able to address these issues, then he stands a good chance of gaining custody."

Said another family court judge, "I like to see a child's school and attendance record to show that even though the mother works, the children are still performing as they should. For many children, a good school record is their only shot at getting a chance in life. When a child tests normally but is failing in school, this is a sign that the custodial parent is not doing a good job."

If you work, every other aspect of your life must be analyzed so you are seen as a good role model, a nurturing parent, and someone physically and emotionally available for your child. Check your work schedule to make sure there is enough good time for the children. Any independent people—teachers, neighbors, clergy, colleagues, not family members or new boyfriends—may make good witnesses on your behalf.

Something else you might try: Make a video of you and the children immersed in an art project together or sailing, let's say, that could be brought to court to show the judge. While some judges, already short on time, may get turned off by a video, photographs, or handmade drawings, some lawyers have found it is effective. The point is to convince the court that even though you work, you still make great time for the children and have a special bond with them.

"Judges have a terrible time making custody decisions and like to know that they have made the right decision," said one appellate court judge. If you are able to make them feel better by "presenting a wonderful picture," as the judge put it, it will be to your advantage. That means explaining to the court that even if you work, you will have enough energy to still read to and play with your child, help with the homework, do art projects together, or if the kids are older, shuttle them around and "be there" for them.

If you don't have flexibility at work, be prepared to show the court what alternative child care arrangements you've made. If your sister lives nearby, will she pick up the children at school if you are late one day? Courts like it when a parent has a family member, such as a grandmother or aunt, available to care for the children while you are at work. In lieu of family, courts view a loving, consistent caretaker as the next best solution. This is especially important if you travel for your work. Make sure your caretaker has a sterling record, because your husband's lawyer will point it out if she doesn't, and it will be held against you. If you can't afford in-house care, check to see if your child's school has an after-school program that would let you pay on an ad hoc basis, or if there is a community or day care center with a similar arrangement. But realize that a lot of judges don't like the sound of day care, so you might want to think about finding a different arrangement, at least while the custody issue is pending. That probably seems ridiculous in light of recent studies, which show that children exposed to day care fare just as well socially and academically as their stay-at-home counterparts. But judges are not always au courant with child development.

Others with whom your children will be interacting in both households will also be judged by the courts: your new husband, his children, your ex-husband's girlfriend or wife, and her children. If you work and your ex-husband has a girlfriend who might care for your children, you will want to investigate her character and size up her ability to take care of your children. Does she behave in any way that could prove her unfit or make her less likely to provide a secure environment for your children? (A detective may be in order for this one.) Your chances of gaining custody are riskier if you work full time and your ex-husband has remarried a woman who is not employed.

Warning to Working Mothers

- **Never leave a child alone when you are at work unless it is age-appropriate.** Make sure you err on the overprotective side to show your exquisite care of your child. A court could consider you derelict in your parental duties if you leave your son or daughter unattended. While youngsters vary in their maturity, and some younger children may be capable of staying by themselves briefly, there is a general rule of thumb: Children eleven years of age or older may be left alone for up to a couple of hours but not for longer stretches of time, such as when they're home sick from school.

   Many experts don't recommend leaving children ages twelve or younger at home alone at night. If you do have a thirteen- or fourteen-year-old stay home at night, don't come in too late. Of course, some fourteen-year olds are also immature and not ready to be left alone. Then they shouldn't be. Children of any age who are fearful should have a baby-sitter.

   It's possible for a well-adjusted child who had no problems staying alone to suddenly feel scared. The uncertainty and stress of a divorce, coupled with a contentious custody case, can do that. Be sensitive to your child's needs. Having fearful children leads to insecurity, which could be interpreted by the courts to mean you are not nurturing or have created an unstable environment for your child.

- **Make sure your paycheck will cover child care costs.** If you are retraining for a new job to become a beautician, going to school to become an emergency medical technician, or pursuing an advanced degree, then you will probably be able to make more money in the long run. The courts will most likely see your work situation as a plus, and even if you're not making much money now, will not use your present circumstances against you. If, however, at the end of retraining or reeducation you still won't be able to pay child care costs, you might want to reconsider your career move. Any job that includes medical insurance might be an important factor in a custody suit if your ex-husband doesn't receive medical benefits. Usually, the parent whose job covers medical benefits will be ordered to pay the costs of the children's medical insurance.

· **Cut down or cut out other aspects of your life that might impinge upon your ability to spend time and maintain the "proper" contact with your child.** Try not to schedule many after-work meetings which would take you away from your kids. Look at every added event or meeting, and question whether it is really necessary to attend. Keep a detailed diary of your schedule. If you can show a judge you are devoted to your children and have made sacrifices (for instance, the meetings you *did not* attend on your children's time), it will strengthen your case and protect you from the accusation that you take too little interest in your children—an easy charge to hurl at a working mother.

POTENTIAL RISK FACTOR: OTHER RELATIONSHIPS

A New Boyfriend

You have to use common sense, patience, and discretion when dealing with sex during a custody debate. "How will it look in court if I sleep with my boyfriend?" mothers often wonder and ask their attorneys. And they should, since every aspect of your life becomes potential ammunition for your husband and his attorney when custody is at issue.

You may feel sexually insecure after the breakup of your marriage, miss having a physical relationship, need reassurance that men are still attracted to you, and/or want to move on. There is no problem with any of those feelings, but they turn out to be problematic if acted upon in a way in which a court might disapprove.

Women are expected to put their children first, but everyone's definition is different. Since sexuality is such a flash point in the courts, you will need to be particularly careful that you are not charged with creating an unwholesome environment for the children. Believe it or not, you can lose custody if you have unprotected sex. How will anyone find out? You might wonder. They probably won't, but if somehow that information slips out, it can be damaging. "Unprotected sex is outrageous conduct," said one practicing matrimonial attorney and former family court judge from the Southwest. "It speaks to character, deceit, and lies. Do you want the child to be brought up this way? Unprotected sex is illustrative of that character."

There is another potential problem with boyfriends: A mother can be so wrapped up in her relationship that she doesn't attend to the needs of her child. Not paying emotional attention to your child could be a custody risk factor, and you need to be aware of it.

Strategies

To appear faultless, think about not having a man in your bed when you are going through a custody dispute. As one Pennsylvania judge candidly advises mothers, "Refrain from sexual activity during a custody battle. Be like Caesar's wife: above reproach. A woman has to have an aura of sanctity." This advice also applies if you think your ex-husband, who shares custody with you or is the noncustodial parent, may want to seek primary custody.

In determining custody, a mother's sex life is usually weighed so that if she is perceived to be harming her children's healthy sexual development, it's a major strike against her. Repeat: A woman's sexual behavior is not always judged by the same standard as a man's. Said one Southwest court of appeals judge who rules on custody cases, "From a practical standpoint, women today are having sex as much as men. It's part of life. But judges have their own sanctimonious ways. A judge can have a girlfriend and screw around but then come to court and be totally outraged when a woman is having an affair. Even though everyone knows that openness in sexual relations is the thing today, we still have a world where judges put a standard on women that is different from that for men." One judge from the South explained why he thought male overnight visitors were more a problem than female: "There's no question mothers get hit harder than dads on overnight visitors. A child is more likely to be harmed by an unrelated male than female. There is a perception by the courts that men are capable of doing more damage to a child. Therefore, mothers should be pure and careful!" And yet another opinion from the bench, this time from a former female family court judge: "A man could go out with a twenty-year-old belly dancer and it would not be difficult for him to retain custody. Hopefully, with more women getting on the bench, things will change."

If you are going to have a new partner sleep over, save it for when your children are out of the house. Typical visitation gives your ex-husband every other weekend with the children, so plan your rendez-vous then. (In some states, overnight guests of the opposite sex are not permitted when the children are home.)

Even if the children are sleeping, they could wake up, come into your bedroom, and then tell Daddy. (Remember *The Good Mother*?) They could think you were having sex when you were just sleeping. Regardless of its veracity, the report could trigger a lawsuit.

The longer your relationship with your boyfriend, the more accepting the court is likely to be. But judges look anything but favorably on a succession of male "roommates."

Here are some questions to ask yourself, because your husband's lawyer certainly will. Again, the point is to come across as a thoughtful adult in a long-term relationship rather than as a promiscuous woman.

- **How long have I been separated?** You risk the judgment of the courts if you jump into bed with any guy, but particularly if you start sleeping around immediately after you separate. Your conduct could be viewed as impulsive, reckless, and irresponsible, especially if it's done in your home with the children present. If you are having an intimate relationship, you still want to be discreet and not share that with many others.

- **How long have I known this man?** Many judges consider six months a respectable amount of time. Others believe you should not be intimate with a man until you are legally divorced. Again, there are no standard rules.

- **Is my ex-husband sleeping with someone, too?** If the answer is yes, is it when the children are around? You could always turn the tables on him, charging that *he* is creating an unfit environment for the children. Does your former spouse have more than one sexual partner? If you have a long-term relationship, the courts are likely to look more kindly on your sex life.

- **How old are the children?** Sexuality around younger children who could be confused about what is occurring and adolescents who are usually obsessed with sex themselves, could be viewed negatively by the court.

- **Will a live-in boyfriend hurt my chances?** Now is not the time, but if you decide to do it anyway, make sure your relationship is long-term and solid, and your boyfriend's behavior is beyond reproach. An engagement ring on your finger would not hurt because it would show commitment and stability. Living together in itself is usually not reason enough to lose custody, but it could be one of the factors. "What I look for is the impact of the new male on the child," said one judge. If the boyfriend is responsible, decent, and caring toward the children, then it will not prejudice this judge. But, he added, "cohabiting shows a total lack of discretion. Just because you are separated doesn't give you the right to live with someone else." Other judges see cohabitation as a nonissue. In some jurisdictions, court orders prohibit a parent from living with a "significant other."

A Gay Mother

Being a lesbian can be a huge obstacle for mothers seeking custody. In 1996, a Florida judge took away custody of an eleven-year-old girl from a lesbian mother and gave it to the father, a convicted killer who had murdered his first wife. How could this happen? The judge said he wanted to give the girl a chance to live in a "nonlesbian world." He ruled against the mother, even though the child had lived with her for three years. The father, now married to his fourth wife, fought for custody only after his lesbian ex-wife sued for more child support. In 1995, the Virginia Supreme Court refused to give a lesbian custody of her three-year-old son, saying that her lesbianism could negatively impact the boy.

These decisions come more than twenty years after the first documented gay and lesbian custody cases. In those days, there were a spate of custody cases where gay mothers lost and had visitation restrictions that were not imposed on heterosexual parents. These included forbidding overnights with same-sex partners, supervised visitation, and in some custody agreements, a prohibition from having a lesbian relationship if they wanted to see their children. These verdicts discouraged many gay mothers from seeking custody. Terrified that they would be cut off from their children if they went to court and lost, many settled out of court.

The attitude reflected in the recent Florida case is beginning to change, however, and lesbian mothers are getting as serious, and often equal, consideration as their straight counterparts. Many courts around the country are heeding the favorable studies on lesbian and gay parenting brought to the court's attention by attorneys hired by homosexuals. The research shows that children reared in lesbian households are not adversely affected, do just as well in school, don't have any more psychological problems, and aren't more likely to become gay adults than the children of straight parents.

A December 1996 decision by a Hawaiian circuit court judge to consider issuing marriage licenses to same-sex couples has been a tremendous boost for gay and lesbian parents. The judge said that the state could not convince him that children raised by same sex parents fare worse than those who grow up in heterosexual households. Judge Kevin Chang also wrote that allowing same sex partners to marry would help their children "obtain certain protections and benefits that come with or become available as a result of marriage." Among the marriage benefits are access to family health insurance, inheritance rights, and retaining custody if their partner dies. Whether or not Judge Chang's decision is upheld on appeal, it is certain to provide encouragement to other gay couples seeking legal status for their relationship.

Courts are increasingly deciding custody on the basis of which parent can provide a better household environment for the child, rather than on his or her sexual orientation. Today, many courts require proof that sexual persuasion is harmful to the child. Other judges view being gay or lesbian as a negative, but not determinative. That means that your sexual preference will not determine whether or not you receive custody, but the court will consider if you are generally a fit parent and the other parent is not. Still other judges flatly deny custody because of a parent's homosexuality, but they may pin it on other factors.

You and your lawyer have to know and understand the track record of the judge assigned to your case. As one Southwest judge confided, "Homosexuality is probably a factor for judges, but they don't state it." A Boston lawyer put it more bluntly: "The law is trying to appear neutral on the issue of homosexuality. You have to show the relationship would adversely impact the kids, and absent that showing, it doesn't matter. But put a sixty-four-year-old male judge on the bench whose wife stayed home raising the kids and say, 'My lesbian lover and I want to raise my ex-husband's child.' What's a judge going to think?"

Approximately forty states that have reported gay or lesbian custody decisions have based them on whether their homosexuality harmed their children. Only a few states have a virtual ban on gay parents gaining custody; Mississippi is one. Most states don't have such explicit prohibitions; however, some states won't grant custody to a gay parent but use a "best interests" test to hide the real reason. In those states, the courts might use sexuality along with other characteristics deemed to be unfavorable and declare a parent unfit. In 1995, the Virginia courts held that certain conduct (sodomy) involved in lesbianism is punishable as a felony. The courts used this criminal behavior as an important consideration in denying custody to lesbian Sharon Bottoms.

Make sure to research the custody laws in your state and know how these statutes are interpreted and applied. But remember: *The standard is supposed to be "the best interests of the child," so if there aren't other factors going against you and you can show you are able to provide a loving environment for your child, you may be okay.* If you can also prove there is no harm arising from your relationship, your sexual orientation, at least theoretically, shouldn't matter.

With the lesbian and gay baby boom of the 1980s, custody battles have expanded to include a new frontier of separating lesbian mothers or gay fathers. In these cases, the courts tend to view the situation as a dispute between a parent and a nonparent, rather than between two parents, as in heterosexual relationships.

The courts will almost always award custody to the legal parent, who will be the biological or adoptive parent. In other words, if your life partner is artificially inseminated (also known as alternative insemination) or has adopted the children, you are in the weaker legal position to win custody. If you and your lover break up and she is the biological or adoptive parent, unless you legally contest the situation, she can decide when and if you can see your child. You will have to find another way to show the courts that you are also the parent. Legally, this could be by arguing that you are in loco parentis, a de facto parent, an equitable parent, or a psychological parent. Courts will often say a lesbian coparent or nonparent has no standing or that the court has no grounds for holding a custody or visitation hearing, but that has begun to be successfully challenged.

Other custody and visitation disputes have emerged involving lesbians who have conceived with donors who had initially agreed to act as a friend rather than a parent and then changed their mind, or relatives, such as grandparents, who seek custody of their grandchildren after their own child's death, rather than allow the lover to raise the children. They would have to prove that the legal parent is unfit, which they might do by raising the issue of your homosexuality. However, if you are a good mother, you have a sound argument because a biological parent is always preferred by the courts.

Strategies

First, find an attorney who is knowledgeable about family law in this area and supportive of your lifestyle. If you have already retained another lawyer, it's a smart idea to confer with someone expert in the field of lesbian custody. You can contact the Lambda Legal Defense and Education Fund, 666 Broadway, New York, NY 10012; 212-995-8585, the National Center for Lesbian Rights, 1663 Mission St., San Francisco, CA 94103; 415-621-0674, the American Civil Liberties Union, 132 West 43rd St., New York, NY 10036; 212-944-9800; or other lesbian mothers to get a referral in your area. Cities with active gay communities also have legal clinics.

An attorney should know what strategies work and don't work in these types of cases and how to combat homophobia in the courts. He or she should be able to address and debunk gay myths: that children reared by lesbians will also be gay when they grow up, that homosexuals sexually molest children more than straights, or that the child reared in a lesbian household will suffer psychological harm. If you want to use your own lawyer and he's not familiar with the research, the material is available from Lambda Legal Defense or the National Center for Lesbian Rights.

If you are HIV positive or have AIDS, this lawyer may know the mental health professionals and physicians knowledgeable with the disease who can explain to the court if the illness will affect your ability to care for your child. Clearly, these delicate issues must be addressed by a lawyer who has experience with similar cases and knows the fears and prejudices of the court. Your attorney should be able to anticipate any custody conditions your ex-husband may want to include. These may be forbidding you to see your child in your own home, being in the company of other lesbians, or cohabiting.

To play it safe, don't hold hands with your lover in public or hug her in front of the children because it could be considered poor modeling of what some still view as an aberrant relationship. It could also reinforce the notion that gay parents are creating an immoral environment for their children. If your ex-husband is heterosexual, the courts could say his lifestyle is healthier for your child. So if you are gay, you may have to hide the fact that you are a lesbian from the courts and your family if you are embroiled in a custody contest, or you may not. But it's important to know that the court may use your homosexuality to deprive you of custody, while relying on other, less politically charged reasons for the decision.

If you are a lesbian, your lawyer might advise you to address the issue directly with the court and to portray your household as being as balanced as a heterosexual's. Like winning a suit between two straight parents, you will have to show your excellent parenting skills and dedication. You want to prove there is consistency for your child and that he is happy with the arrangement. The point you want to make is that your child's needs come before your own. Instead of spending your evenings organizing gay rights meetings, devote them to your son or daughter. You don't want to be accused of putting yourself first or branded a strident feminist. Be careful. Using your lifestyle as a political statement is a good way to lose custody. Although you may feel strongly that people shouldn't discriminate on the basis of sexual orientation, you must still behave like a sensible, levelheaded parent, not a shrill parent who has just found herself and her cause. Remember, your children are not asking to have the spotlight thrust on them because of your beliefs. They are still struggling with the breakup of their parents and the loss of their family.

Like any other dating couple, try not to have your new friend stay over when you have the children. If it's a live-in situation, you will have to make sure your partner has an unblemished past, because if she doesn't, your husband's lawyer will bring it to the court's attention.

In many ways, "selling" your alternative lifestyle to a judge is no different than any other divorce issue involving children. Your strategy is the same: to show that your children's feelings matter most to you and that you are always thinking of their needs. It's particularly important you convey this message to a court when you are in the middle of a custody battle. Your straight ex-husband will be looking for ammunition to use against you to show he is the better parent. You are already at a disadvantage if you are in front of a conservative judge.

You will have to focus on the positive aspect of your role as primary caretaker. When they consider the impact of a mother's lesbian lifestyle on her child, courts don't just have to find that the relationship has had a negative effect on the children in order to give custody to the father. They can also base their decision on myriad other factors described in this chapter.

You may want to ask your lawyer about hiring a guardian ad litem trained in the dynamics of divorce. The G.A.L. is hired by the court as an unbiased advocate for the child and will investigate and report his or her view on custody to the court. You never know which parent the G.A.L. will recommend for custody, but at least he or she can observe you and then testify that the children are not being damaged by your alternative lifestyle.

When you are dealing with adoption, in most states, only one gay parent is allowed to adopt a child. Try to have that be you. (If it's too late for this child, but you plan to adopt more children, it's to your advantage to be the adoptive parent.) If your partner is the biological parent, see if your state allows you to legally adopt your partner's biological or adopted children so that you will have the same legal rights. This is called second-parent adoption. You have to have the consent of the legal parent. Once you both adopt the child you are raising together, your child is covered with either parent's health insurance. They also have inheritance rights. Most states have no laws that address whether homosexuals can be adoptive parents, although some specifically don't allow gay partners to adopt their lover's child. If it is permitted, this is also custody "insurance" in case your partner dies.

Sometimes, the family of the biological lesbian parent who dies seeks custody of her child. There are ways to try to safeguard against this, but they are not foolproof. If you are the biological or adoptive parent, draw up a will naming your lover as your guardian. Include a document that says you believe it is in your child's best interests to remain with your partner in the event of your death. If you have AIDS, make sure you get a certified letter from your doctor stating that you are of sound mind when you signed your will in order to make a legal challenge difficult later on.

If you are the legal parent and you want your partner to be able to make major financial, medical, or educational decisions for you about your child and yourself should you become medically incapacitated, you should sign a durable power of attorney. Ask your lawyer to draw up this document. This is a legally binding document in some states, but not all. Nevertheless, it will register your intent with the courts. Request two separate documents, one for medical powers of attorney and the other for making other important financial or educational decisions. Some states mandate that medical powers of attorney be separate from other kinds. If you choose, you could list different people for different functions.

Consider establishing a trust fund for your child to show the courts you are a responsible, caring parent making a responsible, caring decision about your child's future.

You should also think about drawing up a parenting agreement with your lover in case your relationship ends. If you are the "nonparent," you are definitely at a disadvantage should you have a custody dispute. Although parenting agreements (see chapter 7) between a legal and nonlegal parent are not legally binding, they may convince a judge what your mutual child rearing intentions were before the breakup. A parenting agreement is better than nothing, and it may be added ammunition in a custody case. This would also apply to custody litigation brought by the family after you or your lover died.

If you or your partner were artificially inseminated, there are statutes that can impact your custody. This is a changing field, but currently, more than half the states have laws that distinguish between a sperm bank donor inseminated by a physician and an informal donor. A sperm bank donor has no legal parental rights or responsibilities, including custody or visitation; an informal donor, or someone you know or have chosen, is entitled to full parental rights and can call himself "Dad."

Some mothers want their child to have a father in their lives and therefore may choose a friend to be the donor and also the coparent. If you go this route, understand that this donor has legal rights and responsibilities to the child and that you will all have an ongoing relationship. In essence, you become a family even if you live separately from your child's father.

You will want to enter into a signed contract called a donor-recipient agreement with the donor. It will state his free-will decision to sell his semen and give up all parental rights. The sperm bank or physician can have the donor sign if he is unknown to you; if you know the donor, have him take the semen to the doctor and sign the contract. Whether or not a court will honor a donor-recipient agreement is unclear and will depend on the judge, because, like the parenting agreement, it is not legally binding. But it does indicate your intentions. Some experts advise drawing up a second agreement between you and the donor stating what, if any, relationship he will have with the child. It should stipulate that you have full discretion in deciding the time the donor and your child spend together. Avoid words like *custody, visitation,* and *father* so that it doesn't appear to be a parental relationship. Again, this document is nonenforceable in court, but it could conceivably prevent a successful paternity suit.

Unless you and the known donor decide to coparent, you won't want to put his name on the birth certificate. You can write *unknown* or *name withheld* in the space reserved for the father's name. If you put your lesbian lover's name in that space, it has no legal validity.

POTENTIAL RISK FACTOR: MOVING OUT OF TOWN OR STATE

Today, this is the hottest issue facing separated and divorced couples. More mothers than fathers want to relocate with their children. A custody suit is almost always brought in the home state, the place where the children live or have lived for the last six months to a year. It is also the place where judges like to see children stay, especially when they have equal access to both parents. The goal of every court is to provide children with stability, continuity, and the ability to provide a loving relationship and contact with *both* the mother and father.

You may have no choice but to relocate. You or your new spouse may have gotten a job offer in another state, or you may have to accept a transfer just to keep your present job. You also may be offered a promotion or believe that being closer to your own parents and siblings, who can help out with child care, will benefit your children. But these days, if you do want to relocate with the kids, there is no guarantee you will get primary physical custody, especially if your ex-husband plans to stay in the same neighborhood, town, or school system and he has a good relationship with the children. Judges weigh heavily the rights of fathers, the impact of separating from the children and losing that steady, ongoing relationship, and the child's loss of continuity in his or her community. As one judge from the Southwest stated, "Courts favor stability. Sometimes the emotional stability with one parent may outweigh the stability of the location. But sometimes the child's whole world is that one location, and then I am extremely reluctant to have the child move." Said a judge from Illinois, "I consider whether moving will increase the experience for the child, whether it is beneficial, and if there will be meaningful visitation. It's hard to have meaningful visitation when you live four hundred miles away. A person can't be chained to the community, but if a mother falls in love and wants to move, she may have to make a choice."

The old rationale was that if the mother was moving because of a better job, life, or support system, she would be a happier person and a better mother and the children would be happier. Today, the courts are concerned about the father's happiness, too.

"I like to see parents who can support their move long before a court date and are not doing it for revenge following a divorce," said one Mid-Atlantic judge. "The truth is, a move is a radical change for a child. That child's life will never be the same. Even if the child were to spend the summer with his remaining parent, it's different than living in the same city. Schedules change, routines change, and it's difficult to lead a normal life when a child is merely visiting the other party for short periods. By the time a case goes to court, the party who is moving should present options for visitation for the other parent."

Realize that if you are successful in relocating with your child, a judge may penalize you financially and reduce your child support. That's because your husband could argue that his expenses will rise. When you and the child lived close by, it was just a local call to keep in touch. Now he has to make long distance calls, and perhaps take a plane and sleep in a hotel to keep up a close relationship with his child. Judges are increasingly agreeing with this argument and awarding reduced financial support.

In relocation cases, attorneys are finding that there can be a lawsuit in two states regarding custody. How? Let's say you and your husband were divorced in Utah, where you were awarded sole custody. You move with the children to Colorado, and two years later, your ex-husband decides he wants custody. Your children have friends in the new state. They're enrolled in school and activities there. You argue that Colorado should have jurisdiction because it knows your child better than Utah.

A federal statute called the Uniform Child Custody Jurisdiction Act, enacted in all states and the District of Columbia, addresses the issue of jurisdiction and when a court may make a custody determination or defer to an existing decree from another state. This uniform law helps standardize custody determinations. Here's how it works: The child must have lived in the home state for six months prior to the custody determination or until a parent wrongfully removed or retained a child in another state. (A judge will not make the new state the home state if it is done for devious purposes.) The child must have significant connections in the state with such people as teachers, grandparents, and doctors. (Again, you can't unlawfully remove a child from one state to create significant connections in another.) Another provision of the UCCJA stipulates that even if you have not lived in a state for six months, that state could have jurisdiction if the child has been abandoned or is in danger of being abused or neglected. Only one state can make a custody decision. So once a state awards custody, another state is expected not to interfere.

You may wonder how this affects you. The UCCJA is helpful in case you have custody problems later on. It will tell you where custody can and should be resolved. It also means you don't have to keep running back to the home state where the original custody decision was rendered if you now have your roots in say, Colorado.

In what may prove to be a significant decision in relocation cases for single women, a California family law commissioner in 1997 ruled that an unmarried mother who wanted to move to Massachusetts to reclaim a full scholarship at Harvard University could take her infant daughter with her. Gina Ocon, who was on welfare, had planned to bring her daughter Bailey to Harvard with her, but her former boyfriend, Tommoaso Maggiore, who also lived in California, had sought custody of the child, arguing that Ocon would not be able to juggle both the baby and her workload. Her lawyers claimed it was in the best interests of the child for her mother to earn an Ivy League degree and that Ocon's boyfriend, a waiter, did not pay court-ordered child support, abused alcohol, and was immature. Maggiore's lawyer argued that Bailey should stay near her grandparents in California and that Ocon could attend a college closer to home. Ocon's attorney said that forcing her client to stay in Lakewood, California, where she and the baby lived with her mother, would relegate her to a life of menial work. Ocon claimed she could not afford medical insurance or day care for her baby. The family law commissioner awarded physical custody to Ocon and generous visitation to Maggiore.

Strategies

Do your homework before any move. Since judges don't like removing children from a situation and location that is working, you will have to prove the move will be a positive one for them. You will have to research the potential advantages of the proposed move from an economic, social, and psychological standpoint. Ideally, you want to be able to show that the move will substantially improve the quality of your life and that the benefit will be passed on to your children. Again, the move must be in "the best interests of the child." You probably don't want to tell your ex-husband you are considering a move until you have done that research.

CHECKMATE

- Have you done your homework on the school system in the new area and does it compare favorably with the one your children currently attend? (If not, you might have a hard argument to make if your husband brings it up.) Did you get a copy of the curriculum? If your children are junior high or high school age, ask for a copy of the new school's college acceptance rate and the students' national test scores. You will want to be able to show a judge the school is solid, and how much you are thinking of your child's welfare.

- Do you have a list of extracurricular activities offered in the new location? If your daughter plays soccer, get information on town teams and deadlines for registration that you can give to the judge.

- Do you have pictures of the new apartment or house? Find out how many other boys on the street are your sons' ages. Know neighborhood demographics. How close is the nearest park and library?

- Come to court armed with the name of the pediatrician and dentist your child will see and his or her credentials. If your new job has a medical and dental plan, supply a list of doctors and dentists.

- Have you made arrangements or thought of how your ex-husband can visit the children? Reminder: One of the criteria that a parent is fit to be a primary physical custodian is that he or she will provide access to the other parent. If you want to relocate, you must come up with an alternate visitation plan. Offer to drive the children to visit their father or, if it's too far, have travel arrangements worked out. Judges tend to deny custody to a parent who is unwilling to share the children. Show you are not one of those.

Moving away without the children, even briefly, can imperil your custody case. You may feel you need time alone to reclaim your life and retrench so you can be a better parent. It's unlikely the courts will see it that way. They may view this action as running away from your family and abandoning your children. Your husband's lawyer will certainly claim this. "I take into consideration who is there for the child and who isn't," said one Texas judge, whose state is one of only two in the country that has jury trials in litigated custody cases. "If she changes her mind and comes back, juries and judges tend to hold it against her."

POTENTIAL RISK FACTOR: ALLEGATIONS OF ABUSE

The courts are witnessing tremendous increases in the number of allegations of sexual and physical abuse in custody cases. The National Committee for the Prevention of Child Abuse reports that more than 90 percent of abuse charges can be substantiated, except in divorce and custody cases, when the figure of unproveable claims jumps to as high as 70 percent. Psychologists have identified a phenomenon called Sexual Abuse In Divorce Syndrome (SAID), which they use to determine whether the charge is real or trumped up in contested custody contests. Some of the factors used to identify SAID include: a bitter custody and divorce battle; no allegations of abuse during the marriage or in court proceedings; a new, serious relationship for the father; and a hostile relationship between the parents. If the child acts relaxed around the alleged perpetrator, volunteers information about the abuse before being asked, or uses vocabulary and phrases that are too sophisticated for her age, then it's possible the claims are false.

While you are unlikely to be accused of sexually abusing your child, you never know what your husband can say if he wants to play dirty. It's possible he could claim you physically abused your child. Allegations of abuse frequently come up when fathers don't get as much visitation as they would like, after their ex-wives report the child support checks are late, or when they want sole custody.

In today's custody climate, normal behavior in an intact marriage may suddenly become "abusive behavior" when divorce and children are at issue. If you spank a child, it can be called "child abuse." Permissible displays of affection, such as hugging a child, may be miscon-strued or mislabeled in a bitter dispute, making the parent who is acting "incorrectly" suddenly look unfit.

The way the system now works in many states, anyone, a disgrun-tled father included, can pick up the phone and call the Department of Social Services and anonymously report that he or she has heard some-one is beating, neglecting, or sexually abusing a child. Neglect could mean the accuser's ex-wife went away for a weekend and had the chil-dren stay with a baby-sitter or left older children home alone for a short period. At times, it has meant the mother was fifteen minutes late to pick up the child at school and he had to walk home.

Remember that children are impressionable, and the difference be-tween roughhousing, let's say, and abuse can become blurred. A child may want to please the parent who is claiming abuse. Youngsters have been known to say that the other parent hit or punched them in the stomach when the adult was merely playing or horsing around.

Also, be careful about any male you bring into the house. He must be told how to behave around the children because his conduct, in-nocent though it may be, could prompt your ex-husband to claim your new partner acted improperly toward the children or that the two of you exposed them to immoral or violent conduct. Speak candidly with him and tell him the passion will be kept in the bedroom and to keep the disciplining of your children to you. Let your husband or boyfriend know that even if he grew up where kissing on the lips or spanking was acceptable, he should only kiss your children on the cheek or give them a hug, and never, ever touch them on any part of the body considered sexual: the breast, behind, thighs, or genitals.

Mothers also hurl abuse charges when they are not merited. (Of course, if you suspect they are true and/or so does your pediatrician, you need to report your husband to the district attorney's office or your state Department of Social Services—look in the White Pages under "District Attorney" or in the Government Pages possibly under "Abuse" or call information—as well as find a lawyer well-versed in the field to represent you.) If you or your new husband make these claims just to harm the other parent's reputation, to get your ex-spouse out of the marital home, or to win a custody battle, it will backfire and cause you to lose custody. More importantly, your children will suffer.

Strategies

Many times, false allegations are caused by frustration. For that reason, an equitable custody arrangement is the best insurance against outrageous allegations. Once an arrangement is in place, don't do anything that will set off your ex-husband. Don't withhold the children, even if he is late with child support payments. (You are not legally entitled to; you can lose custody for this behavior.) And don't go back to court unless there is a serious, legitimate issue that can't be worked out any other way. Judges have enormous workloads and don't like being bothered with matters that are mundane or petty or could be dealt with amicably out of the courtroom.

If your husband makes claims about abuse, you are likely to be in a situation where it is your word, or your boyfriend's or new husband's, against your ex-husband's. To soften the impact of these allegations, get some type of independent verification that these charges of abuse are manufactured. Make sure the mental health professional you see has experience in abuse. An abuse investigation will consist of separate interviews with you, your husband, and each of you with your child, a meeting with both attorneys and court staff to discern where the case stood when the allegations were brought, and interviews with doctors, teachers, friends, and others who have recently spent time with your child. The investigator will probably meet twice alone with your child. If the charge seems serious enough, the court may prohibit you from seeing your child during the investigation. In that case, ask for supervised visitation so you can try to maintain your relationship.

Take your child to the pediatrician. If the kids are age three or older, get them counseling with a therapist familiar with custody issues who can provide independent, objective documentation that the abuse is not happening. Skilled mental health experts trained in play therapy can work with very young children. The purpose of hiring a therapist should be that it is in the child's best interests, rather than simply as ammunition in a custody battle. Remember that refuting false charges of abuse *is* in your child's best interest.

Once the allegations are proven false, your husband will be at a legal disadvantage. What judge will think your spouse has his child's best interests at heart if he has concocted these twisted charges? If he does make accusations and you can refute them, you have a better chance of prevailing. Criminal charges can also be brought against him.

Ask your lawyer if a court-appointed guardian ad litem or an expert witness should be brought in on the case. These experts will be able to evaluate your children and your family environment. In particularly bitter custody cases, another attorney may be hired to represent the children. This may be merited in cases where there may be false allegations of abuse.

POTENTIAL RISK FACTOR: LEAVING THE FAMILY HOME

In awarding custody, judges usually look to see who historically has been the primary caretaker, including which parent has stayed in the family home, the place most familiar to the children. If you leave and your husband stays with the children, the court could consider your spouse to be the de facto primary custodial parent.

Strategies

If at all possible, your children should stay in the family home with you so you can be considered the primary physical custodian. If your husband also insists on remaining in the house, be as civil as possible, but use your knowledge of his weaknesses to make him feel uncomfortable and unwelcome. Your goal is to get him to vacate the house. You can explain to him that if he leaves the house, the situation may calm down and be less tense. He may agree, not realizing he is making an unwise legal move.

Of course, it's not always possible to stay in the family house for financial or safety reasons. If the living situation becomes intolerable, your second choice is to take the children and get out. You have a much stronger chance of gaining temporary custody if the children are with you. But even then, you will have to give the court a compelling reason for removing them from the marital home. If you leave them with your husband, be prepared to have a difficult time convincing the judge that you did not just walk out. If you fear violence, take your children with you to a shelter or new residence, but make sure you file a custody petition simultaneously and, if necessary, a protection order, so that you are not accused of concealing or abducting the children.

A custody petition is a legal document you file with the court. It requests legal confirmation or validation that you are the child's guardian. If you have a custody order, you can ask police to help you get your child back.

POTENTIAL RISK FACTOR: NOT SHARING THE CHILDREN

"The number one way to lose custody," claims a Wisconsin judge, "is to not respect the other party's rights." Judges don't want to hear that a parent is uncooperative around issues relating to the children. When there is evidence of this, they will frequently rule against the obstructor. Uncooperative parents are many judges' pet peeve.

If you interfere with visitation, you can also be held in contempt of court and even jailed. You could also be fined and lose custody. Your ex-husband could argue convincingly that there was a change of circumstances—parental alienation—and try to overturn your custody award (for more on parental alienation, see p. 88). In most states, withholding the child or hiding a child out of state is considered parental kidnapping and is a felony.

Strategies

Be cooperative or be willing to take the consequences. If you make it difficult for him to see the children, it could hurt both you and your children.

POTENTIAL RISK FACTOR: GIVING YOUR HUSBAND TOO MANY CHILD CARE RESPONSIBILITIES

When mothers and fathers get relatively equal scores as capable custodians, courts consider who the primary caretaker has been prior to the separation. This is considered particularly important when children are of preschool age.

Judges don't like to uproot a child from the parent who has provided the most nurturing. If that has been your husband, he has a leg up in a custody fight.

Strategies

Make sure you keep control of primary custodial activities: arranging and making the children's meals, helping with schoolwork, keeping in touch with teachers and attending parent conferences, confirming birthday party invitations and buying the present, getting involved in your child's school and extracurricular activities, and making and accompanying your child to dental and medical appointments (don't have a sitter do it if you can help it). Keep a copy of all school correspondence, even your notes on carpool arrangements for play dates. In a custody contest, attorneys will ask who does these day-to-day child chores, and you want to prove that it is you. Keeping a daily log for a couple of months of all the "jobs" and duties you perform as a mother will provide a court with this kind of reliable evidence.

If you and your husband divide activities equally and you are offered the chance to take on more responsibilities, do it. While it will be an extra burden in the short run, it will show a judge you have been the primary custodian.

Keep a calendar that records the visits between your children and your ex-husband. That way, if he claims he spends an equal amount of time with them, you have proof to refute it.

POTENTIAL RISK FACTOR: HAVING YOUR CHILD EXPRESS AN INTEREST IN LIVING WITH YOUR HUSBAND

Many judges do take this into consideration, especially when children are around age twelve or older. Boys, in particular, may decide they want full-time exposure to their fathers. Adolescent girls, who bridle at your rules, may conclude their fathers will be more permissive.

If your income is far less than your husband's, the children may think their father can offer more materially and decide his home is more appealing. In some states, judges will question the child to get a better sense of where he wants to live. If it is determined that the arrangement is in the child's best interest, the judge may agree.

Strategies

You have little leverage. Even if you believe the children would be better off with you, if they are teenagers, it will be hard to dissuade them. In this case, your smartest tactic is to remain loving and involved in their life and not make them feel guilty about their choice. It would be unnatural for you not to feel sad and hurt, but try not to act it, because it could impact on your relationship. That doesn't mean you have to pretend you are happy that they chose living with their father, but you do need to give them permission to have a good relationship with him and give the situation a chance. It frequently happens that children change their minds, and they may decide to return to you. If you have given them a hard time, they may not consider it.

POTENTIAL RISK FACTOR: BAD-MOUTHING THEIR FATHER

This is not an insignificant risk factor. Apart from being destructive and giving you little or no advantage with your children—they may eventually resent your barbs—talking disparagingly about your husband to them is dangerous. Judges don't like to hear that one parent is putting down the other. "If everything else is equal, a parent may lose custody for doing this," said one judge from New Mexico, "and women are more inclined to alienate children than men. Bad-mouthing is parental alienation. What you are doing is alienating the child on purpose. Parental alienation is perceived as a woman's weapon."

The term *parental alienation syndrome* was created by Harvard University psychiatrist Richard Gardner, who, in the 1970s, began seeing a disorder in children involved in custody disputes. It is where the child views one parent as flawless and the other as full of faults; one is idolized, the other is criticized. In 80 to 90 percent of the cases, Gardner believes the mother is the preferred parent, and the father the hated one. He attributes some of the children's attitude to brainwashing by the mother. Gardner also feels the adversarial courtroom system has made some women so desperate to win that they bad-mouth their husbands in an effort to gain favor.

Strategy

Bite your tongue! Don't make derogatory comments about your children's father to them. It doesn't mean you can't think them! Besides being bad for your child, she could repeat these statements to her father, and he could tell his lawyer.

If you have already taken one of these risks, consult an attorney to see if she can advise you on how to rectify your situation so that a judge will not feel you are trying to manipulate the court but rather trying to be a good parent.

Now that you know what the courts find offensive, make sure to behave accordingly. It will also be best for your children.

· 5 ·

Choosing a Lawyer

BELOW-THE-BELT TACTICS

Did you know that if you meet with a lawyer for an initial consultation but decide not to hire her, that lawyer is not permitted to then represent your husband? The ethical rules governing lawyers consider that to be a conflict of interest. It's not uncommon for one spouse to consult with all the "good" divorce lawyers in the area to disqualify them from representing the other. This tactic can be an expensive way to disqualify an attorney the other side might have wanted to use. The point? If there is a lawyer you are considering hiring, contact her immediately so your husband doesn't get to her first. It also works the other way. If there is an attorney in town known as the "shark" you are afraid your husband might use, consult the shark before he does.

FINDING A LAWYER

You might be impressed by a smooth-talking television attorney who is advertising his services. People can speak before a camera (or hire an excellent scriptwriter), but that doesn't make them good lawyers. It's the same with newspaper advertisements that promise to handle divorces for a few hundred dollars. It can't possibly be that great a deal! Expect extra costs that will increase your bill significantly.

There are lawyers who take on a range of legal matters, including divorce and custody, and others who concentrate in family law. Some of that may be determined by the size of your community. It is usually best to hire an attorney who specializes in family law because she will be familiar with what needs to be done. To specialize in family law can mean a lawyer's practice is primarily or exclusively made up of divorce and custody cases, or that he was accepted into an elite group such as the American Academy of Matrimonial Lawyers (312-263-6477). This organization certifies attorneys who specialize in family law. Members must devote at least 75 percent of their practice to matrimonial law for at least ten years; they may charge more than other attorneys. Six states actually certify specialists in family law. They are Florida, California, Arizona, New Mexico, Texas, and North Carolina. The requirements for specialization differ from state to state. Even if a state does not provide for specialization, an attorney may choose to concentrate in one area of law and spend most of her practice in one specific field. At the very least, you want a lawyer who is a member of the local bar association and takes continuing legal education courses (ask her).

Forget finding a lawyer through the Yellow Pages. Ask a friend who has gone through a divorce, or her husband's divorce lawyer or her friends' attorneys. Do you have a family member or attorney friend who can give you a referral? Who do you know who has recently done well in a settlement and custody dispute and ended up with the custody arrangement you want? Who were their lawyers? You might also ask your pediatrician or parents at your children's school.

You can contact the local, county, or state bar association (check with their grievance committee to see if complaints have been filed against your initial picks), the Women's Bar Association (check the Yellow Pages), or the American Bar Association's Family Law Section (312-988-5613) to obtain a list of divorce lawyers in your area. Some states allow lawyers to be certified in domestic relations law. These reference services share lawyers' names but don't offer their opinion about them. Attorneys simply pay a fee to get on the lists. It's critical that you check their credentials to make sure they are experienced in matrimonial law. You could also try *The Martindale-Hubbell Law Dictionary*, which lists lawyers by their geographic location and specialty, the year they were admitted to the bar, and their college and law school alma mater. It doesn't list any complaints against them; Martindale-Hubbell should be available at your local library. It also has an on-line Web site at <http://www.martindale.com/maps/../locator/home/html>.

If the referral does not come from a client, ask the lawyer for the names of some of her clients.

WHAT DO YOU WANT IN A LAWYER?

Having a skilled attorney is crucial. Even if all the facts are in your favor, if you have an ineffective lawyer, those facts and legal arguments will not be presented well and your risk of losing soars.

Your lawyer must gather the facts, counsel you on your options, speak persuasively on your behalf in negotiations with your spouse, and champion your cause effectively in court if negotiations fail. These tasks require a high level of competence, dedication, and experience, and define the characteristics you want in a lawyer.

The Top Four Traits Your Attorney Should Have

1. Experience
2. Skill as a negotiator
3. Good listening skills
4. Compassion

Gathering the facts requires a lawyer who listens carefully to your concerns and then digs in to find out everything there is to know about your case. The attorney you pick should never intimidate or bully you or make you feel as if you're not sophisticated enough to understand the divorce and custody process. "I wanted a lawyer who could educate me, someone I could ask questions of and who would repeat what I didn't understand as many times as it took," said one Massachusetts mother who did not use the first divorce attorney she met. "Often, lawyers assume you know what they know about the law. I wanted someone to walk me through it and be patient, like an excellent doctor. Sometimes lawyers think they're doing you a favor by being brief. They think you'll be happy they're not taking up too much of your time because it will cost less."

You want a lawyer who will listen and defer to you within reason, but will also be candid and tell you what she really thinks your chances are of winning. Use your instincts; if you don't want a slug-out custody fight or to use dirty tactics, say so. Still, your attorney may feel she has to use some strategies you don't like. Find out why she wants to do them. If you still can't sleep at night, say so. Don't forget: *You* are the client and it is *your* case and your lawyer works for *you*. Don't give up control.

You might be questioning your ability to choose a lawyer. After all, you chose your husband, and look what happened with that! But you need to use your intuition to decide whether the relationship will work. "I went to one of the most highly respected lawyers in Oregon," said the mother of two young children when she decided to leave her husband. "I had a sense from him he was much more sympathetic to my husband than to me. It didn't feel right. I thought he was someone who should represent the husband, not the wife. I asked him about money my husband had inherited when we were married. Without listening to what I had to say, he said, 'Of course you're not entitled.' He was very dismissive, and I thought it was an important issue he was unwilling to discuss. I probably wasn't entitled to the money, but I wanted to know why. I didn't hire him."

Advising you on your options requires a lawyer with experience, compassion, and wisdom. An inexperienced lawyer is unlikely to know all your options. An attorney without compassion won't understand the impact of those options on your lives, and a lawyer who lacks wisdom may get caught up in the battle of the moment without considering your family's long-term well-being.

You don't have to choose the most expensive attorney, but find someone who concentrates in divorce work and has experience. Don't be a guinea pig and hire a lawyer just beginning a divorce practice. (Realize, however, that there's no such thing as the perfect practitioner. An American Bar Association study conducted from 1981 to 1985 analyzed 290,227 malpractice claims and found that divorce lawyers with the most experience were subject to more claims than their less-seasoned counterparts.)

The lawyer you choose should not only specialize in the divorce field but know about valuing business and real estate, taxes and accounting, pension laws, and children and child support issues. The tax laws are complicated and will be an integral component of the negotiation process. Having an attorney who understands the tax implications in terms of alimony, child support, and property is critical because it will impact your divorce settlement (see chapter 9). Your lawyer may be able to access computer data banks to sniff out your husband's hidden assets or know which forensic accountants get results. If you have been a stay-at-home mother, an expert financial consultant can figure out your financial contribution to the marriage from economic data and government indicators. A forensic psychiatrist will provide a psychiatric profile of your ex-spouse or conduct an investigation if emotional stability is an issue. A skilled domestic relations lawyer will have a cadre of top-notch outside experts lined up to consult when necessary.

A good lawyer will know her way around the courthouse and the system. If she tells you that she has been offered a settlement that is at least as good, if not better, than the terms you would have been offered at trial, she will be speaking from experience and could spare you a costly and emotionally draining court contest. In bitter custody cases, a guardian ad litem may be assigned to be an advocate for the child. (This is either a mental health professional or an attorney who interviews both parents, the child, family friends, and others who interact regularly with your child. He or she will make a custody recommendation to the judge.) The lawyers for both sides must agree on a G.A.L. or the judge will assign one. "I try to make sure I don't get a G.A.L. who is a dud," said one seasoned lawyer from the Northeast. "I don't leave it up to the court which G.A.L. I get. If I have a working alcoholic mother, that's one G.A.L. If I've got a stay-at-home mom, another G.A.L. If I want custody of two teenage boys or two teenage girls, another G.A.L. I keep a bio in my computer of the G.A.L.s and know who is good for what. They all have predilections and leanings."

If your case is going to be tried in front of a master (a lawyer who hears the case before there is a trial in front of a judge) or a judge, a *really* good, experienced lawyer knows the biases of the judges and masters. They may not like women or working women or gay women, for instance. Be prepared. Know who your judge is. "How you present the case will depend on who your judge is," advises one Philadelphia judge. Your attorney should have appeared before most of these judges many times, or at least be able to tell you how specific judges are likely to react in certain situations. Some male judges, for example, may lean toward giving a father more custodial time; others may feel every other weekend is the norm. Ask your lawyer which judges are sitting in custody court. If she says she doesn't know, you're in trouble. But if she tells you the judges have just changed rotations, you know you've found someone tuned in.

In some counties you can get a case brought before a specific judge; in other jurisdictions, judges are assigned randomly and there is no way to "judge shop." But that still doesn't stop some divorce attorneys who may be unethical and feign illness or a work conflict on the day of their court case rather than go before a judge they don't feel will be sympathetic to their client. At any rate, if you can't choose a judge, your attorney will at least know which one will be presiding that day, as well as that judge's opinions on certain issues. That way you will be able to prepare yourself accordingly. If your husband's lawyer doesn't do his homework on the judge, it can put you way ahead.

A top-drawer lawyer will tell you what information she needs, as well as what you need to know. She will help you reach the decisions you must make. Of course, it's possible to have a great lawyer and still lose, but odds are more in your favor with a well-trained, seasoned advocate.

To represent you in negotiations, your attorney must, at a minimum, be articulate and convincing. The lawyer's reputation as an effective advocate should better your chances of reaching a satisfactory agreement. At the same time, his negotiating demeanor and style must be calculated to solve your divorce and custody issues. What does this mean? A shy, mealy-mouthed lawyer or a Rambo type are not your best bets. You need someone who will settle your case if you are presented with a reasonable offer and will not go to court for the sake of winning (and higher attorneys' fees). The difference between winning and losing could depend on your lawyer's negotiation skills.

To advocate for you at a trial, your lawyer needs solid courtroom skills, which usually come with years of experience. But there also must be the right chemistry between the two of you. You will have to be totally honest and not forget to mention facts that might upset you or make your cause look bad. Your conversation with an attorney is confidential because it is protected by the lawyer-client privilege. Candor and openness are essential, and because of the privilege, what you say can't come back to haunt you.

CONTACTING AN ATTORNEY

For many women, making the call to a lawyer is frightening because it is an acknowledgment that the marriage is in trouble or has ended. Don't feel guilty about picking up the phone. You should know your rights and act fast so you will be able to make educated, intelligent decisions. What you do before the divorce can have significant implications during the divorce process.

Many lawyers won't come to the telephone or will speak with you only briefly and then have you make an appointment with their secretary. Before you book the meeting, ask if it will be a free consultation or if there will be a fee (typically at their hourly rate). Both ways of doing business are standard, and just because you are charged for the first visit doesn't mean the attorney will cost more for the case than someone who doesn't bill for the consult.

Be prepared for a long first meeting. A competent lawyer will tell you about the divorce and custody laws in your state and give you an action plan. Your attorney is the ultimate strategist in your case and must fully understand all of the issues involved, from the legal to the psychological to the financial. Even though she's not your therapist, she must understand your emotional state and thinking. You can get a sense if she gets the emotional piece by the questions she asks and her responses to what you tell her. For instance, if you tell her custody is your major concern and she seems to dismiss it and steer the conversation toward the property settlement, she might not be the lawyer for you. (That does not diminish the importance of the financial aspects of the case.)

At the consult, expect her to grill you about your marriage. She is not stepping out of line, that's her job. She might ask you: What kind of personalities do your children have? What is their reaction to the separation? Do they have special needs or physical or emotional therapy that might be required? Who was the primary caretaker during the marriage? If your husband is the authoritarian type, do you think he will try to control the money? Has he discussed giving you less money if you ask for custody or contest joint custody? Did you ever have a good marriage? Why do you think the relationship dissolved? What part did each of you have in its demise? Has your husband ever threatened to steal the children? Was there violence in the marriage? Your attorney will be trying to get a psychological read on your husband and a good description of your "opponent." If you decide to retain this lawyer, she will be better able to advise you and help you combat moves your husband might make.

You must communicate what you want from the divorce. It might be primary physical custody, the marital home, including mortgage payments, a share of the investment account, certain possessions, including wedding gifts and purchases, a car since you and your husband needed only one during the marriage, or alimony. Put this down on paper, along with this question: How do I go about getting it so I can afford to feed the children, pay the bills, and carry on adequately?

Your lawyer can't work effectively for you if you don't make it clear exactly what your objectives are. You may not be clear at the first meeting, but you should have some idea of what is on your wish list.

It's difficult for a lawyer to predict how long your case will take, but it is reasonable to expect an estimate. You can be a tremendous help to your attorney. The better prepared you are, the better guess your attorney will have about cost and/or other marital assets. The lawyer will want some information about your marriage: how long it has lasted; your educational backgrounds; employment history; financial situation; and whether or not you have children. Write down your children's names and ages, the names and telephone numbers of their teachers, principals, guidance counselors, therapists, pediatrician, dentist, and favorite baby-sitter, their extracurricular activities, hobbies, religious affiliation, clothing sizes, any health problems they may have, and their likes and dislikes. You will want to include anything that will help give the lawyer a complete picture of who did what in the marriage. This information should help your cause. Your husband may say he is Father of the Year and claim he knows the intimate details of his child's day-to-day life, but if he can't tell a court the name of his child's pediatrician or his daughter's soccer practice schedule, or his son's allergies, it may show that he is not as involved with the child as he says he is. "I want to know as much about the kid as I can," said one attorney, "to test the father to see what he really knows."

You will also want to give your lawyer some financial documents. Some of these would be:

- Your social security number, as well as your husband's
- The names of the businesses and addresses where you both work
- Both of your salaries
- Work benefits for the two of you
- Assets owned jointly and separately and their approximate value
- Your debts
- Tax returns from the past few years
- Copies of the pension plan
- Income and expenses
- Any related court matters such as an abuse action or bankruptcy
- Any written documentation or retirement plans for you or your spouse

If you have it, bring your marriage certificate (necessary to file a complaint). Have the list ready so you can hand it to the attorney if she requests it. She will need it for court, so you might as well complete it. Still, not having all the items on the list should not stop you from calling.

While your attorney will not know exactly how your case will go, she should be able to give you some idea based on the facts you have given her.

Questions to Ask Your Prospective Lawyer

How long have you been practicing family law? What percentage of your work is matrimonial law? (The answer should be at least 50 percent.)

How long have you been practicing matrimonial law in this area? (The longer, the better; it could give you some idea if she is, or should be, well-connected.)

Do you represent men, women, or both, and in what proportion? (You don't necessarily want an attorney with an all female clientele. A lawyer who also has male clients will understand the issues from both sides and may be helpful in psyching out your husband. It doesn't matter if you have a male or female lawyer. What matters is the quality of that lawyer.)

What is your success rate? (If he says, "I've won every case since I started practicing twenty years ago," that may not tell you all you need to know. His record may be the result of settling all of the tough cases. What you really want to know is his success rate in cases he has tried to conclusion and the percentage of cases he has settled. A good figure would be trying close to 75 percent of all cases to conclusion and settling 70 to 80 percent.)

Do you try settling cases before taking them to court? (If she says, "Not usually," move right along. The attorney you hire should try to work out issues first. At the same time, you don't want a lawyer who wants you to settle too quickly. Ask what percentage of her cases go to court. You are looking for a low percentage unless you are convinced your case can't be settled any other way. Follow up by asking if she will be able to go to court if the case can't be settled. Find out how many cases the attorney has tried in the last year. You're looking for a low percentage, but you also need someone with real-life trial experience. If the attorney says she doesn't believe in trying these kinds of cases, it could mean she doesn't know how. It could also mean she believes that a trial is too uncertain and/or costly. A family with limited resources could end up depleting its money in a court fight.)

May I contact you, or will I have to speak with an associate? Is there someone available on weekends if I have an immediate problem? (You want to know there is someone knowledgeable on call, whether it is an associate or partner. If you want to talk to the partner only, make sure he takes weekend calls and is accessible most of the time.)

Who will be responsible for my case? (You may hire a name attorney and find out that the big gun only comes in to handle your case for the court hearing. You may not be happy with the associate and/or paralegal assigned to deal with you the rest of the time, although it may be cheaper.)

Are you familiar with tax and accounting issues? Do you work with any particular accountants or tax specialists? (This will be particularly important if your case involves property transfers, maintenance or spousal support, or business valuations.)

Do you recommend psychological evaluations when custody is contested? Do you work with certain psychiatrists, psychologists, or other mental health evaluators? (You want your attorney to be familiar with therapists' work and their biases.)

What kind of child support and property division am I likely to get? (The attorney might not be able to provide specifics but should be familiar with the state support guidelines and know ballpark numbers in property division.)

What do you think of mediation in general and for my case specifically? (You want someone who respects the process of mediation and has had experience with mediators, even if she's not in favor of it in your case.)

How much will it cost? (Your case may appear simple, but if your husband's attorney piles on the paperwork, your attorney's fees will increase. Also, find out if there is a retainer fee, or up-front money usually required by the client, and if so, how much.) How will my retainer be spent?

Do you know anything about my husband's lawyer? (The strategies your lawyer will use may depend on opposing counsel's style. *Remember: You have two adversaries: your husband and his lawyer.* Who your husband hires will also affect your legal bills. Some attorneys like to fight and escalate costs. If he's chosen one of those, expect a hike in your legal fees.)

How do you feel about asking the judge to order my husband to pay my legal bill? (You would have to prove you can't afford legal counsel, but he can.) If you don't think it's a good idea, are you willing to wait until the end of the case for your payment?

How do you bill? (Request regular, detailed statements so that you don't end up with one incomprehensible, enormous bill. Most lawyers bill monthly. Ask for an itemized monthly or bimonthly—every sixty days—bill so you know exactly what you are paying for. Once you are working with a lawyer and receive an itemized bill, read it carefully. If something on the bill doesn't make sense, ask your attorney to clarify it. If you still want to dispute it, contest the fee in a written, certified letter to your lawyer and request a prompt explanation. Lawyers do make mistakes. Keep track of all your correspondence and calls—the date, length, and purpose of each conversation with your lawyer—so you can refer to them when you check the bill.)

What will I be expected to do as your client? (There is tremendous work involved in winning a custody case. Your attorney should be clear at the outset about how responsibilities will be allocated and what information is important and what isn't.)

Have you had experience before the judges I am likely to encounter? (Knowing how to play the judge is crucial in winning adversarial custody cases, so you want someone with a good track record before your judge. If he has won before that judge, the judge is likely to have respect for your lawyer.)

After you have met with the attorney and you decide you want him to take your case, he should draft a retainer letter that explains the terms of the legal relationship, including lawyers' fees, office expenses such as telephone calls and photocopying, and fees for other services, such as filing with the court or serving a complaint. It's a good idea to interview two to three lawyers before hiring one.

THE MONEY

Mothers are often surprised to learn they will have to pay their own legal expenses. There are circumstances, however, where a court will order one spouse to pick up the legal fees of the other. This happens if you have no money and your case would be harmed if a court didn't order your husband to pay. Legally, if you can prove you are the needy spouse, you can get the moneyed spouse to foot your lawyer's bill. Hopefully, you will get enough from your property settlement to help cover those bills. You might consider requesting alimony pendente lite, or alimony pending a divorce, so that you can get some money to live on before the divorce and earmark some for your attorney's fees. Some lawyers use court-awarded legal fees as a way to run up a client's legal bills and don't act in his best interest.

Husbands may threaten a custody fight as leverage for something they want, knowing their wives can't afford large legal bills. Don't let him scare you that way. (If you can't afford legal fees, have your attorney file a motion, or a legal request, for interim legal fees that will allow you to get the case started. Your husband must be able to afford it, though.) You might want to mention that scare tactic in your motion. You also must decide if he's using custody as an idle threat or if he's serious. Another alternative is to ask your attorney to present a motion to advance legal fees against the future division of property. Sometimes this money is advanced against the settlement. With a custody modification, however, there would be no assets to divide, so you could ask your lawyer to request an allowance for fees.

Just as it is hard to estimate how much time your case will take, the cost may also be unknown. But there are ranges your lawyer should be able to provide depending on how simple or complex the case is. If it goes to trial, it could run you $20,000 or more. Generally, family lawyers charge on an hourly basis. Hourly rates differ greatly from attorney to attorney and state to state, but are typically anywhere from $150 to $350, with lawyers in urban areas charging more than in smaller towns. An attorney who specializes in divorce may charge more for that specialty than a general practitioner.

Family lawyers are not allowed to charge on a contingency fee basis, which means the bill would be based on the final outcome of the case. Contingent fee agreements are most often used in personal injury cases where a lawyer will take a percentage of the recovery as a fee. It is unethical in divorce cases to use this method of payment. However, contingent fee agreements can be used for recovery of past debts under any contracts you might have made with your husband in writing during the period of separation or even after, such as support obligations or property.

Realize that if a lawyer has to wait two hours to speak with a judge for five minutes, you pay for the waiting time (as well as her commuting time). Since there aren't nearly enough matrimonial judges for divorce cases, judges often have a staggering workload. Arguing a simple motion or having a conference with the judge can take the entire day, as your lawyer waits for your case to be called. Some lawyers bill in fifteen-minute increments. That means that even if you speak with them for only two minutes, you will be billed for fifteen minutes of their time. Check with your lawyer on that and keep track of the date and amount of time you are on the phone together.

One reason why you need to find out who (partner, associate, paralegal) will be handling your case is because divorce lawyers generally charge an hourly fee and your bill depends on your attorney's rate. If you hire a sole practitioner, or someone who is in business alone, you can assume that you will be paying for that lawyer's time only, unless she has a paralegal working with her, and the paralegal's hourly rate might be different (and lower). If you are thinking of using someone from a large firm, understand that more than one attorney may handle your case. Ask the lawyer whether she will be the only attorney on your case. If not, find out what the billable hours are of everyone who will work on your behalf. Will more than one attorney be accompanying you to a hearing or drafting documents? If so, you could be paying multiple billable hourly rates, which could add up to hundreds of dollars per hour. You are in charge, so you can insist on single coverage, and who will be present. If your lawyer will not agree to these ground rules, you may want to look elsewhere.

A Point to Remember: Fighting Is Expensive

The more you and your spouse spar, the more issues the lawyers will have to tackle, and the more it's going to cost you. Usually, lawyers are the ones who cash in on long, drawn-out custody fights.

The more experienced your lawyer is in divorce law, the less time it should take her to understand your case. Don't select someone who has to research an entire field of family law at your expense. Don't hire a lawyer who charges less but is learning on your case. That learning curve could prove costly and dangerous.

The more you can educate yourself about the issues, the more you can help your lawyer, which should translate into savings. Once you have a handle on the case, ask your attorney how she feels about mediating or arbitrating specific issues. Also discuss ways you can lower your bill. Some firms, for example, have standard divorce documents, such as separation agreements, that they customize for clients. They simply enter the appropriate information into their computer and print it out. Theoretically, at least, it saves them from having to reinvent the wheel.

A TIP ON KEEPING YOUR COSTS DOWN

If your lawyer bills in fifteen-minute increments and you need to ask her a question, go through her secretary instead. Ask her to ask her boss your questions, and have her get back to you. You could also save up all your questions and ask them all at once instead of calling each time there is an issue. Keep a list in a special lawyer notebook of the questions you want to pose and write down the answers so you can refer to them.

Besides a bill for legal services, you will be charged for other costs connected to the divorce. These might include:

· **Court fees.** It costs money to file a complaint and other documents such as subpoena fees. There may also be a charge for a court reporter or an independent expert who could testify on your behalf. A suggestion: Read all the pleadings and correspondence carefully; even the best attorneys make mistakes and your catching them can save time, money, and problems later on.

· **Fees to serve the complaint.** Sometimes a complaint is mailed to the other attorney, if there is one. But if your husband needs to be personally served, you will have to pay for a process server.

· **Expert witness fees** for such professionals as a forensic accountant, a psychologist or psychiatrist, or a pension or business valuator. You may also hire a mental health professional who will evaluate your child's emotional state and be available to testify on your behalf. If the court orders a custody evaluation, the fee may be paid for by both parents, who would split the fee unless one parent makes significantly more money than the other. If neither of you can afford the evaluation, the court will usually cover the cost.

· **Photocopying, telephone expenses, and postage.**

· **Travel expenses** if your lawyer has to travel for the case.

Retainers

Usually, family lawyers ask for an advance of fees or a retainer, generally $5,000 to $25,000, but it can be even more. This sum acts as a down payment in your case. Most attorneys charge hourly against this retainer or will bill you hourly and apply the down payment. Some lawyers will request a nonrefundable retainer. This means that regardless of how little time your lawyer spends on the case, you won't get your money back. Attorneys justify this by saying they have held time open for your case. The cost could be prohibitive. A strategy: If you want the option of getting back your money if the case is settled quickly, you change lawyers, or reconcile with your husband, place a provision in the retainer agreement stating that the unused portion of the retainer will be returned to you. Your attorney may not agree to this, and then you will have to decide what you want to do, but she might and it could save you thousands of dollars. Ask to put in a clause stating that if you contest any legal costs, your lawyer will not charge you for straightening out the bill. Also, see if you can insert a provision stating your lawyer won't leave the case if you can't pay his bill as you go along. (He may not agree to this.) Along this line, request a clause saying your lawyer will not withdraw from your case without just cause and that he must get approval from the judge to remove himself.

Make sure your lawyer sends you a retainer letter, which spells out the terms of your representation. It will state what services she will provide, how much it will cost, your lawyer's hourly billing rate and the fees of others in the firm who will work on your case, and a payment schedule. Don't sign it until you understand everything that is in it and you agree with it all. Those agreements are negotiable, so you may be able to better the terms originally offered to you.

BEWARE OF LAWYERS WHO . . .

- Ask you to sign a Confession of Judgment. This is a form that says you admit a sum of money is owed and will not contest that amount in court. Don't sign it! You lose your right to contest the lawyer's fees if you do.

- Refuse to give up your file if you decide to switch attorneys. In most jurisdictions, it is unethical for a lawyer to keep your file if you owe her money and want to change counsel. Holding on to your file could also delay your divorce action.

- Tell you they expect a bonus at the end of the case or that the fee is based on results obtained. Do not agree to this!

- Claim they are overwhelmed and overworked.

- Interrupt constantly. If they do it to you, they might do it to the judge, who could find it irritating, and it may prejudice your case.

- Act as if they are "in bed" with your husband's lawyer and are not taking your case seriously.

CHANGING LAWYERS

In general, it is best to keep the same lawyer throughout your proceedings. It will keep the costs down and provide continuity. If you make a change, you will have to essentially start your case from the beginning and bring your new attorney up to speed. She will have to establish a relationship with the experts and other witnesses.

Judges are wary of litigants who continually switch counsel. They may view this as a sign that you are taking an unreasonable position, or it may lead the judge to believe you are emotionally unstable. And remember: Judges won't want to place a child with an emotionally unstable parent.

Don't change simply because you dislike the advice you are getting. If you think your attorney is really off base, get a second opinion. But if you find the other lawyer tells you the same thing, or if during a hearing, the judge confirms the advice your attorney has given you, realize you just may not like what you're hearing. Don't shoot the messenger.

Still, you don't want to stay with a lawyer you can't stand. You will want to examine the reasons for your displeasure and make sure they are valid. Here are some legitimate reasons to consider a change:

- **Your lawyer refuses to return your telephone calls.** You have to be able to communicate with her. But you also have to be reasonable. There are times you will call and she may be on another call, in court, at a meeting, or out of town. Don't expect to be put through immediately. A good lawyer, however, will return your call promptly. That might not be until the next day. You should not have to wait several days. If you have an emergency, tell the secretary or your lawyer's voice mail that the call is urgent and you need immediate help. If she's unresponsive, let her know you expect better attention. If the situation is not rectified, start looking around.

· **Your attorney fails to meet deadlines.** There is never an excuse for a lawyer to miss filing deadlines. Doing so can prejudice your rights and put you in a poor legal position. Also, your lawyer should be prepared for meetings and hearings. If she doesn't know the facts and is not responding to letters or pleadings (court filings) filed by your ex-husband, you need to hire a new mouthpiece.

· **You are uncomfortable with your counsel and feel you can't be honest.** When you aren't candid with your attorney, it hurts your case. If you clam up and can't relate to your lawyer, you won't be able to help her get you what you want.

· **Your legal bill is going up but you don't see any progress in the case.** Ask why. There might be behind-the-scenes negotiations that could actually save you money and be getting results. But you want to make sure your attorney is not running up fees and socializing with your husband's lawyer at your expense.

· **Your lawyer is not listening to you.** She ignores your input. Of course, there may be a good reason why she wants to take a different tack, but she should explain her rationale. Without realizing it, you may be looking for revenge. If that is the case and your lawyer suggests a more sensible approach or one that is likely to bring you success, you may think she is weak or incompetent or even in cahoots with your husband's lawyer. All those things may or may not be accurate, and you have to sort them out carefully.

Don't fire your attorney until you have found a replacement. The second lawyer will want to know you are no longer working with your original attorney so you will need to hire and fire in quick succession. You will be expected to pay your first lawyer promptly, particularly if you want your new lawyer to receive the file. The first lawyer can ask for a lien on the documents, called a retaining lien. You must give written authorization in order for your first lawyer to withdraw from the case. This should be a letter stating that you no longer need her services and expect her to withdraw from the case and release your files. The second lawyer will be responsible for coordinating the transfer.

THINGS YOU SHOULD NEVER DO

Use the same attorney as your husband. He may say to you, "Listen, it will be cheaper if we use just one lawyer. I'll pay for it." It may sound like a great deal, but you will get what you pay for: *his* attorney. Get your own. You need an advocate for your side. For the same reason, don't use an attorney who is referred to you by your husband's family or friends.

Sign anything before conferring with a lawyer. You and your husband may be on good terms and he may have made certain promises to you. Even though you both have hired counsel, you may begin talking about the settlement without lawyers present. The terms may seem fair. If you haven't retained an attorney yet, make sure you wait to hire one before formally agreeing to any important terms.

Abuse your lawyer. You are under a lot of pressure and you may be frustrated by your case. But don't use your lawyer as your whipping boy (or girl). Your lawyer may not be able to work well on your behalf if you are rude or harass her. Some clients get mad because their attorneys deliver bad news. Instead, use your energy to gather the information she needs to fight for you. Yelling at times may be warranted, but think carefully before you do that. Said one female Boston matrimonial attorney, "Male clients yell at their lawyers all the time, especially if they feel their lawyer isn't giving them the kind of service they want. Why shouldn't you? It's no different than going to a car repair shop and saying, 'Take your time.' But if you tell them you need the car by 3 P.M. to do a car pool, you get it. Yelling is a form of communication and if you think it will get your lawyer to pay more attention to your case, then do it."

Sleep with your lawyer. You may be feeling unattractive, perhaps like a failure. As one male lawyer puts it, "I know many matrimonial lawyers who have slept with their clients. It's an opportunity that some men can't pass up. It's easy for an attorney to become the male figure in the woman's life. It's hard, because you're in this position of power and control." It does happen, even if it isn't supposed to. Lawyers who are sexually involved with their clients risk being sanctioned, which could include disbarment. They are ethically bound not to make advances toward a client or sleep with one, but they sometimes break that rule. Divorce is a vulnerable time, but don't even think about it! If the possibility exists, switch attorneys.

REPRESENTING YOURSELF

Statistics from local courts around the country show a tremendous increase in the number of people who represent themselves in divorce cases. Connecticut family courts have seen a 20 percent rise in this area compared to twenty years ago. A survey by a judge from Placer County, California, revealed in eight or nine out of ten cases today in several California counties, one of the parents, if not both, don't have a lawyer.

It's perfectly legal to represent yourself, but it is very difficult. Unless you have an ability to grasp legal concepts, it will be hard to master such issues as the rules of procedure, discovery, and evidence. You not only have to be able to argue your case persuasively in front of a judge but, armed with strategies and legal facts, be able to confront your husband and his attorney. It's also hard to emotionally distance yourself so you can be objective. It takes enormous discipline to act calm and rational when you are overwrought, but falling apart or blowing up will only hurt your case. The best representation generally comes from a dispassionate third party, like an attorney.

If you can, hire a lawyer rather than represent yourself in a custody case. Judges don't view it as their job to protect a party who represents himself. If you don't have a lawyer but your husband does, his lawyer can ask you whatever questions he wants and there is no one to object to those questions except you. If you don't know when to object, you might answer questions you don't have to and damage your case.

Don't consider representing yourself if you are frightened of your husband. There are legal aid groups (call your local or state bar association or community legal services) that may take your case free of charge. Mediation is another way to cut your legal costs, but again, you will want to confer with a lawyer to get some guidance.

Even if you are thinking of representing yourself, consult with an attorney to find out what your legal rights are and what action you should take to protect those rights. A couple of hours of a lawyer's time could save you a lot later. Many parent orientation and education programs required by the courts also provide legal pointers on how to put yourself in the best legal position. These programs are gaining momentum nationwide and are either offered by the courts or privately.

Some programs have what are called legal technicians. Ask your court what, if any, resources they have for parents who represent themselves and how they suggest you proceed. The bar association in Florida, for instance, provides forms for filing child support, visitation, divorce, and protective orders. In Arizona, computers in the courthouses offer all legal forms necessary for a divorce proceeding, as well as information on how to fill out the forms.

Knowing what choosing and retaining a lawyer entails will put you in a better position to decide if you want to be represented by professional counsel or by yourself.

Which Route to Take? Mediation versus a Courtroom Battle

Should you try to work it out or go for your gun? Basically, that is the philosophical difference between mediation and court. With mediation, you, your husband, and a mediator—who does not represent either of you and is neutral—craft or revise a custody agreement. The two of you make all the decisions and resolve your conflicts with the help of a mediator, often without representation by a lawyer. *The mediator doesn't make the decisions for you.* You may not get every provision you want, but you have control over the process and are forced to really think about what you are doing and why. You gather the information, evaluate your position, and then decide. And if you don't like the final agreement, you don't sign it. With mediation, you can always change your mind and go to trial.

The court route is different. Rather than your husband and you being in charge, a judge, who is a stranger, gets to decide with whom your children will live. You have little control over the outcome and have to gamble on the personal biases of the judge you are assigned. It's possible your judge has never practiced family law or had any psychology training. The process can also take far longer and be more expensive. Instead of communicating directly, you talk to your attorney, who talks to your husband's attorney, who confers with your husband, and then both lawyers talk. It's not a time-efficient approach, and the court docket may be so crowded it could take several months, or even years, before a judge hears your case.

Regardless of how well-intentioned either you or your husband are, the courtroom is adversarial by nature. It is your lawyer's job to represent you and make you look like the better parent, and it is the same for his lawyer. So, even if you and your husband want to keep the contest clean, don't count on it. Before deciding whether to litigate your case, one judge advises mothers to ask themselves, "Am I doing this because I hate the S.O.B. or because it's the best thing for my child?"

Mediation has become a popular way to resolve custody, child support, and visitation issues. In 1996, the U.S. Commission on Child and Family Welfare recommended that all courts require mediation as a way to resolve parenting disputes and craft parenting plans for the future.

CHECKMATE

- Mediation is permitted in all states, and thirty-nine states require it before going to court, while others order it in contested cases. Call your local bar association; it will be listed in the phone book.

- Twenty-seven states allow or require it as an option, and five states (California, Florida, Maine, North Carolina, and Wisconsin) order mediation if parents can't agree on parenting arrangements.

- More than half the states have some type of court-mediated program (where a mental health professional or attorney acting as a mediator is hired by a divorcing couple to help work out a settlement that is later brought before a judge) for divorce cases.

- Depending on where you live, court-supervised mediation is either confidential or a mediator can make a recommendation to the judge if a couple can't reach consensus.

- Private mediation is confidential in thirty-eight states unless you and your husband waive this or agree that the mediator can do a follow-up evaluation for custody and testify on the findings.

NOT EVERYONE IS A CANDIDATE

Mediation is not advised for all parents. If your husband has abused you or been violent, you probably don't want to mediate your case. Fifteen states either provide court waivers if there has been spousal abuse or prohibit mediation if a judge believes one of the parents or a child has been battered. Why? You could be frightened, and that fear might put you in a poor negotiating position. You might feel you have to give in to your husband's requests instead of standing up for your rights. Still, some experts believe that battered women can have success in mediation if their mediator is skilled in handling domestic violence disputes.

Mediation is not usually recommended if there is drug or alcohol abuse, mental impairment, or such a hostile relationship between you and your husband that you can't communicate or you feel bullied by him. It may be hard, but not impossible, to mediate if one of you made all the decisions, or if you have trouble expressing your needs and wishes. Don't forget: If you choose mediation, you must be able to represent yourself against your husband in his presence. You will have to deal with him face to face with no buffer, except the mediator, who is neutral and, therefore, doesn't take sides. The mediator will help you both articulate your position and address your concerns.

If you feel you are overwhelmed, overpowered, or in the weaker position, and you can't advocate well for yourself, think about bringing in an expert, such as an accountant, financial planner, or lawyer who could accompany you to one or two of the mediation sessions when the discussions are about the property settlement.

MEDIATION

Mediation is a process where you and your soon-to-be ex-spouse try to work out your differences with a trained third party. Some of these differences are how much time each of you spends with your child, where your child will live, and which of you (it could be both) makes the decisions. Other issues that are mediated include child support, alimony, and property.

Mediators may be attorneys but often have a mental health or probation background and are trained in child development and mediation skills. A mediator will be able to tell you about the laws in your state, how the court might rule on a specific issue, and the legal consequences of your decisions. He can also identify problems you might have with your custody agreement. Warning: Mediators are not required to be licensed.

You can go to a mediator to draft a separation agreement that would include your custody arrangements, or you could seek one at the time of the divorce. Mediators prefer to meet with both parents together, but when that won't work, the mediator can have separate meetings with each of you and shuttle back and forth. This is called caucusing and is not the preferred choice of mediating.

The focus of mediation is problem solving, not winning a battle. Parents meet with a mediator for as long as it takes to reach an agreement, typically four to ten sessions, for an hour or so each, over two to several months. In simple terms, the mediator will first ask you both to describe your children and the kind of custody plan you envision. You may need to compile information, such as financial records and facts relating to your children. Then you meet several more times to hash out your agreement. Once you are both satisfied with the terms, the mediator will draft the document to be filed with the court, or you can hire a lawyer to redraft the agreement as a legal document. The final agreement is a binding legal contract and can be enforced the same way any other legal agreement is.

You can use a mediator in a number of ways: for the entire custody agreement, to get you going in the right direction, or intermittently when you and your husband reach an impasse. It is most efficient and cost-effective to retain a mediator to handle most, if not all, aspects of your divorce.

What transpires in mediation may be confidential, depending on the state. When it is, the mediator can't go into court at a later date (if you end up in a litigated contest) and testify about what was discussed in the sessions. But a mediator would be required to testify if he were subpoenaed by a court because he made a recommendation to the court that the other parent contested. (Most states that require mediation don't require the mediator to make a recommendation.) It's a good idea to sign an agreement with the mediator that clarifies the terms of your agreement, just as you would with an attorney in a retainer letter. One provision you might want to include is a confidentiality clause.

Find out if the mediator will make a recommendation to the court. Regardless, you will need to impress the mediator with your parenting ability. *The points you will want to make are that your child's best interests come first, that you are open to trying a variety of options if it will benefit your child, and that you are willing to share your child with your husband and be a cooperative parent.*

FINDING A MEDIATOR

Since no license is required to be a mediator, make sure the person you hire has one. You might try the Yellow Pages of the telephone directory under "Mediation," the local bar association, a therapist, a parent who has gone through a divorce, local social service agencies, or your minister or rabbi.

Or you could contact the following groups, which could provide a referral in your area. Warning: A referral service will offer a list of mediators who have requested and/or paid to be on that list. It is not based on credentials or reputation, so you need to do your own homework.

The Academy of Family Mediators
4 Militia Drive
Lexington, MA 02173
Phone: 617-674-2663
E-mail: afmoffice@igc.apc.org

Association of Family and Conciliation Courts
329 West Wilson
Madison, WI 53703-3612
Phone: 608-251-0604
E-mail: affcc@afccnet.org

(To receive a referral, you must become a member of the organization, which costs $125 and entitles you to a quarterly journal and newsletter; recommended mediators will be members of the organization.)

Conflict Resolution Center, Inc.
204 37th Street
Pittsburgh, PA 15201-1859
Phone: 412-687-6210
E-mail: crcii@conflictnet.org

(There is a mediator search fee of $15.)

Society of Professionals In Dispute Resolution
1621 Connecticut Avenue NW
Washington, DC 20009
Phone: 202-265-1927
E-mail: spidr@spidr.org

WHAT YOU CAN EXPECT

In the first session, the mediator will set the ground rules and explain his or her role and your roles. You and your husband will identify what issues you have to mediate. This process can help clarify your thinking, and the two of you will hear why certain issues are so meaningful to the other. Some of the questions the mediator will ask include with whom you think the children should live, what school they should attend, what kind of relationship you want to have with them, how your children can maintain their friendships, and what arrangement would work best for all of you. If the children are old enough, you will also want to get their opinion on at least some of these issues. You can decide how you will gather this information, whether it is by meeting together with your husband and children, each of you meeting separately with your children, or getting together with one child at a time and possibly one parent.

Once a mediator has this information, you will be able to see where you and your husband disagree. Expect a good deal of conflict. The mediator will try to get you to communicate in a healthy way: without intimidation, interrupting, threats, attacks, or coercion. That may be by getting you to recognize your typical pattern of communicating. (This awareness has the potential to change the way you relate to your husband on future issues.)

If you choose mediation, you have to be able to communicate your position without backing down. Be firm. Your husband will state his position. Listen well. If you have heard his argument and decide that his position has merit, you may want to change your position. In any event, your husband may appreciate the fact that you are at least listening to him with an open mind, and that may make him less adversarial. If, however, you feel you are being pressured into making concessions, step back. Don't be afraid to say you need to think your position over and will address it in the next session. That will buy you time to act rationally rather than impulsively.

CHILDREN AND MEDIATION

Some mediators and parents like to include children in at least part of the process. It can help keep the focus on the children's needs, allows them to feel involved and their opinions considered, and provides input to proposed options.

If children do participate, they may be interviewed separately from their parents to determine their wishes and concerns, and/or with their parents for meetings on topics that affect them. *They should not be present during negotiations involving finances and assets.* Sometimes children are brought in at the final session after the agreement has been reached. This may be a good way to explain the arrangement to them and answer their questions.

Mediation with children will not work if you and your husband are hostile toward each other or one of you can't be trusted to act civil. Experts agree that youngsters under the age of eight should probably not participate in any meetings. Whether or not your child engages in mediation will depend upon his emotional maturity and personality; not all children eight and older are good candidates. Children should not be involved if it's going to make them feel they have to choose between parents. (Mediators will certainly not put them in this position, but kids might feel it, anyway.) If you decide to have your children participate, make sure the mediator has a strong background in child development, family dynamics, and the impact of divorce on children, as well as training in interviewing techniques for children.

DOES MEDIATION WORK?

Much of the time, it does. After researching fifteen projects that included seventy-five courts in four states where mediation was either mandated or chosen, Jessica Pearson, director for the Center for Policy Research, discovered that parents reached an agreement half to three-quarters of the time. Pearson also found that 70 to 90 percent of parents who participate in mediation are satisfied with the outcome. Who can say that about custody cases that go to trial? Mediation also cuts down on litigated custody cases. In California, mediation, which is required, has slashed the number of trials from 20 percent to just 5 percent of all litigated cases. There is also apparently a higher compliance rate for mediated agreements than for those that have been reached through court.

Mediation can reduce the anger between you and your husband. There can be less frustration because you become part of the decision-making process. But there is another reason why it works: It allows you to confront your husband face-to-face and explain why you feel wronged (and vice versa). That can be cathartic and allow you to give up some of the anger and focus on the resolution, which is really what you want, anyway. You can listen to each other, have your say, learn your husband's point of view, and hopefully, move on.

When mediation doesn't work, the court may ask a custody evaluator to make a custody finding to the judge. Much of what the custody evaluator does is similar to a mediator. He is likely to be a mental health professional. Courts sometimes pick up the fee for this service, but usually the parents must pay.

If you do end up going to court after mediation, at least you will have addressed some of the thornier issues and may have come to an agreement on some sticking points. That will free you up to resolve the remainder of the custody issues. The process of mediation may have also enhanced your communication skills outside of this negotiation and could help you be more effective in your day-to-day dealings in other areas of your life, like with your children or work colleagues.

THE COST OF MEDIATION

It definitely costs less to mediate than to go to court. Most mediators charge on a sliding scale and bill on an hourly basis, usually $100 to $350. Mediators usually don't require retainers, although some will, especially if they are lawyers. But the retainer fee may be ten times less than what a lawyer litigating your case would charge, perhaps $1,500 compared to $15,000. Depending on how long it takes you to reach an agreement, mediation generally costs $1,500 to $5,000 and another $1,000 if you decide to have an attorney draft the agreement. The fee is rarely higher than $10,000. Mediators will also charge for work done outside a session, which might include writing notes on the meetings or drafting the agreement.

A litigated custody contest, in contrast, typically requires at least a $5,000 retainer, usually more, from both you and your husband, and another $10,000 to $40,000 per person on average after the retainer. Why not put the money that would have been spent on litigation into college tuition?

DON'T RULE OUT A LAWYER OR OTHER EXPERTS WHEN YOU USE MEDIATION

Even if you opt for mediation, it is smart to hire an attorney to review the relevant issues that should be decided during the mediation and ways for you to present your case. Also have her review the custody agreement after it is drafted but before it is signed so she can point out anything that is to your disadvantage or won't stand up in court.

Reviewing sensitive information with a lawyer is a good idea, such as how to respond if your husband brings up your new boyfriend or your new job that has longer hours. Your lawyer will be able to tell you what to say or not to say and how to say it to placate your husband and get the best deal possible. Your case may be so inflammatory that your lawyer may advise you not to use mediation.

Don't be surprised if the lawyer asks you to supply more information before deciding whether to recommend mediation. If she does, you can enter mediation armed with the facts and advice you have been given, as well as confidence in your ability to negotiate well.

If you can't afford a lawyer, check to see if your jurisdiction provides a mediation program through the courts. If so, speak with the people in the mediation program to learn what factors mediators consider important in making their recommendations. For instance, do they usually rule for the parent who is more willing to negotiate and share the children? Find out as much as you can about the program, or look for a private mediation program through a referral.

IS A MALE OR FEMALE MEDIATOR BETTER?

There is no right answer, but it's worth thinking about. You will either have two males on one side or two females, depending on the gender of the mediator. You may feel outnumbered if the mediator is a male. If that's the case, you may be able to convince your husband to meet with the mediator before you agree to use him to see if you feel he will be sympathetic to you as a woman. You could do this by saying you wanted to see what he was like without explaining the gender angle. No reputable mediator will allow you to interview him without your husband. (Even though you can't meet alone with a mediator, you can find out which ones are the best by asking friends or colleagues who have used one, your lawyer, therapist, or clergyperson. Then you can ask your husband if he would be willing to interview the top two or three with you. What you are trying to do is learn how experienced the mediator is and get a sense of whether he will understand and manage the issues well.)

If you feel comfortable with the mediator, his gender is a nonissue. Gender is far less important than the individual. You also want to make sure your husband is comfortable. If he feels like he is being ganged up on because the mediator is another female, he might be less inclined to open up, discuss the situation, and make decisions that will benefit you. So, if having a male mediator means less to you than having a female does to him, defer to him.

SHOULD YOU USE A PRIVATE MEDIATOR OR ONE PROVIDED BY THE COURT?

Usually you will have a choice, and if you can afford it, you will want to find someone on your own. In many jurisdictions, the court may have its own mediation program. These mediators usually have an undergraduate degree in social work or psychology, as well as at least twenty hours of mediation training. They typically don't have extensive legal training. In some states, there are staff mediators; others use court-appointed programs, and still others have volunteers. Usually, court-appointed mediators spend less time with you than those you hire privately, on average one to six hours, and you rarely get to choose whom you get.

Private mediation costs more, but you may find you have more success when you have more choices. Get it right: You will be working *very* closely with your mediator.

CHECKMATE

Some questions to ask a mediator:

- How long have you been a mediator?
- What is your training? (Remember: In most states you don't need a license to be a mediator, and anyone can go into the business, so this is a critical question.) Do you have a background in child development?
- How much experience have you had working with families around the issue of custody?
- Do you have any preferences about which parent should get custody?
- Do you prefer to see me with my husband or separately? Will you involve our children?
- How do you see your role in our case?
- How do you handle stalemates?
- How long do you see my case taking?
- What kind of money can I expect to pay? How frequently do you bill?

IN THE WORDS OF ONE MEDIATOR

A New York mediator, who is a psychotherapist by training and a member of the Academy of Family Mediators, has this to say about the process:

"There is no such thing as being impartial, and yet that is the premise of mediation. No one is completely capable of being impartial. Bias is natural. I don't believe there exists anything in the universe where people interact without an opinion. However, I make myself completely conscious and aware of what my bias is and try to work toward the role of being impartial.

"I find mediation can empower people, especially women. They are making decisions about their future, versus court, where the focus is on blame, conflict, and bringing up the dirt, all under the threat of going to trial and being pressured into reaching an agreement. I've noticed that women often presume that the kids belong to them.

"I tell the husband and wife that since they both love the children and want what is best for them, it is in the kids' best interests to have contact and an ongoing relationship with both parents. I tell women, 'No matter what your feelings are for your husband, if you love your kids, you will want him to be the best father he can be, or your kids will suffer. You can hate him if you choose, but don't try to create a wedge between the children and their father.'

"If a man initiated the divorce, a common response for the mother is to align herself with the children, particularly if they are girls. They identify with the mother more than boys. Sometimes the mothers influence their children to hate their father by brainwashing and poisoning them against their dads. Pretend that you are married for twenty-five years and your husband left you for a younger woman. You might pull the kids to you to give you comfort. I tell mothers, 'If you get your children to hate their father, your daughter will have problems establishing relationships with men when she is an adult. You say you love your daughter. Do you want this to happen? If you say you love your daughter, let's see your behavior conform to it.'

"I focus on what we need to do to reach an agreement rather than finger-pointing. There's an expression in mediation: 'Let's not rehash the past.' When I hear blame coming up, I refocus and say, 'This isn't helpful in reaching an agreement. This is not a therapy session. Let's refocus toward our goal without blame.' I try to demilitarize the fight so that both parents can become more rational and focus on their love for the kids.

"Most men are scared stiff to leave home and their children, even if they are the ones who want the marriage to end. Most have never been without a woman. They had their mother, a girlfriend, and then a wife. They desperately fear they will become visitors to their children and lose them completely. Men are not raised to be in touch with their feelings. They are trained to show anger but not fear. Anger is a mask for fear. If you and your husband can acknowledge that you are both afraid, you can get somewhere and perhaps mediate instead of litigate.

"Women sometimes create a fixed posture going into mediation. It's a control issue as well as fear. They're afraid they may lose whatever it is—custody or alimony—and they need to feel in control. They may think they are entitled to a certain amount of money in alimony, let's say. I say, 'There's no such thing as being entitled. Give up that presumption and trust in the mediation process.' Mothers should not have a presumption about what they're going to wind up with. In fact, sometimes they can actually do better in their agreement than they expected.

"I also see a lot of unequal situations, where the mother might be a stay-at-home mom and the husband a high-powered financier. If I think it could affect mediation because it's not a level playing field, then I advise the woman to bring in an expert who is a financial adviser either in the session or outside. You need a reasonably even, level playing field to mediate."

ARBITRATION

Sometimes people confuse mediation and arbitration. In mediation, both you and your husband decide on an agreement. In arbitration, an arbitrator, who is like a judge but is usually a lawyer (and can be in the mental health field), listens to both of you argue your case and decides the outcome. Arbitration is used to resolve custody and visitation disputes in ten states. One Florida jurist describes arbitrators as hired judges.

Arbitration may either be binding or nonbinding. If it is binding, you are stuck with the decision (unless you can prove the arbitrator was biased, exceeded his or her powers as defined in the arbitration agreement, or made a gross mistake of law). Nonbinding arbitration means you can appeal the decision. If you do, however, and the court reaches the same decision, you may be saddled with your husband's court costs. Arbitration is less formal than going before a judge, and it also costs less. It is usually comparable to an attorney's fees. Like mediators, arbitrators may be appointed by the court or selected privately. Sometimes a court will have each parent or the lawyers submit a list of three names and if they can't agree on one, the judge will choose.

Finding an Arbitrator

Arbitrators also don't need a license to practice, so check to make sure the one you choose has one. You could try to find one the way you would a mediator—through friends, therapists, local social service agencies, or the Yellow Pages under "Arbitration."

The American Arbitration Association has branches in most large cities that might be able to make a referral. If there isn't one where you live, you could call the New York headquarters and find the AAA closest to you.

American Arbitration Association
140 West 51st Street
New York, NY 10020-1203
Phone: 212-484-4000

THE COURTROOM APPROACH: WHAT YOU SHOULD KNOW

Do whatever you can to avoid a courtroom battle. It will almost always cause you and your family anguish, cost a great deal of money, and not necessarily give you the outcome you want. You know better than any judge what is best for your kids. You also know specifics about their personalities that will help you craft an agreement that addresses their needs.

It is possible your situation can't be resolved any other way. In that case, you should understand the process before embarking on this course.

Realize *you* will be the target of the custody battle. There is no such thing as getting the benefit of the doubt in a custody dispute. All of your quirks and worst traits will be exaggerated, and your actions will be taken out of context and distorted. The goal of your husband's attorney will be to make you look bad and your spouse look good. There are no secrets in a litigated custody case. Your husband and his lawyer will stoop to unsavory tactics and so will you and your attorney. You are trying to prove you are the more fit parent, or that your husband is the less fit. If you *really* want to win, this is what you have to do, your lawyer will tell you. You will not like the person you are, and certainly you will not like how your ex-husband portrays you. You will be paying an exorbitant amount of money for the least fun you have ever experienced.

And then there are the children. Even if you swear you don't want to, you will be pitting one parent against the other and forcing your children to choose. While you may not believe you are doing this, they will interpret the battle this way. Experts agree that contested custody can only be detrimental to children. The day-to-day life during a custody battle could well be intolerable for them.

When you give a judge permission to decide on the fate of your children, you are participating in a crap shoot. A judge can't listen to just a few hours or days of testimony and fully appreciate who you are or what your life is like. As one judge in Philadelphia tells the parties who come before him, "You are asking me to make a very important decision, and I hardly know you. It would be much wiser for you to decide these issues between the two of you."

Before you embark on a trial, understand you will have little control over who hears your case. It could be a judge who is enlightened and educated about family law and the impact of divorce on children, but it could just as easily be someone who has never practiced matrimonial law. Divorce judges may have no qualifications for their seat; they may be appointed for political reasons.

In some jurisdictions, there are no designated matrimonial judges. Sometimes the case is not even heard by a judge, but by a judicial hearing officer, who may be a retired judge or someone else trained to hear cases, or by special referees (attorneys who work for judges).

Divorce court is emotional, sad, and messy—not exactly what most seasoned judges consider a plum position and not one they often choose. You may not be getting the cream of the crop. In an effort to rid the courts of judges who have sat in divorce court too long and make harsh rulings based on their prejudice—they rule for fathers or for mothers, almost without hearing the facts of a case—the courts sometimes rotate judges. It's a good concept, but cases become assigned and reassigned because new judges come on the bench. You may have explained your case to one judge, only to have to essentially begin all over. That translates into lost time and money.

There are many legal costs that you may not anticipate. You will have to pay your attorney to wait around the courtroom and argue a motion on your behalf or have a conference with the judge. Your bill depends not only on your attorney and her strategy but whom your husband hires. If he is a fighter who files interminable motions that your attorney must answer, it will jack up your legal fees.

Neither mediation nor litigation is appealing, but if you know what to expect from each, you will be better prepared to make your choice. If it is your ex-partner who forces your hand, you will be ready.

7

What Does a Good Custody Agreement Contain?

If you are pleased with your custody agreement or at least feel you can live with it, you've probably got a good one. You will want to compromise to come up with a legal document that will satisfy you both. It must be precise and detailed so that everyone understands the plan. You also want there to be enough time built into it for both you and your ex-spouse to be with your child.

The agreement can deal with as many or as few issues as you choose. *It should always focus on what will work best for your children*. In crafting it, think about how you can make the situation the least stressful for them. The agreement will contain your legal and physical custody arrangement. It will be tailored to the needs and requests of you and your ex-husband. It should not only spell out what each of you agrees to, but what happens if one of you breaches the agreement. You will need to define what constitutes a breach. A big mistake many parents make is not putting in a provision to address changing the agreement. Stipulate that your agreement is effective for a certain amount of time, and that if needs change, it may be renegotiated at a later date to address your children's future growth and other circumstances. A good custody agreement may also state what conditions would call for a change. It should never be viewed as the final plan. You will want to have a clause saying you will meet with each other, say once a year at a specific time, to review the agreement. You should also agree how you will disagree. If you can't reach consensus on a nonemergency matter, you will want to clarify how it will be resolved. Perhaps you will use a mediator. If so, put in writing how that mediator will be chosen and what will happen, such as arbitration, if mediation doesn't work.

It's a good idea to try out a temporary agreement and not make any major decisions at the beginning when you both may be over-wrought. According to mediators and lawyers, large numbers of parents reevaluate their permanent agreements a couple of years after signing them.

If you and your husband live in nearby towns, you might mutually decide your children will live primarily with you for the next two years until they reach middle school and high school. You could agree that you will be responsible for making the school decisions during that time, but that the arrangement would be reassessed in a couple of years. That could give you both time to research the school districts to see which one might be better for the children. (You would have a legal advantage because the children would have already settled in with you.) Having these clauses gives you flexibility, provided you and your ex-husband really have the children's best interests at heart and your husband is not using a change of custody as a means of control.

Your agreement should clearly define the roles of your husband and you. Realize that the situation could change—your ex-husband might get remarried and have more children or stepchildren, or change jobs, or receive a substantial raise, which spurs him to hire a nanny and seek sole custody. Even if things feel easy between the two of you today, you will want to have enough details in the agreement in case goodwill dissipates or circumstances change.

Make sure you include any issues that you anticipate the two of you could fight over. This should eliminate the "But I thought it was okay if I . . ." line. When it's in writing, the agreement has a better chance of being followed. And if it isn't, you may have to go to court to have the judge decide the issue.

PARENTING PLANS

All states require a custody agreement, but some also ask that a parenting plan be filed with the court. This plan implements the custody arrangement and is sometimes, but not always, identical to the custody agreement. Its purpose is the same: to formally reach an understanding about what each parent's responsibilities are for the child, from who makes which decisions to the hours each of you gets to spend with your children and where they will live. Some parents write plans that are less detailed than those ordered by the court. The best part of a parenting plan is that you are in control and can negotiate the terms of the agreement with your husband.

Presently, thirty states recognize parenting plans and make parents incorporate them into the court order. That means the court reviews them and they are enforceable should there be a problem. In ten out of fifteen states, these plans are only required when there is joint custody. Washington is the only state to insist on a parenting plan regardless of the custody arrangement, and fifteen others recognize some kind of a parental agreement. Some states demand parents address specific issues.

The kinds of issues you put in your agreement or parenting plan depend on your arrangement. (If you have sole custody, you are legally allowed to make all of the decisions dealing with your child's medical care, schooling, and religious training. If you have opted for joint legal custody, then both of you can have an equal say in these issues.) In the agreement, address which decisions each of you will make and when. You may feel strongly that your children should go to a single-sex school and want to call the shots about their education. Your husband may feel equally strongly about their religious upbringing. If you practice different religions and can't agree on which you want for your children, you might put in writing that they will be exposed to both religions and can choose when they reach age eighteen. You could divide all the big decisions and choices by category (schools, religion, child care, insurance). If your relationship is amicable, you may both want to be involved in making all major decisions within each category. In part, how you structure it will depend on how well you and your husband get along.

After establishing which decisions each of you will make, break them down further. Some parents delegate the day-to-day details to the primary caretaker. If the children live with you during the week and alternate weekends, your husband may allow you to be the boss about after-school activities, especially since you are the one doing the transporting. If he sees the children for extended periods during the week, he may insist on having a say in those choices. If that is the case, think about including a transportation schedule. This lets each parent know from the beginning what his and her obligations will be. The list may also help make some of the decisions.

Here are some issues to address in your document:

Finances

1. Who pays for what?
2. What happens if the expenses are substantially higher at one house? Will the other parent be compensated?

Schools

1. Who decides which school the children attend: day care, public, private, or home schooling? Will it be single-sex or coed?
2. Will the child be in a special education or gifted program?
3. Which parent or parents will be responsible for monitoring the child's performance?
4. Will the parents attend parent-teacher conferences separately or together? If it is separate, which one will go?
5. Who will be involved in Parent-Teacher Association activities?
6. Will both parents receive report cards and other school records and notices?
7. Who will choose the children's after-school activities?

Medical Issues

1. Which pediatrician, dentist, or therapist will the children see? What if the parents don't agree that a counselor is necessary? What if one doesn't want to pay for orthodontia? Orthodontia can run a family between $3,000 and $5,000. Many parents insert a clause about who will pay for braces. Sometimes it says both parents must agree on the choice of the orthodontist or that there has to be a second opinion before any cost is incurred. At the least, you should include a clause saying that the parent who

receives medical, dental, and/or eye care benefits will be responsible for these payments.

2. Who will take them to their regular visits?

3. What is the plan if there is a medical emergency? Will the custodial parent notify the noncustodial parent before the child is treated? What if there is no time to wait? Will the doctor make the ultimate decision, and if not, who will?

4. What responsibility does the custodial parent have toward the other parent when the child is sick with a virus or cold? Is the custodial parent required to tell the noncustodial parent about every cold? Will visitation time be made up if the child is too sick to switch houses? Who makes that call? If the child needs medicine, how will one parent communicate instructions to the other parent?

5. How do the parents decide on elective surgery?

Some of these questions probably seem unnecessary. If you have a good relationship or trust your husband's judgment on these issues, you may decide not to include them, or you might want to make your agreement more flexible. You may want to see how it goes and stipulate that you will renegotiate specific issues every year or two and build in time to review the agreement unless a problem arises that needs immediate attention. These times may coincide with milestones in your children's lives, such as graduation from elementary or junior high school, or at specific ages. In the initial stages of your divorce, your plan should be more rigid. At a time when you are trying to establish a new life for yourself, it will let you and your ex-spouse know when you will be free. A strict schedule can also be good for you and your child. It will provide structure and let her know when she can expect to see you both. The longer the period of time that you have been divorced, the more likely it is that you and your ex-husband can be flexible. But it might not be the case if you or he remarries and has more children. You may want to renegotiate your custody agreement at this time to develop a more concrete schedule. There are no prescribed times for modifying an agreement, but some attorneys advise considering it when there is a major life change such as remarriage or relocation (see chapter 8).

Living Arrangements

As in other areas of custody, the more problems you have with your ex-spouse, the more detailed you will want your plan. The agreement must state with which parent your child will live and when. You might want to list drop-off and pickup schedules and a provision stating that you and your ex-husband will notify each other before your child is taken out of the area or state. (If you fear your husband may steal your child, see chapter 17.)

Child Care

If you live close to each other, think about writing a clause that says if either parent can't be home, the other will get the first option to "baby-sit." You might want to provide a list of acceptable baby-sitters or agencies or state how baby-sitters will be chosen. One mother's solution to the baby-sitter issue was to offer to find her husband sitters when their daughter was at his house. He didn't have to scramble for a sitter, and his ex-wife got peace of mind.

If you are afraid your husband might leave your child alone, you could put in a clause forbidding it. But whether you could prevent his girlfriend from baby-sitting is questionable.

You will also have to decide who will pay for child care if one parent or both work. If your office is at home, you might want to stipulate that you will have help during your work hours.

Access

This entails how you and your ex-spouse will communicate with your child when she is with the other parent. The agreement should discuss when it's acceptable to call your child and how often (probably no more than once a day unless there is a logistical problem or an emergency). You could stipulate that when the children are with one parent, the other will be allowed unencumbered contact. This may mean via telephone, fax, regular mail, or E-mail. Some agreements provide times when this communication is to take place.

Even if you and your husband currently have a good relationship, this provision is a way to protect yourself should your circumstances change: He remarries and his new wife doesn't approve of the contact on "her time," or, for unanticipated reasons, communication with your husband becomes strained.

Transportation Between Houses

One Eloise in Paris–type nine-year-old from the East Coast who shuttled between parents told her divorce attorney, "I take cabs so often, I even know the names of all of the cab drivers!" Few parents have those kinds of resources. Transportation might not even be an issue if you live close to your ex-husband and your children are old enough to walk, bike, or take buses. But if it is, you might want to be responsible for taking your child one way and have your husband handle the trip back. The farther away you live from your ex-husband, the more complicated the plan might be, and you will need to address this in the agreement. If there are costs attached to transportation, like plane fare, spell out which parent will pay. If you are uncomfortable having your child fly alone but your husband thinks it's fine, or vice versa, decide what to do and include the decision in the agreement (see chapter 12).

Vacations and Holidays

Besides the day-to-day schedule, you should address holidays, which tend to be emotional issues and can lead to fighting if they are not decided in advance or formalized. Sit down with a calendar and circle all holidays, including those at school. Decide which ones you really want to spend with your child, and think about which holidays you would be willing to trade off. This will put you in a better bargaining position. The farther in advance you can plan, the more bargaining power you may have. You also won't have to spoil a special occasion with a fight beforehand. It may save you in other ways, too. If you live far apart, it gives you time to research the least expensive plane, train, or bus fares.

Some schools have special days for children and parents. Find out what days they are and allocate them so your son or daughter will not end up spending the day alone. It may also eliminate any embarrassment your child might feel if you and your husband both attend and are not civil to each other. Request a school schedule as soon as it is published.

Parents split holidays in various ways. You might want to alternate years, spending Christmas, Kwanza, or the first night of Hanukkah with the children in even years and Thanksgiving in odd years. If you observe a two-day holiday, you could stipulate you will split it, if that's feasible, or switch every year. Or if you are able, divide the day, with your children spending 8 A.M. to 3 P.M. with one parent, and the rest of the day and evening with the other. Some parents celebrate important holidays together with their children. Usually, this happens when neither parent has remarried.

Occasions such as Mother's Day and Father's Day are typically celebrated with the appropriate parent. If your weekend falls on Father's Day, you may have to give up part of your time with your child. If that's the case and you want to make up the time later, find out if your ex-husband will consent, and if so, put it in writing.

You will also need to schedule school vacations. Depending on your custody arrangement, you may split the time with the children or have the noncustodial parent get the whole vacation. To cut down on baby-sitting costs, consider making it required that you split their vacation time equally. Because it is longer, summer might not be given to just one parent. You will also want to specify how much advance notice is needed to request summer vacation time with the children. As a couple, you will have to decide about camp, teen tours, community service programs, or a job at home or elsewhere.

Birthdays

Your child's birthday is likely to be a sticking point. You will probably both want to be with her on that day, but if you don't live close, it may not be an issue. If her birthday is in the summer, that could change the custody schedule. You may choose to celebrate your child's birthday separately and have two different parties or celebrate jointly with one family party. Some parents pick a date when they will be with their child to formally celebrate the occasion.

Permissible Activities

If you have strong feelings about a specific activity or sport, you could address it in your custody agreement or parenting plan. Let's say you oppose ice hockey, snowboarding, or in-line skating, but your husband doesn't. You could impose certain restrictions if the kids did do them. The agreement might require your child to wear a protective helmet for all three activities, for example. This level of detail may seem like overkill, but if you decide on the rules and follow them, your husband can't later turn around and say you are trying to control how he parents. At the same time, if he refuses to have your child put on the helmet, you could charge he is violating the agreement and being neglectful.

Moving

Can you or your husband move out of the jurisdiction, and if so, how far? That is a question you might want to answer in your agreement. If you think it's a possibility, add a clause outlining what would happen if you or your husband were to move. It could say you would retain primary custody but accept financial responsibility for transporting your children to see their father. Or it might say you would split the cost. Or the deal might be that if either one of you moves, the other would receive custody, or at least primary physical custody. Another possibility would be that you continue to be the primary custodian but have the children spend a good part of the summer, as well as other vacations, with your husband.

If you feel you can get a good agreement on moving now, you may want to include it. But if you think you won't get the kind of clause you want, don't bring up the topic (see chapter 4).

Insurance Coverage and Medical Expenses

Medical insurance coverage is usually addressed in the child support order but may also be included in the custody agreement. Besides basic health insurance, think about a provision for dental and eye care. If your ex-spouse is covered through work, make sure he provides coverage for the children; if he is self-employed and your job offers coverage, you might be responsible. Depending on your financial standing, you could try to get your ex-husband to pick up the tab for the whole thing or split it fifty-fifty. These items can be expensive, so clarify it in writing so you don't get stuck if your husband suddenly decides not to pay.

Life insurance should also be addressed. If your ex-spouse agrees to pay for educational costs, medical benefits, extracurricular activities, or other child care costs, try to negotiate a clause saying he will carry life insurance to fund these costs. If he were to die and not leave enough money to cover these costs, money provided through life insurance could help you pay them. Consult an insurance agent for available plans and terms; the agent can help you figure out what kind of plan and what amount would be adequate.

Income Tax Exemption

Also include in your agreement which parent will get the income tax exemption for the children or if you will split the exemption. By law, if you have physical custody at least 51 percent of the time, you are entitled to file as head of the household and qualify for the tax exemption. If you split custody, the parent who has the children most during the year can claim this exemption. Parents can change this rule by signing the IRS form 8332. This will let the noncustodial parent take the exemption. The exemption is sometimes used as a bargaining chip, so you might think about trading it for a concession on another issue that is important to you.

Child Support

Some parenting plans address child support. This issue, however, is often covered in a child support order (see chapter 9 for information on child support).

CHECKMATE

Ingredients of a Good Custody Agreement
- Think about having a temporary agreement first.
- Make sure the focus is on what works best for your child.
- Agree to exchange all educational and medical information pertaining to your kids.
- Define your role and your husband's, including which decisions each of you will make.
- Include issues you anticipate might be the basis for a later disagreement and work them out in advance.
- Address what happens if one of you breaks the agreement, what you do if circumstances change, and what constitutes a change.
- Specify an annual time to review the agreement.

Remember that when you sit down to negotiate your first custody agreement, emotions and tempers may be strained. Increasing the number of issues on the table may make reaching any agreement more difficult. The key is reasonableness and compromise. The more you win at this stage, the more difficult it may be to work cooperatively with your ex-husband in the implementation of the plan. Decide what is really important to you and focus on achieving those goals. At the same time, recognize what is most important to your former spouse. There may be points on which you decide to compromise. Your life, and the lives of your children, will be less stressful if both you and your ex-husband feel that the plan is fair.

8

What to Do if Your Custody Plan Is Not Working

It's likely that your ex-husband will be the one to decide he wants to modify or change the custody agreement. Perhaps he was not set up to take the children at the time of the divorce; he might have had a demanding or inflexible job, or no job. Now he has remarried, has more flexibility in his work, or found work. Your teenager may have decided that Dad is more relaxed and she'd rather live with him. Your ex-husband has also come to the same conclusion. What are the chances he will prevail?

The courts have the authority to change a custody agreement when needs change—yours, your children's, or your ex-husband's. Legally, to modify custody, you have to prove a "change in circumstances."

Many judges claim the real test for determining whether to modify an existing order is whether there factually is a change in circumstances that will impact negatively or positively on the child. Jurists usually look favorably on a petition to change when the needs of the child change, such as when they grow older and the situation no longer seems to be working for them. Often there is a negative reason for seeking the modification: A parent may be abusing alcohol or neglecting the children under his care, or a child who has been a straight A or B student may suddenly start failing courses. The circumstances must arise out of actual, verifiable events and can't be simply because you are not happy with your custody hours or think your husband is not acting like the parent you want him to be.

Some jurisdictions require you to prove your child is seriously endangered by the present arrangement (such as abuse) in order to modify a custody decree within the first year of the order.

If you want to modify a custody arrangement, you will not only be asked to prove that the situation has greatly changed since the last time the custody award was made but also that the arrangement you propose is better than the current one. Reminder: Courts don't like to rock the boat and change a situation that is working, so the parent who requests a change will have to show it isn't working.

Like everything else about custody, there is little uniformity on this issue. In an effort to discourage parents from going back to court frequently, some states have added another hurdle when there is a custody modification request within the first year or two after an initial award. Besides a change of circumstances, parents must prove that the present situation is dangerous for the child.

If you and your husband mutually agree that you want to change custody or the visitation schedule, you will not have to prove a change of circumstances. Although it is not required, it's a smart idea to formalize the new arrangement by going back to court. That way, your husband will not be able to revert to the old setup without a lot of effort, time, and money, should he change his mind.

What is a change of circumstances? The issue is subjective, and there is no one definition. It may differ from jurisdiction to jurisdiction and is likely to have a different meaning depending on the judge. You can have the same set of facts and one judge may rule there is a legitimate change of circumstances, but another may find there isn't. There are some situations, however, that most judges will agree are grounds for a custody modification.

WHAT MIGHT CONVINCE THE COURT

· The most common reason parents give for changing or terminating an arrangement is that one parent wants to move. You might be able to argue successfully that you want to move closer to your family so your children will get to know their aunts, uncles, cousins, and grandparents, but certain jurisdictions have begun to make it harder for women to win with this argument. Judges hate having to decide this issue. They don't like depriving a child of contact with the other parent, which is what moving usually does. If either of you wants to move with your child, the courts will be reluctant to consent unless there are compelling reasons to do so (see chapter 4.) Know that some courts make the parent who is relocating pay transportation costs when the children visit the noncustodian.

· Any change in lifestyle that is detrimental to the children would also be a reason to alter a custody agreement. Let's say your husband begins to drink or take drugs. If he picks up the children or drops them off and you realize he is driving under the influence, you could have grounds for changing custody.

   Your children might be able to confirm his inappropriate behavior, but if they are too young to testify, you are going to have to find other ways to prove he has a drinking or drug problem. This might be by calling friends or colleagues to the stand or examining medical and work records. If the court is convinced, it will decide how his abuse impacts your children. The judge might order supervised visitation, forbid him to drive with the children, or even stop visits altogether until he is clean. But the judge may also decide that your husband's problem does not affect the children and refuse to modify a decree.

   If your former spouse begins to leave your children with his new girlfriend, with neighbors, or alone, instead of spending time with them, this could also be the basis for a changed circumstances argument. If he leaves them with a grandparent, though, the court may say this time is important and does not merit a change in the arrangement.

   If his girlfriend moves in with him and you think that is setting a bad example for your children, you may be able to cut out their overnight stays with him, but don't count on terminating all visitation. Some judges are not fazed by cohabitation, although others view it as grounds for modification. If your ex-husband's new girlfriend or wife mistreats or abuses your children, this changed circumstance would sway most judges.

· Your child's desire to move in with the noncustodial parent is another reason for a change of agreement. This may be a legitimate reason to change physical custody, but only if it does not look as if there was pressure from the noncustodial parent. Whether it qualifies for grounds will depend on the judge, the state, and your situation. Sometimes children say they want to move out when a parent finds a new partner. Your child might not like or want to be with your ex-husband's live-in girlfriend or wife or your live-in boyfriend or new husband. These feelings alone are probably not enough to convince most judges that a change in custody arrangements is warranted. To prevail, you would have to show that the new relationship is harmful to your child in some way.

· If you truly suspect physical or sexual abuse of your children, the courts will treat your allegations seriously. Your children may be too young to testify. At any rate, the judge will call mental health professionals and possibly neighbors or teachers, and will not rely on your word alone. If the charges prove true, the judge will either modify, restrict, or stop visitation or custody.

Just as some fathers threaten to seek custody if their ex-wives ask for more child support, some mothers charge their ex-husbands with physical or sexual abuse of their children to deprive them of time with the kids. When these claims are false everyone suffers and you could lose custody.

· You might want to renegotiate if your working hours or your husband's have changed. That could mean he works longer hours or travels more frequently, for instance, or you have a new, flexible schedule that would be more conducive to having the children with you. By the same token, your ex-husband might have recently remarried a stay-at-home wife who is willing to take care of your children, while you have a more demanding work schedule. With more women in the workforce having more responsible jobs, this is an increasingly common basis for seeking a custody modification. Courts today look hard at the schedules of both working parents in deciding who has enough time to be a hands-on parent.

· Your children are older and their needs and schedules have changed, so the current agreement doesn't work for them. They may have lots of friends at one home and very few near the other, or their after-school activities might be concentrated closer to one parent. Convenience may not be a sufficient basis for modifying a custody decree.

Today, the biggest changes divorce lawyers are seeing is from joint custody to sole custody. Many couples who thought they could work out their differences and share the children are realizing that they can't or have found the logistics of switching back and forth between households too difficult. Many of the bloodiest custody cases involve modification because couples may still be full of anger and resentment and willing to fight to the death over the children. To change from joint to sole custody would require a good reason, such as parental alienation, noncooperation by a parent, bad-mouthing, or the factors discussed above as changed circumstances. Similarly, any altering of a custody arrangement, whether it is to increase or decrease time, would also require the proponent to prove a change of circumstances.

If you want to change from sole to joint custody, and both you and your husband have agreed to that modification, the legal hurdles are much easier to overcome. You won't be asked to prove that your circumstances have changed. Rather, if both you and your ex-husband agree that you want to share custody and can show that this new plan is in the best interests of your child, a court will essentially rubber-stamp your decision.

REASONS THAT MIGHT NOT BE SUFFICIENT

The following do not constitute a change in circumstances and thus a valid reason to modify a custody agreement: your husband's request to reduce child support or failure to make payments, his new wife's smoking habit when your child is healthy and other factors are equal, or your daughter's desire to live with her father simply because she likes his rules better. Judges don't like to make changes for two reasons: It upsets the stability in the house, which they are trying to achieve, and they have too many cases on their dockets to have to hear your case over and over. Therefore, a parent seeking modification has a large obstacle to surmount. Don't start down that road unless there is a very important reason to do it. You don't want to be viewed as a mom who cried wolf. When you truly need the assistance of the court, you don't want a judge to think, "Here she comes again."

TAKING ACTION TO AMEND THE PLAN

You have to analyze why your situation is not working and decide whether your reasons for seeking modification would constitute a legally sufficient change in circumstances. Your attorney should be able to give you her read on your chances of prevailing in court. Among other things, she can tell you about the judge's past record in dealing with such requests and what that jurist finds persuasive or unpersuasive. If your lawyer thinks you have grounds for modification, you should at least try to negotiate a change in custody with your husband before you seek the assistance of the court. Even if you believe the request will be futile, make the effort so your lawyer can tell the judge that you are before him because your husband turned down your reasonable request.

If you have to go before a judge, you will have to prepare your case the same way you did the first time. You are going to need to prove your allegations by lining up witnesses, compiling documentation to back you up, and sharing your diary or journal, if you kept one. If your children are older and no longer want the same custody schedule, you might want to bring them into court. Think about this carefully, though, because putting children on the stand where they would essentially be choosing one parent over the other could have psychological repercussions for them. You will also need to be prepared for what they might say, which could be that they want to live with their father. Sure, it could be because their friends live nearer to Dad's, but the truth is they have still made their choice. Make sure that you know your case well—what you want, and what your children want—and don't act precipitously.

If you understand what the courts consider grounds for modification—and what they don't—you will know realistically what your or your ex-spouse's chances are of changing custody.

Mothers and Money

The world of balancing budgets, making investments, planning for retirement, collecting child support and alimony, and filing taxes may seem mysterious to you. The prospect of having to master that world can be frightening and overwhelming. During marriage, many of the brightest women don't take care of the day-to-day finances of their families. Mothers may manage a house and a job, but not necessarily the money. In many households, that is a man's job. But remember, men handle finances because they have learned to, and you will do the same. Keep in mind, however, that money management is not learned overnight.

You need to have this knowledge so that you will be able to live independently. How you handle your financial situation may even impact on whether or not you keep custody. Ignorance and naïveté can cause you and your children to be financially shortchanged for years, if not forever.

WHAT DO I HAVE?

The first step is to gather your family's financial records. Your goal is to create a complete picture of your family's assets, liabilities, income sources, and expenses. Your husband may voluntarily give you financial documents. However, he is not required to surrender these documents. That is done through discovery, a formal legal process that requires him to produce all relevant information, and which your attorney should request.

In the meantime, start by making sure you open the mail and record all bills and account numbers, even if you aren't the one who pays them. Look around your house for any financial records and photocopy them. These could include bank and stock account statements; loan documents; income tax returns (W-2 and K-1 forms); pension, profit-sharing, and bonus plans; royalties; patents and copyrights; work expense account statements; statements for in-kind donations or payments for services rendered; work contracts for deferred pay and bonuses; payment vouchers; trust funds or annuities; income-producing property; and life insurance, especially whole life. You should also catalog your valuables such as art, jewelry, and silver, real estate owned and mortgages against it, separate property, and property received as a gift or inheritance.

You often find out what your assets are by going over your financial records. Next, make a list of all your *assets*, which is everything you own jointly (the two of you) or separately (in one of your names only). Assets include personal property (cash, jewelry, furniture, electronic equipment, artwork, computers), real property, which would be homes or rental properties, cars, a portfolio including stocks and bonds (write down certificate numbers), pension or retirement plans belonging to you or your husband or that you might be entitled to in the future, all bank accounts, life insurance policies, and cash.

Should I Sell the House?

Your home is often the largest asset in the marital pot. You will need to answer the following questions:

What is my house worth? Get a real estate appraiser to value your home. Find out the recent selling price of comparable homes in your neighborhood.

How much profit would I make if I sold the house? Check your closing statement to determine the costs related to your purchase and the actual purchase price. Did you make any improvements, such as renovating the kitchen, adding a family room, or updating a bathroom that could hike the selling price? Compile receipts and check stubs.

What are the possible tax implications? Will I have to pay a capital gains tax? You may be required to pay a substantial tax bill if you sell your house or other property that you receive as part of your divorce settlement. Before you agree on a settlement, make sure you understand the tax implications of any sale of property or stocks. Keep in mind that if you sell your home to your spouse while you are still married, there are no tax consequences.

Take this information to an accountant.

Can I afford to stay in my house? How much will I get from the sale? Refer to the section on renting versus buying on page 152.

TAXING QUESTIONS

What is my tax liability?

Can I afford to keep my house?

Do I want to keep it?

How much have we put into the house?

When should I/we sell it?

What does my accountant think?

Real Property or Real Estate

The next assets to write down are any other property or real estate that you or your husband own. This would include a vacation home, real estate either of you might own as part of a business, or real estate bought as an investment (office buildings or a duplex apartment, for example).

At the same time that you collect other information about household expenses, make a list of all of the personal property or furniture and belongings in the house.

Investment Accounts

These would be with a stock brokerage or discount brokerage firm, money markets, or a bank. There can be more than one account. Find out what kind of assets are there, how much income they generate, and how they are titled. Call the brokerage houses to try to obtain copies of the statements or a listing of the accounts. If possible, you want to do this without your husband's knowledge. If your name is not on the account, you may have to go through him or hire a forensic expert who can help locate these assets. Ask your attorney for a referral.

Pensions

The largest asset after the family home is a pension plan or retirement account. Many wives have no idea what type of retirement accounts their husbands have. It's important to find out, because you may be entitled to a portion of the pension that accrued during the marriage. Some businesses will divulge this information if you call the personnel department and ask about your husband's retirement plan.

There are many different types of retirement plans. They include individual retirement accounts (IRAs), 401(K) plans, tax savings annuities (TSAs), employee savings plans, and 403(b) plans. Don't let them scare you. They should be easy to value. You can get the statements from your husband by looking through the mail or having your attorney request them. Your husband's attorney is supposed to provide statements or copies of his pension plan, including whether or not the pension is vested and what it is worth. Most statements also reveal what your spouse is entitled to on a certain date in the future, generally at retirement age. Some plans will need to be valued by an actuary or pension evaluator. Tip: For any retirement plan, find out who the identified beneficiary is. It could be more than one person. Under certain types of plans you are not automatically entitled to be the beneficiary. In fact, you may not be the beneficiary now. Make sure the beneficiary is covered under the divorce agreement. The underlying asset—that is, the retirement plan in question—should be considered part of the divorce settlement.

Pension or retirement plans can be split by the courts through an instrument, or document, called a Qualified Domestic Relations Order or QDRO. This will allow you to get a portion of your husband's retirement plan, or vice versa, without any tax consequences if you don't withdraw it. If it is your husband's pension, this will let you transfer the allowable part of the pension into your name if he has retired, or it can be distributed according to the terms at the time of his retirement.

Family-Owned Businesses

If your husband has a family-owned business, you need to be extra vigilant and think about hiring an expert. Why? One of the most difficult assets on which to place a value is a family-owned business. For one thing, it's easy to hide income and assets. Therefore, get all financial statements that pertain to the business, such as tax returns. A certified public accountant could try to determine if your husband is hiding any assets, but your attorney would most likely have to subpoena these records.

Make sure you don't throw out any of your husband's business papers. They may reveal an unknown tax return (or even a love letter) that could help your case.

If your husband has a family business, scrutinize this checklist:

- All federal, state, and local tax returns, including individual, corporate, and/or partnership returns
- Bank statements and canceled checks
- Financial statements
- Buy/sell agreements
- Loan applications
- Retirement plans
- Life insurance policies
- Refinancing statements

Why Having Cash Is Crucial

The one asset that many women don't have is cash. Cash is not just paper money. It is also balances in your checking account, your money market fund, or even passbook savings accounts. It's important to save cash because you will need it to hire an excellent lawyer, to pay his or her fees, including a retainer, as well as for living expenses. If you can, figure out how much you will need for a worst case scenario: If you have prolonged litigation, you could have to pay fees for your attorney, a guardian ad litem, custody evaluator, mental health professional, a forensic psychiatrist, and therapists for you and your children.

Sometimes you can get your husband to pay your legal fees during the divorce by petitioning the court. You would have to have a good reason to do this (you can't afford the bill and your husband earns substantially more than you, for example), and prove you would be at a disadvantage if you had to pay. If there are any strategic delays in your case, you will need to pay your bills while you await a resolution.

You are going to need cash for deposits on new utility accounts, for instance, and everyday living expenses. It's difficult to save at a time when you will probably have less money than you did in the marriage. It will take planning, but it is necessary. Keep a record of all your available cash in the different accounts (money market funds, safe deposit boxes, and bank accounts).

If you decide to withdraw money from your joint bank account or a safe deposit box, keep careful records because by law you are required to deduct them when you and your husband eventually settle your case. If you take out the money from your joint bank account and place it in another account in your name only, keep track of how you spend that money. You don't want to be accused of stealing or squandering your husband's portion. Your attorney is going to ask you about any money you have withdrawn, and eventually you will need to give your husband what he is owed.

WHAT DO I NEED?

1. Do a budget.
2. Decide whether to stay, move, rent, or buy.

Unless you are independently wealthy or your husband has already offered a generous settlement, assume that divorce will have a negative financial impact on you. Most studies report the standard of living for divorced women drops on average by 30 percent. Some reveal figures as high as 37 percent for mothers and children—while the standard of living for their ex-husbands often rises 10 to 15 percent. Regardless of the figure you use, the reality is that two separate households cost more than one. Be prepared for a different lifestyle that will probably involve cutting back on your expenses, making it even more important for you to master your finances.

Your attorney will ask you how much you are currently spending and how much money you need to live. If it is a low figure and you seem to be getting by, the courts might decide to maintain the status quo, so make sure you don't shortchange yourself.

If you don't have a job, chances are you will need to go back to work either part-time or full-time, if not immediately, then some time in the future. Don't do anything precipitously; if you want to stay home with your young children, then do so, unless the court requires you to find a job. Child care may cost more than your job pays, and once you begin, the court may hold you to your new position and expect you to stay. Be strategic and use this time to examine your options. Figure out how much you need to earn and know what your costs are. You must learn what kind of bills you get, what has to be paid, and about paying on a regular basis.

How to Do a Budget

Until you have a budget, you won't know what your financial needs are and what you need to do. You must figure out how much it costs to run your household. This means what it will cost for your needs and expenses as well as your children's. The best way to figure this out is to make a budget. It's also important to know what your budget is when it comes time to negotiate a divorce agreement and child support. If your expenses are well-documented, it will be harder for your husband to claim the money you are requesting is inflated. The court will demand this as well.

First, consider your housing, which will be your biggest cost. If you rent, write down how much you pay your landlord monthly. If you own, put down your monthly mortgage cost. Add monthly fees attached to the mortgage payment, such as a condominium or co-op fee. Real estate taxes should also be on the list.

Next, figure out how much your monthly utilities cost. These are gas or oil bills, electric bills, and water and sewer costs. If you pay quarterly for any of these items, take the amount of your check and divide it by three for the monthly amount. If your husband keeps the checkbook and it is a joint account, you are legally entitled to any information in it. If you don't have access to it or your past statements, call the various utility companies and get copies of your bills. (Write down all account numbers and telephone numbers of the companies for future reference.) Add your telephone expenses to the list of monthly utilities and extras such as cable TV costs, any yard work, or household maintenance you pay for. To estimate your monthly telephone expenses, call the phone company and ask for your records for the last year. If they are similar to what you can expect to spend next year, add them up, divide by twelve, and put that number on your running list. If you're planning for the following year, add a 2 to 3 percent adjustment for unknown or unanticipated cost increases.

If you own a car and pay monthly, add that figure. Car insurance (you can calculate it annually or divide the payments by twelve and make it monthly) and car maintenance and repairs need to be included, along with an estimate of your weekly gas costs.

Next, list your weekly expenses. These will include items such as groceries, prescription or nonprescription medication, toiletries, and any additional costs, such as meals at work, entertainment, eating out, therapy, or extracurricular expenses. Begin saving all the receipts from your activities so you can get a complete account of your spending. Some items will not have receipts, so write these down in a notebook and add them to your list. If you use credit cards to pay for some of your monthly expenses, be sure to include them. Also write down any home equity loans, second mortgages, and school or business loans that you may have.

Make separate lists for your needs and your children's. For example, write down your clothing costs and then make another list for your children. Include all expenses, such as sporting equipment and uniforms, extracurricular activities, books and reference material, tutors, school supplies, lunch money, school trips, diapers, and any other regular costs. If you have younger children and use a baby-sitter, add that monthly expense to your list. The same for day care expenses or a play group. Don't forget the monthly costs of haircuts and presents for birthday parties your children may attend.

Your next figure will be for medical insurance. Your children's coverage will be part of the negotiation process, and there's no reason it can't continue under your husband's policy if that is the way it is currently structured. You can't expect to continue your personal insurance coverage through your husband after divorce. If he has been the one to have health insurance coverage through work, you may worry that divorce means the end of that insurance. No and yes. You will have to find out how much the monthly premium is, which portion of that premium covers your portion of the insurance, and which part covers your child's health insurance. Often a court will order the parent who has health insurance through work to cover the costs during the divorce proceeding until the divorce becomes final. After the divorce, there is a federal law called the Consolidated Omnibus Budget Reconciliation Act of 1985 or COBRA, which allows you to continue the coverage for up to thirty-six months on whatever policy you are currently covered under, although it's usually at a higher cost. This is not ideal, but it will give you time to check into other insurance coverage.

Don't wait until the divorce is final to start looking into individual insurance coverage. Check out small business associations or civic organizations to see if they offer group coverage. Call the medical benefits department at your office, if that is where you are covered, or your husband's office, if he is the one who carries the insurance, and find out about the company's policy after divorce. Also find out if dental insurance is covered by the health insurance, and if so, if it includes orthodontia.

Once you figure out what goes out of the house (the expenses you must pay), it is time to calculate money coming into the house: your salary, your husband's salary, business profits, self-employment income, commissions, workers' compensation, disability benefits, tips, pension distributions attributable to the employer's contribution, and Social Security. These are all sources of income. Pay attention here, because alimony and child support are based on different factors, but the most important one is income. That's why you want to nail down all compensation (salary plus bonus, possibly stock options plus perks) your husband has. When the courts calculate income for alimony and child support, they look to the hidden sources of income. If your husband gets perks from his job, such as a free car, country club, health club or dining club memberships, travel and entertainment expenses, or company charge cards, the costs of these extras can be added on to his income and that, theoretically, is more money for you. Also, don't forget investment income, such as dividends and interest.

Renting versus Buying

One of the most important decisions you will have to make is whether you want to stay in your home, buy a new house, rent, or, if you are already renting, move to a less expensive or smaller house or apartment. If you can help it, it's best not to make major financial decisions immediately after you separate. You will need time to decide whether it makes more sense to remain in the marital home or to move. If you opt to leave your house, you will want to research the advantages of renting versus buying. This can be a complicated issue and may not be immediately obvious. You may be in a rent-controlled apartment, for example, that may be decontrolled in the next couple of years with a huge increase. On the other hand, you may own a house with a fixed mortgage that will remain constant over the coming years.

Think about whether you might need to relocate for your job. Will you be able to get a family member to cosign a bank loan, lend, or give you money for a down payment on a house? Can you handle the responsibilities, emotional and financial, of owning a house now? Do you want to keep the marital home to preserve a sense of security and stability for your children if it's at all possible? If you have to move, you might want to rent for a few months while you decide whether it's financially feasible to purchase a home or condominium or continue to rent and where you want to be.

Think about your needs. Must you have all of your current space? How much of the time will the children be with you? How many bedrooms are required? If you are the noncustodial parent or the joint legal custodian, do you really need those extra bedrooms for the children? What will you do about extended visits during vacations, particularly the summer, if you feel you don't? What are your minimum requirements? What and where would you live if you had a bigger settlement?

After you have figured out what you need or want, confer with someone knowledgeable about money: a banker, an accountant, or a financial planner. If the divorce settlement is not finalized, you will not know how much money you will have to spend on anything, including housing. Here's where it helps to have a competent attorney who can make an educated guess on what you are likely to receive in a settlement so you can at least make tentative plans about buying or renting.

There are some basic financial concepts that you must know:

· It's ordinarily not good fiscal planning to spend more than 30 percent of your household income on housing. In fact, a bank may not approve of a mortgage loan if you allot more than 30 to 32 percent of your gross annual income to mortgage costs. These include principal and interest on your mortgage, property taxes, and insurance.

· To decide if it is more feasible to rent or buy, calculate on a monthly basis what each would cost. With a house, add the property tax, maintenance costs (a reasonable figure is usually 1 percent of the cost of the house divided by 12), and the monthly mortgage. Compare that figure to your monthly rent, noting whether you think it will increase, and by how much, in the future.

You will want to consider the tax consequences of renting versus buying, how much you could earn by investing money instead of using it as a down payment on a house, and whether you have the money to buy a home in an area that will appreciate in value.

· If you plan to stay in your new house for five to ten years, it makes sense to buy.

· If you are in a rent-controlled unit, try to determine how long rent control will be in place. Call the housing authority or housing office at your local Town or City Hall to get an official opinion.

· There are different types of mortgages, and the monthly costs can vary greatly. Ask a banker what type of mortgage is best for you.

WHAT CAN I EXPECT TO GET OR GIVE?

Child Support

Child support refers to financial payments made by the noncustodial parent to the custodian for child-related issues. Occasionally, the custodial parent is ordered to pay child support to a poor, noncustodial parent so there is money when the child visits. Unlike alimony (support money paid to a spouse), child support is mandatory in almost all cases until your child reaches the age of majority. That age varies, depending on the state, but the norm is graduation from high school. Check the laws in your state with an attorney or at your local law library to find out at what age your child is no longer considered a minor. Some states extend a parent's support duty to the child's twenty-third birthday.

Typically, child support is given on a biweekly or monthly basis, depending on when the payer receives his paycheck, or by agreement of the two parties. Even if you earn or have enough money to support your children and make more than your ex-husband, by law he must still help out financially. By the same token, the court will expect you to contribute to their care, regardless of how much or how little you make. Of course, if you have absolutely no money and no ability to earn money with young children at home, you may not have to chip in. For most people, child support payments don't really cover all child care expenses, especially as the children get older and their needs increase. There are many unanticipated purchases, such as a field trip out of state, transportation to and from day care, or growth spurts that require new clothing.

In 1988, Congress passed the Family Support Act, which took effect in October 1989. It is a federal law that guides states in developing their own guidelines for child support. There are no uniform national guidelines. They set out formulas that determine what factors are to be considered when deriving child support figures. Until 1989, support payments were inconsistent among the states and the payments were low. This law required all states to adopt a uniform, statewide formula that set out support payments. All states now incorporate these guidelines into their support laws. The laws determine, as best they can, how much it will cost to raise a child and how much the noncustodial parent will pay to the custodian.

Currently, there are three ways to calculate child support. One way, used by more than thirty states, determines the income of both parents and prorates the amount of support based on their incomes. This prorated formula compares the income, considers the number of children, and assigns a dollar amount. Fewer than fifteen states award child support based on a fixed percentage of the payer's income. It amounts to 17 percent of the paying parent's income if there is only one child, 25 percent for two children, 29 percent for three, and up to 35 percent for five children. Percentages are on the first $80,000 a year of the paying parent's income, and more support money is awarded if the court chooses to deviate. These guidelines are only recommended amounts to be paid. In most states, couples can agree to deviate from the guidelines. They can also come to an agreement about how to handle college expenses. As long as this agreement meets the requirements of a legally binding contract, it is enforceable. The third way to calculate child support is the Delaware Melson formula, which is used in a few states. It is based on the net income of both parents and sets a minimum figure for support while still allowing a child to receive the benefits of the parents' available income.

Remember, however, if your husband loses his job or finds he has no money, the best-written child support order in the world will only be good on paper.

Child Support Statistics

· Child support is not taxable to the person who receives it, nor deductible by the person who pays it.

· It is provided until a child reaches the age of majority (between eighteen and twenty-one, depending on the state), is emancipated, or dies.

· Some states require parents to pay for college expenses.

· It is based on state guidelines and the current income of the payer and payee.

· Child support can't be discharged in bankruptcy.

· You don't have to be divorced or ever married to receive child support in most states.

· Child support is expected to begin on the day of separation, not when the order is signed.

· A parent may not withhold visitation if the other parent is behind in child support payments; by the same token, you can't withhold money because your ex-spouse is blocking visitation.

· The payer is obligated to give the full amount of child support awarded to the payee even if the child spends vacations or summers with the payer.

There can always be deviations from these guidelines. If you can negotiate with your husband, ask that salary increases or other added revenue (bonuses, stock options, trust funds) be addressed in a private agreement, such as a trust fund for your child, in which a percentage of his salary increases automatically go into the fund. You will also want to research the cost of taking care of your child (ask an accountant) or calculate food, clothing, housing, school, medical and dental bills, therapy, camp, vacations, extracurricular activities, video rentals, and birthday party presents so you know you are in the ballpark. The court may award child support above the guidelines for a variety of reasons. They include:

· Special education needs such as private school tuition or a tutor
· Extra needs, such as psychological counseling, speech lessons, or physical therapy
· Medical or dental bills that insurance does not cover
· Extracurricular activities or summer programs
· Child care or preschool expenses (Some states deduct the costs of child care from the parents' gross income before calculating the guidelines; others add on these costs after a guideline amount is established.)
· Income from overtime, second jobs, and/or bonuses

At other times, judges may decide on child support payments that are below the guidelines. This usually happens when:

· There is a custody arrangement where the child spends an unusual amount of time with one parent.
· The custodial parent has remarried, and the new spouse has a large income.
· The noncustodial parent has a low income.
· There was a high debt incurred during the marriage, which the noncustodial parent is still paying off.

· There has been a large division of property where one spouse has received a large percentage of assets free and clear of any debts.

Most courts determine child support by using net income, although there are exceptions that calculate on gross income. What are they? Gross income is a person's income without any deductions taken out. To get your net income, you take the figure for gross income and subtract federal and state income taxes, Social Security taxes, Medicare tax, and any deductions for health insurance. Other deductions may include those mandatory from retirement accounts, although not 401 (k), or voluntary payments made to retirement accounts, union dues, other child support orders to more of your children from other families, and payments of any family debts that have accrued and benefited the family. Check with the law of your state to see whether it uses net or gross income. Beware: States may vary on their interpretation of these two types of income.

It's easier to determine the income of a person who works for someone else and receives a salary. The salary is usually a fixed amount, and so are the deductions. It is far more difficult to get an accurate number for someone who is self-employed. Someone who works for himself can easily hide income, especially if it's predominately a cash business. Normally, the court will disregard unusually high expenses the person claims as deductions and determine a true monetary number, not one simply set by a self-employed person. Many times, the courts will carefully scrutinize the lifestyle of the business owner. They will determine the value of his assets, his cost of living, and any perks received. For instance, if your husband claims to be poverty-stricken but has just leased a BMW convertible, the courts may reconsider his financial records. An accountant or an attorney trained in the field of forensic accounting can unearth hidden deductions. Also, many items that may be deductible for the government may not be for child support.

Adding a Provision to Your Child Support Agreement

Consider adding a provision to your child support agreement that provides for life insurance or an annuity that will guarantee you will have money to support the children if your ex-husband dies (providing he is paying you child support). Sometimes, insurance is provided through an employer, but the policy doesn't necessarily stay in effect if your husband leaves the company. Some people opt to buy life insurance. If your spouse dies prematurely, then you will become the full custodian with sole financial responsibility for your children.

Child Support Modifications

Child support orders can be changed at any time. If either you or your ex-husband want to modify the support, you must petition for a change and show there is a change in circumstances. For the noncustodial parent, the change may include a decrease or complete loss of income, a provable increase in expenses, a substantial hike in the income of the custodian, or a change of needs by the children. If a custodial parent expects the support payments to increase, she must show a decrease in her income, increased expenses due to such circumstances as prohibitive medical needs, a major increase in the salary of the noncustodial parent, or changed needs on the part of the children. If your ex-husband receives a salary increase while your expenses have increased, you might ask your lawyer to file a petition to increase child support. Chances are, it's not going to be your ex-husband's idea to give you more money.

What are the chances of getting more money? If your income level is above the designated guideline amount, you will have to show your husband that your expenses have increased for taking care of your child. Save receipts from big-ticket items, such as a winter coat for your daughter, sports equipment, computer software, or medical and dental bills. You could argue that the children's needs have increased as they have gotten older. If you have been saddled with unexpected bills for household repairs for a home you share with the children—a bathroom flood or a replaced roof, for example—you might be able to convince the courts that you truly need more money. If it applies, you could also point out that your salary has not kept pace with inflation.

If you are making a good salary, the courts may not approve a child support increase. If your ex-husband makes so much money that the amount he pays is already way above the average child support or guidelines, it will also be hard to win additional child support.

If you want to change your support order and file with the court, you are still required to adhere to the existing support order until the issue is resolved. If you are the one who makes the support payments but can't pay in full, pay as much as you can during the period you are awaiting a court hearing.

When He Doesn't Pay

As of January 1, 1994, all child support orders allow the state to automatically deduct the money from the payer's paycheck. If your ex-husband is the one paying child support, his employer must deduct the child support payments from his wages and send it to the court. Under this new law, automatic wage withholding begins immediately, and you don't have to wait until your ex-spouse is late with payments before the support is deducted from his paycheck. This system works well if your ex-husband draws a salary from a company, but it is more problematic when he is self-employed or switches jobs often and doesn't send the support payments to the court. The courts have recently given more power to state departments of revenue and federal agencies to enforce payments. If a noncustodial father is out of work and doesn't make an effort to get a job, a judge could hold him in contempt of court, meaning he is in violation of a court order. When parents don't pay without good reason (they have no money), a court could place a lien on their property or bank account or threaten or impose a jail sentence and/or a fine. If your ex-husband has a good reason why he hasn't paid, like loss of a job, then the support obligation will likely be reduced without any consequences.

If your ex-husband is behind in his child support payments, there are other ways to try to collect the money, but it can be a slow process. One is through the federal tax intercept program. If, for example, your ex-husband is due a tax refund from the federal government for over-paying his taxes, the state that wants the support money can notify Uncle Sam to take that refund and send it to the state to apply to past due child support. State governments also have the authority to place liens on property owned by your ex-husband. The state could foreclose on his property and force the proceeds to be applied to the past due child support.

If you live in a different state than your ex-husband, there are state and federal laws designed for this situation. Among them are the Uniform Reciprocal Enforcement of Support Act (URESA) and the Uniform Interstate Family Support Act (UIFSA). They help enforce support orders entered in one state when the party obligated to pay lives in another.

It's difficult to collect past due child support if your ex-husband goes to extremes to buck the system. Remember Jeffrey A. Nichols, the "deadbeat dad" from New York who made national headlines in 1996 when he was imprisoned twice for failing to pay $640,000 in child support? Nichols was the first person to be convicted in New York of violating the Child Support Recovery Act, the 1992 law that made it a misdemeanor to fail to pay child support for children living in another state. The investment adviser not only neglected to pay his ex-wife $9,000 a month of child support but moved from Canada to Florida to Vermont to avoid this obligation.

While child support and custody may be two separate issues, the bottom line is that you shouldn't prevent or hinder visitation by your ex-husband. You will have a better chance of collecting support money from him if you don't deny him visitation or make it difficult for him to see the children. Money aside, you are also potentially hurting your children by not giving them important access to their father.

A 1996 report to the President and Congress submitted by the U.S. Commission on Child and Family Welfare, entitled *Parenting Our Children: In The Best Interest of the Nation*, states that about 60 percent of the 9.9 million women and 80 percent of the 1.6 million men who are custodial parents received no child support. This figure includes people who had no child support orders or had orders but did not receive the money. Interestingly, these figures show that more often it is the men who don't receive child support, yet the impact on the 5.9 million women is probably greater than on the 1.3 million men who don't receive child support.

What Is the Real Impact of Child Support on Women?

Most often, women don't earn as much as men. The effect of receiving no child support has a tremendous impact on a mother's household. One study revealed that custodial mothers who received no child support in 1991 had an average annual income of $11,140, compared to $27,221 for custodial fathers receiving no child support.

As men have gotten more custody rights, they can now assert these rights to threaten women—and often they do. Your husband might say, "If you want more money, I will be forced to ask for sole custody, and I'll be the primary caretaker." Faced with this situation, women often agree to accept less child support money so they can get more time with their children. Many women consider this "custody blackmail." It's important to try to figure out whether your husband plans to force your hand and seek custody or if he is simply threatening you because he doesn't want to pay more. You know your husband and might be able to determine his motives and his possible actions. Still, it can be helpful to discuss this problem with your lawyer or a neutral third party, like a mediator, who might be able to flesh out whether he is serious about seeking custody. This is also a good time to have a thorough picture of your financial needs. If you know how much you need to live on, you will be better able to judge what you are, or are not, willing to give up economically and what you absolutely need to have. Preparation here, as in all areas of the divorce process, is the key to getting what you want.

ALIMONY, SPOUSAL SUPPORT, AND MAINTENANCE

Alimony, spousal support, and *maintenance* are the three terms that refer to money payments made by one spouse to another. Here the term *alimony* will be used generically for all of these payments. (Many courts refer to alimony as maintenance.) Alimony is intended to provide economic support to a dependent spouse—husband or wife—during or after divorce. It doesn't include child support, noncash property settlements, payments that are your spouse's part of community income, use of property, or payments for the purpose of keeping up the payer's property.

Here are the factors courts consider when deciding on alimony:

- How long you and your husband were married
- If you have devoted many years to staying home with your children and managing the household instead of working
- Your needs
- The amount and sources of income of you and your husband and the liabilities or debts of each

- How much each of you is capable of earning now and in the future
- If there are young children at home
- The health of both parties
- Your standard of living during the marriage
- Fault

Some states consider fault, or how both of you behaved during the marriage, when deciding whether to give alimony or how much alimony to give, as well as how much property the recipient will get from the divorce settlement. An extramarital affair, for example, may not cancel out alimony but possibly reduce it. That is another reason to conduct yourself with discretion and decorum.

Many judges also factor in the husband's and wife's separate assets. The purpose of the list is to determine a spouse's need for support. Need means what is required to keep the same standard of living as during the marriage. (This is an idealistic notion, since divorce usually has a negative financial impact on both parties, particularly women.)

Don't expect that you will necessarily receive alimony. It is awarded in only about 15 percent of all cases. In general, the shorter the marriage, the less likely you will be to be awarded alimony, and the older the party seeking alimony, the greater the chance of receiving it. If you work, you probably will not receive alimony. If the property division can cover the needs of both parties, a judge may also decide not to award alimony. Typically, the court will give alimony if you have had a fairly long marriage; twenty years or more is considered long, but some judges believe seven years or more may also merit alimony. That might be the case if one partner worked to support the other, who had attended graduate school, let's say. The court might consider that contribution to the spouse's future earning capacity. You could also be a candidate for alimony if the disparity in income or earning capacity between you and your husband is great. In other words, you would have to make a lot less money than your spouse to be considered for alimony, and vice versa.

One option is for the judge to grant you rehabilitative alimony. This means that your husband will give you a certain sum of money for a specified period of time to help get you back on your feet. (You may have to do the same for your husband.) This will give you time to retrain or reeducate yourself. If you are a stay-at-home mom with young children, it could be enough money for you to be able to delay going back to work until after your kids are school age. But beware: Courts today may expect you to go back to work, whether you want to or not, as soon as your children are in school. If you don't, the court has the right to attach a monetary number as an "earning capacity," or what you are capable of earning, to you. The judge or other fact-finder may assign income to a person who is voluntarily unemployed or underemployed or who has hidden his actual earnings. It could be a large figure or just minimum wage. Your earning capacity is contingent upon your education, work experience, the professional opportunities available to you in the community, your age, and your skills. There may be exceptions to this rule if you or your child are disabled, you are taking courses to better yourself and your job prospects, or if you have been downsized or can't find a job commensurate with your skills and geographic location. If you are the breadwinner and your husband is the stay-at-home dad, then maintenance would depend on your income and his earning capacity. The greater your age in a long-term marriage, the more likely a judge will rule for permanent, rather than rehabilitative, alimony. If you make significantly more than your husband, a judge will most likely have you pay maintenance.

Another possibility is alimony pendente lite, which is alimony pending divorce or during the separation. This money is designed to help put the parties on equal financial footing until the divorce is final. One of you would have to earn far more than the other, who would have little cash.

There is also permanent alimony. This situation usually only occurs when there has been a long marriage, the difference in income or earning capacity between you and your spouse is great, and one spouse's income is large enough to support an alimony order. Your lifestyle during the marriage is usually studied, as are the responsibilities of the spouse asking for alimony, whether you worked to support your husband while he gained an education or helped to enhance his business. Again, your age, educational level, health, and earning capacity are taken into account. Since alimony is determined largely on incomes and to a lesser degree on expenses, you must keep a complete record of these items.

Permanent alimony is not always permanent. It can stop when the spouse receiving alimony gets remarried or one of the two of you dies. In some states, alimony may be terminated when the person receiving alimony cohabits or lives with another person. These terms could be written into your agreement. It is important that you know the laws of your state on this last fact.

Three Alimony Scenarios

Steve and Louise have been married for five years. Both are teachers who have earned approximately $30,000 a year. For the past five years, Louise has been at home with their two sons, ages five and two. Steve and Louise have separated, and Louise wants to continue to stay home with the children. The courts will probably not give Louise alimony because she and Steve have the same level of education and their earning capacity is similar. It would be difficult for Steve to support two households on his income, they have not been married for a long time, and the court will most likely say they can put the boys in day care, split the cost, and better support two households that way.

Don and Marlene, who have had a ten-year marriage, met through work. Don is the CEO of a marketing company and earns close to $200,000 a year. Marlene used to be a receptionist for Don's company but has not worked since they were married. Her lawyer is arguing that she helped enhance her husband's career by entertaining and running the household. They have one six-year-old daughter. Marlene will probably receive rehabilitative alimony unless she receives an adequate distribution when their assets are divided. There is a huge earning disparity between Don and Marlene. While Marlene didn't work, she helped nurture Don professionally and they had a handsome lifestyle during their marriage.

Louise and Harry produced two children, Andrew, thirteen, and Elise, fifteen, during their twenty-one-year marriage. Louise is an obstetrician and Harry is a scientist. They moved from Wisconsin to California so that Harry could work at a lab where he had gotten a grant. For the last year, he has tailored his schedule to get home when the children's after-school sports are over. Louise has been the primary financial provider. Her career is more lucrative than Harry's, who wanted to stay in the research field and also liked being home for the kids. Harry has asked for the divorce, primary custody, as well as alimony; Louise's salary is three times more than his. Louise is not able to change her schedule because with managed health care, she has to work more hours to make up for staff cuts. Since Harry has been the primary caretaker over the last year, the courts may grant him primary physical custody, and since Louise earns more than Harry, he could receive alimony for several years, depending on the state and the judge.

DID YOU KNOW?

According to the Department of Labor Statistics, nearly 30 percent of working wives earn more than their husbands. If you fit the bill and get divorced, you may have to pay alimony to your ex-husband if you meet the criteria and live in a state that awards alimony. Let's say you are finishing your medical residency or aspiring for a top position in a brokerage firm to put your children through college. Your husband is disenchanted with his job and decides to "take off" a few years and be a househusband. Your marriage breaks up and both of you want custody. He also wants alimony. Since he has been the primary caretaker and you have been the breadwinner, he has a good chance of getting both. Therefore, if your marriage is unstable, don't make any major job changes or reverse your child care roles without thinking of the custody implications.

EQUITABLE DISTRIBUTION AND COMMUNITY PROPERTY

Equitable distribution and community property are two laws used to divide up property. Equitable means fair but not necessarily equal. In a state that has equitable distribution, the court will look at all your assets and decide what is an equitable way to divide them.

There are certain factors they consider when trying to figure out what would be a fair split. They are:

- The length of the marriage
- The health, age, sources of income, and employability of both parties
- The contribution by one party to the education of the other
- The sources of income of both
- The value of the property each will receive
- The standard of living established during the marriage
- The economic circumstances the parties are in at the time of divorce

A judge will consider these items, all assets, how much they are worth, and then divide the marital pot.

Some states have community property laws. In these states, spouses are viewed as equal owners of property and the courts may divide assets fifty-fifty or in what they regard as an equitable split.

Ask your attorney or research it yourself at your local library to find out whether your state follows the equitable distribution or community property rules.

What Is Mine and What Is Ours?

Although the law varies from state to state, typically, you are entitled to keep any property you had before you were married or that was given to you as a separate gift or inheritance while you were married, unless you already threw it into the marital pot. Keep in mind that any appreciation or increase in value of this property during the marriage belongs to both of you. If you deposited money in a joint account, it usually makes it part of the marital property and you will have to share it. In some states, the court may allow you to keep any real estate or stocks and bonds that are in your name alone. If your spouse's name has been added to your account, you can try to set up a separate bank account to reclaim your property.

Your Debts and Liabilities

You need to compile a list of all your debts, which are everything you owe separately or jointly to creditors. The most obvious debts are credit cards; mortgages; car, school, and other types of loans; loans against the pension plan; and lines of credit. A good way to figure out what you owe is to pay attention to all of the monthly bills of the household. Spend time investigating all of your bills before you separate, but if you haven't, begin now.

Debt can also be a joint affair. In most states, both you and your husband are responsible for debts either one of you incurred during the marriage or until the marriage is over (when you are separated or divorced, depending on the jurisdiction). That means at some time you will have to pay them off. Try to do this while you are still married so the money will not come out of your pocket only.

If the expense was acquired at the time of the separation, the court will decide if it is a joint or separate debt, depending on its purpose. If it's to pay the mortgage or buy necessary clothing, for example, it will probably be ruled a joint debt. If, however, it is a luxury buy, like a new CD player your husband purchased, the debt will usually go in his column.

You will need to draw up a list of all your debts so you can split them.

What If I Think My Husband May Be Hiding Money?

If you suspect your husband is not leveling with you, you will probably have to hire professional help, such as a private detective or forensic certified public accountant, unless you know and can prove some of the things your husband has been doing. These may include having unreported cash income, running personal expenses through the business, submitting false tax returns, and receiving perks from his work. You may fear he has purchased property secretly or stashed away money in a hidden bank account, but you will need hard evidence to substantiate your hunches. If your husband expects a salary increase or a bonus, he may ask his boss to defer the money so his current income will shrink (in order to pay you less). Realize that if you file a joint tax return and have signed your name to it, then you are equally liable for any of the deception.

It's important not to write off friends or relatives of your husband because they may have information that you need. This might include bank accounts you don't know about, money in different names, possibly even other children. Stay as superficially friendly as you can.

TAX IMPLICATIONS

Obtain a copy of the government's Internal Revenue Service publication 504 on *Divorced or Separated Individuals* from your local IRS branch if you have questions about tax liability.

Review possible tax consequences with an accountant or financial planner.

CHECKMATE

Cost of Getting a Divorce
You can't deduct legal fees and court costs incurred for the divorce itself, but you can deduct the portion of your legal bill connected with tax advice on alimony.

You may be able to deduct fees you pay to appraisers, actuaries, and accountants for services to determine any capital gains you might have to pay.

You are allowed to add certain legal fees incurred when you are dividing up your property with your ex-husband, such as the cost of preparing and filing a deed that transfers the title to your name alone.

Joint and Individual Tax Liability

Both you and your spouse are responsible, jointly and individually, for the tax and any interest and penalty due on your joint return. This means that you may be held liable for all the tax due, even if all the income was earned by your husband.

Property Settlement

If you receive stocks or bonds as part of your property settlement, make sure you find out how much you can expect to pay in capital gains tax when you sell them.

Mortgage Payments

If you make all the mortgage payments (principal and interest) on a jointly owned home and they otherwise qualify, you can deduct one-half of the total payments as alimony.

Taxes and Insurance

If you have to pay all the real estate taxes or insurance on a home held as tenants in common, you can deduct one-half of these payments as alimony and your ex-partner must report one-half.

If your home is held as tenants by the entireties (a half interest in the whole property with right of survivorship), your tax and insurance payments don't count as alimony.

Child Support

A payment that is specifically designated as child support can't be called alimony for tax purposes.

Alimony

When you receive alimony, you must pay taxes on it, and your spouse can deduct it, provided it meets with the Internal Revenue Service guidelines. A payment to or from a spouse under a divorce or separation agreement is alimony if the spouses don't file a joint return and the following conditions are met:

1. The payment is in cash.
2. The agreement doesn't say the payment is not alimony.
3. You don't live in the same house as your spouse.
4. The payment is not treated as child support.
5. There is no liability to make any payment (in cash or property) after the death of the recipient spouse.
6. After the person receiving alimony dies, the payments stop.
7. Payments don't decrease by $15,000 or more from one year to the next for the first three years. If your alimony payments decrease or stop during the first three calendar years, you may be subject to the recapture rule. According to the rule, you have

to count as income all of the previous amounts paid over the first three years as alimony. The three-year period begins with the first calendar year you or your husband make a payment qualifying as alimony.

Your attorney should explain the nuances of alimony and how it can impact your settlement, including child support. Since child support is taxable, your husband (assuming he is the one paying you money) may want to give you more alimony because he can deduct it, and less child support, which he can't. There is nothing wrong with this, but make sure that he gives you enough alimony to cover your taxes. You will want to know that, after you have paid your taxes, you are left with the amount you want. Remember: You will be taxed on alimony. Check your tax bracket and make sure that you're not paying more in alimony taxes just so your husband can pay less child support. But it may be a way to get what you want and also let your husband benefit.

When you are negotiating your divorce settlement, always think about the tax liability. Because you may have to pay income tax on the profit (called capital gains) you make when you sell stocks, bonds, or your home, you must consider the tax consequences as well as the value of assets. Don't agree to anything until you know your tax liability.

Your attorney and your husband's lawyer will try to work on a deal where you both pay as little in taxes as possible. Often that can be accomplished by shifting some of your husband's income (if he earns significantly more than you) to your income through alimony and property payments and taking advantage of the dependency exemptions available for your children.

Alimony is one way to reduce the gross income for the payer, which will cut down on taxes. You are also allowed an exemption for every dependent in your house. Again, you would subtract from your gross income the amount of exemptions to which you are entitled. Currently, the exemption for most people is $2,650. If you and your husband have many deductible expenses, you will want to itemize the deductions. Keep all receipts and records. Some people choose to take a standard deduction, which is a fixed amount you don't need to document. You and your dependents are entitled to exemptions, whether or not you itemize deductions.

Note: If you have doubts about the endurance of your marriage, consider the implications of custody and support before you split. That means being aware of what a promotion could look like to the court. Obviously, if it's a career move you want or need, proceed, but be aware of its possible effect so you can do some damage control if need be. Like any good move on a chess board, consider all your options before moving your pieces.

WHAT'S LEFT TO DO?

Establish Your Own Credit

You have to have a good credit history if you want to rent an apartment or buy a house, take out a loan on a car, or obtain a credit card or charge account after the divorce. A bad credit history can keep you from getting these things. First, you'll have to find out what your credit record looks like. Write to get a credit report. If everything was in your husband's name, you won't have one. But if you cosigned a lease or mortgage with him, then you will. If he was chronically late in paying bills, you may also have a poor credit record and have difficulty getting a home mortgage or business loan. You may need a friend or relative to cosign with you, or wait until you build up your credit.

Find out what your credit history is and begin to build your own, separate from your husband. You can check out your credit history in a variety of ways. If you have applied for and been turned down for credit, you are entitled to a free copy of the credit report. You can also purchase a copy of your report from a credit agency. In either case, if there is incorrect information, you have the right to dispute it. The Consumer Credit Counseling Service (800-388-2227) is a nonprofit association that can help you set a realistic budget and possibly negotiate with credit card companies to pay down your debt.

You are going to want credit card companies to give you a card in your name only and obtain charge accounts, too, just for you. If you aren't working or make significantly less than your husband, you will want to try this while you are still married, when it's going to be easier to get credit. One way to establish credit in your name is to get a secured credit card. You send in a deposit to the credit card company and the deposit will earn interest. The company will issue a card for anywhere between one to three times the amount of your deposit. It allows you to establish a credit history. While you are still married, consider dividing your joint credit card into separate accounts.

Call the credit card company and get your name off your joint card so you are not liable for your husband's debt. This can be done with a telephone call to the company and must be followed up with a letter sent by certified mail, return receipt requested. In the letter state that you are no longer responsible for your husband's charges as of the date of the letter; you are not required to offer a reason for your request. The company will cancel your name on the card and issue you a new one. You will no longer be responsible for future charges on the original card, but you could be for those incurred when it was a joint account. You probably don't have to worry about being denied credit. Usually, a credit card company will issue you a new card even if you aren't working, especially if you and your husband had a solid payment history.

Check with the credit card companies that you and your husband have to make sure he has not suddenly canceled your joint accounts or is running up a huge bill. Ask your lawyer when and how to notify credit card companies and places where you have joint charge accounts that you will not be responsible for your husband's debts.

Inventory Valuables

If you have safe deposit boxes, visit them and inventory their contents. The object is to protect your valuables, not to hide them. Take pictures of the contents if you don't want to remove items or photocopy them when possible. Videotaping is also an efficient method. You might consider having someone else take an inventory, date it, and sign an affidavit attesting to its accuracy, which could then be given to your lawyer. This would work for other possessions you have, such as furniture or antiques, that you feel are valuable. There are businesses that will videotape personal belongings for insurance companies. You can try that route or even take pictures yourself and date them. It will be hard for your husband to prove that you have stolen valuables when you have this kind of concrete evidence. The court will see how well-prepared and honest you are. And your husband? He will probably be upset that you have done your homework and may cave in on other divorce-related issues.

Go Over Your Will

Take a look at your will. If your husband is the beneficiary or executor in the will, redraft the document as soon as possible. Also revisit the issue of guardianship of your children with a lawyer.

Rethink How You File Your Taxes

Obviously, you want to pay as little as you can in taxes. If you are separated or divorced, ask an accountant if it makes more sense to file a separate or a joint tax return with your husband. The difference can be tremendous. You could have more money to divide between the two of you instead of giving it to the government. If you have any question about your husband's honesty or the accuracy of these tax returns, you will want to file a separate return.

If your husband always prepared the tax returns, you may want to get help filing, at least initially. Consult a certified public accountant, go to a large accounting firm, or buy computer software or a book that explains what you need to do. Whatever you decide, you should still know the basics.

To figure what federal taxes you have to pay, first add up your gross income, including salary, dividends, interest, and other items that are taxable, and subtract deductions and exemptions to derive your taxable income. Your taxable income will dictate what tax bracket you are in so you can determine the amount of taxes you owe. The percentage rate at which you are taxed is determined by your income; the larger the taxable income, the higher the percentage.

Act Smart

Be fiscally conservative. Don't move to a more expensive residence solely to increase the amount of money you think your ex-spouse will have to pay because your expenses are now higher. The courts will see through this, and you will be even shorter on cash than you were before. Don't do anything unethical, such as opening an out-of-state bank account or giving big chunks of cash to relatives in order to hide cash and other assets. If you submit false statements or act dishonestly, you may be subject to criminal penalties.

Sleazy Tactics

Be careful. Your husband may be well-intentioned, but don't bank on his doing the right thing financially. If you are the one who ended the marriage, your husband might want to punish you. If he has a new girlfriend, he may try to get extra money from the settlement to support her.

Don't put slimy tactics past him and don't engage in them yourself. These might include hiding personal property and assets, raiding your joint bank account, deferring a raise until after the divorce so he doesn't have to share it, or charging heavily on joint credit cards. The credit card "scam" would raise the debt, lowering the net assets the two of you would split. Watch out: Prior to signing the divorce agreement, your husband may try to reduce his standard of living in an effort to convince a judge that he doesn't have much money so he can end up paying you less.

General Financial Housekeeping Tips

Know where all your records are, from insurance information to mortgage statements and birth certificates. Don't count on your husband or anyone else to hand them over or keep track of them.

Have your attorney act fast to protect your money and other assets.

Keep a record of your current expenses and project what you expect them to be in the future.

If you can afford it, hire an accountant to help you budget and manage your money. If you can't, borrow books on the subject from the library or purchase them at a bookstore (generally found in the personal finance section). Besides how-to books, consider taking an adult education class on finance or getting computer software. Various computer programs, available in computer stores, can help you pay bills electronically and do the math for you.

If you have to reduce your standard of living, start by cutting your major living expense: housing. You might want to go from a large home to a smaller one or to an apartment, or from a smaller house to a smaller apartment in a less expensive area. Try not to spend anything that is not essential and reduce your spending on essentials. Join wholesale ware-house clubs or buy store brands rather than private labels. Again, there are books that can guide you (*The Tightwad Gazette, The Cheapskate's Guide to Living Cheaper and Better,* and *Handbook for Modern Frugality,* to name a few).

If you have to go back to work but don't know what kind of job to pursue, there are books specially designed to deal with reentering the job market. A career counselor might also be helpful. After you are offered the job, ask the prospective company about their pension plan and health benefits, and find out if they pick up any of these costs. But don't do that at the first interview. Ask what other benefits they offer, such as paid sick leave, paid vacations, or emergency child care. Some businesses provide in-house day care on either a regular or temporary basis, and it may be subsidized.

Don't assume child support will cover all your costs for raising your children. In most cases, it will be a fixed sum determined by state guide-lines.

Don't make any rash financial decisions.

Professionals You Should Have on Your Side

An accountant will calculate how much money you have and what you can do with it. Ask your attorney if he or she advises you to use an accountant and to give you a referral. You will want someone with experience in matrimonial law. Always ask for references.

A financial planner will map out your economic future: what your current financial needs are; how to adjust to a postdivorce eco-nomic lifestyle, and how to do tax, retirement, estate, and college plan-ning. He or she may help you restructure your investments, perhaps converting some of them into cash.

Being financially savvy is the key to getting what you want: a bal-anced budget, an effective attorney, and a settlement that will provide you with a secure future.

What to Expect before and in Court

Before going to court, you will have to understand the law and the court's procedures and rules, since the parent who wins is often the one who is best prepared. The more you understand, the better able you will be to help your lawyer and yourself. The trial also should be less stressful if you are legally and psychologically ready for it.

The first thing you will need to do is get ready to take on your ex-husband. You may be dealing with a male-dominated courtroom and a male mentality. Men are used to a good fight and to acting tough, while women tend to cry, blame themselves, and get depressed. But that mode doesn't work in a custody battle. You can and should be polite, but you have to have the stomach, the stamina, and the tenacity to fight for primary custody of your children.

Expect to spend hours with your lawyer preparing for your trial. It can get very expensive, but in a custody contest, you need to put in the time. Your lawyer must know everything about you, your children, and your husband in order to prepare for all contingencies that might arise at trial. For this reason, your attorney will have to prepare all witnesses and review documents and information pertaining to your case. Obviously, the more limited the issues that need to be tried, the less it will cost.

When you or your husband get serious about a divorce and contact an attorney, you start your official involvement with the court system. The party who files the divorce or custody action (if you decide to deal with the issue of your children first) is called the *plaintiff* or *petitioner*. The other spouse becomes the *defendant* or *respondent*.

Although the papers filed by the lawyers vary from state to state, in general, the plaintiff's lawyer begins the process by filing a complaint or petition telling the court the essential facts and requesting specific forms of relief. This can be anything from asking that the court order a schedule of when the children will be with each parent to seeking exclusive possession of your home, or requesting child support or the division of property. In a divorce complaint, you often ask for relief for all your concerns—financial and custody—in one document. The complaint is both filed with the court and delivered (called served) to the other spouse, who must respond to it. The response generally provides the other spouse's view of the essential facts and his or her requests for relief.

If an issue—such as with whom your child should live primarily—addressed in the complaint requires the immediate attention of the court, your attorney may file an emergency petition requesting an immediate hearing. If the facts merit it, your counsel can file a petition asking for temporary custody or a petition to prevent your husband from squandering marital property or to award alimony pending divorce or spousal support, interim counsel fees, or for child support. Make sure you are educated about the divorce process (by speaking with other divorcees, attorneys, attending seminars, and reading up on the subject) so you can discuss the issues and strategies with your lawyer before there is a crisis.

There may be a tactical advantage to moving first and quickly. If you are the one taking the initiative on an emergency issue that requires immediate attention or harm may occur, or you just file first, your husband may not have had time to find an attorney, or at least the most desirable one. (Bear in mind that he is not allowed to use any lawyer with whom you have consulted, even if that lawyer might have been his first choice.) Note, however, that judges will generally give the other party time to hire legal counsel.

You must be fully prepared at any emergency hearing. Why? First of all, there is a psychological advantage to winning the first round. You are showing your husband you are serious about gaining custody and willing to do the necessary work and spend the money to get it. Also, there is always the possibility that the results of the emergency hearing may end up being permanent, especially in custody matters. That's because judges like to maintain the status quo if the arrangement is working well and may be reluctant to contradict an earlier decision. Therefore, make sure you present your best case and cover all of the terms that may be important to you. Review these terms with your lawyer and understand every word before you agree to anything. Realize that the temporary agreement may limit you later on. For instance, if you receive a lesser sum of money for spousal support than you had requested, and at a later hearing your husband's lawyer shows that you are managing on this amount, you may be stuck with the original figure even if you are just getting by.

As the divorce proceedings progress, attorneys for both sides may exchange written documents, some of which will request additional relief from the court or information from the other spouse. These requests for information are known collectively as discovery. In some states, attorneys must ask permission of the court to engage in discovery; in others, discovery is a matter of right. Discovery can take the form of interrogatories (written questions that must be answered by the other side), requests to inspect and copy documents, or requests for depositions, which are formal question and answer sessions taken under oath and transcribed by a court reporter. Discovery is always expensive, because you are paying for your lawyer's time, whether it is to draft the interrogatories or depose your ex-husband, plus additional costs (stenographers transcribing the notes of testimony and reproducing them).

If you need to have a hearing, the attorneys for both sides will present evidence. Evidence includes oral testimony, written affidavits (statements of facts signed by you, your husband, or others, sworn to be true and accurate), or other documentation, such as photographs, bank statements, diaries, or medical records.

Your lawyer may submit interrogatories to secure information from the defendant. For example, your husband's attorney or yours may request information concerning your earning capacity. This may include what level of education you've attained, whether you have any job skills or potential, and if you worked prior to the marriage (if that's the case, what your salary was).

You will need to review the answers to the questions your lawyer prepares for you. *The answers are important and may be the ones you're again asked by your husband's attorney in court, so make sure you answer accurately and in a way that will get you what you want.* For instance, if you are asked what your net income is, make sure you deduct all taxes and any deductions prescribed by state law, so that you give the correct answer. If you are questioned about the hours you work, which may be different shifts, including a night shift once a month, emphasize that the night shift occurs only twelve times a year and you have excellent child care coverage during those times.

The attorney for the other side may ask if you were ever under a doctor's care for an emotional problem. (Your husband could argue your emotional state will interfere with your custodial responsibilities.) Therapy is generally accepted by the courts as a positive method for resolving issues and won't be held against you, but you still need to work with your lawyer to best prepare this kind of answer. (Severe depression is a far greater problem and a major obstacle for winning custody.) Sometimes one party will subpoena documents, such as medical records, to determine if a parent has a physical or emotional problem that could be argued might interfere with custodial responsibilities.

THE DEPOSITION

One of the most useful tools for extracting information is the deposition. The deposition is a minihearing in which both lawyers have the opportunity to ask questions of a party or other witnesses, but no judge is present. Depositions are less formal than a hearing before a judge, but they can be just as intimidating. Careful and thorough preparation is essential. Your lawyer will prepare you to testify. You must make a candid and full disclosure of the facts and then your lawyer will help you formulate honest but positive answers to the questions your husband's attorney is most likely to ask.

There are certain rules to keep in mind when you are deposed or questioned at trial. Listen carefully to the question. Don't answer it if you don't understand the question. If you don't understand, say so; it is not an admission of ignorance. Don't answer a question because you think you'll look smart; it may only get you into trouble. If the question contains a factual assertion with which you disagree, don't answer without correcting that fact. You can say, "Yes, but . . ." and explain what you mean. You are required to answer all questions, even if you don't like them, unless and until your lawyer objects and instructs you not to answer. A judge may later be called upon to rule on whether the objection and the instruction were proper. Answer opposing counsel's questions truthfully, but keep your answers brief. Don't volunteer any additional information. Your husband's lawyer may try to trip you up, so pay attention.

Even though your lawyer has prepared you for the deposition, it is still likely to be grueling and unpredictable. Stay calm and in control. You can't let the other side rattle you. If you need a break, ask your lawyer. Telling the truth is essential. Any discrepancies in your story from the time of the deposition to the time of the trial will be raised by your husband's attorney and will weaken your position. No fact will hurt your case as much as getting caught in a lie. It puts into question the rest of your testimony.

An unsettling part of a deposition is having your husband in the room when you answer the questions. He has a right to be there because he is the other party to the lawsuit. Equally uncomfortable is having to listen to his answers when he is being questioned by your attorney. Make sure you don't interrupt; leave that to your lawyer. Urge your lawyer to take your husband's deposition first. As a strategy, it's often advantageous because you will know what he is claiming and it gives you a chance to prepare your response when his attorney asks you questions. There's an additional benefit to hearing his responses: You will get a sense of how he performs as a witness and how you might compare with him in court.

THE SETTLEMENT CONFERENCE

At any time, including during a trial, your lawyer or his may suggest a settlement conference, where both sides meet in an attorney's office to try to come to a mutual and quick agreement. You and your lawyer will confer before the conference to discuss your case and hone your strategy. This is the time to tell your lawyer what is most important to you. Your wish list might be having primary physical custody, half of your husband's pension, staying in the marital house, or whatever else you want. Think of what compromises you are willing to make, because inevitably you will have to make some. Again, this raises the importance of preparing your case thoroughly. You need to know what there is to give up before you can give it up. In addition, you have to know your options.

The results of a settlement conference are not binding unless it results in an agreement between you and your husband. You are under no obligation to settle, but the legal fees will be far lower if you do. You may escape some of the acrimony you are guaranteed to experience if you go to trial. Remember: What you want to get out of a settlement conference is an agreement that is enforceable.

As a result of the settlement conference, your attorney may make an offer, and your husband's attorney may counter, or the other way around. There will be some issues on which you agree more quickly than others. If you come to an agreement, the lawyers will prepare a formal document, which may look like a court order or a commercial contract. Once that document is signed and, where appropriate, approved by the court, what is said—and not said—in the agreement will become binding on you and your husband.

Just as you scrutinized your temporary agreement, you need to do the same with the permanent order. Make sure you also understand what is not in the agreement and whether you will be bound later on by the omission. The lawyer's job is to work with you until you fully understand the agreement.

You may not reach an agreement, but at least you will have defined which issues will make up the case. You will then need to get ready for your trial.

THINGS YOU AND YOUR LAWYER SHOULD DO BEFORE STEPPING FOOT IN A COURTROOM

1. Prepare for your testimony, both on direct and cross-examination.
2. Interview witnesses and prepare for their testimony.
3. If you know about a potential witness who may hurt your case, take that person's deposition before court to help in preparing cross-examination or to prepare others to rebut the harmful testimony. For example, if a former baby-sitter said she's arrived several times to find your young children in the house unsu-

pervised, your lawyer could take her deposition first. He might determine that unsupervised means that you were on the telephone and your children were in the next room, and that she is a *former* sitter because she let her boyfriend come over when the children were under her care.

4. Understand what the assigned judge typically does, both in terms of how he runs his courtroom and what he likes and does not like to hear.

5. If you've never been in a courtroom, go visit one, preferably when the judge who will hear your case is on the bench.

THE COURTROOM

There are courtroom rules and protocol that must be strictly followed during a trial. It is critical to know what to expect so you don't behave improperly or freeze up when faced with what is guaranteed to be an intimidating and emotional situation.

This is what you can expect at your trial: Both your lawyer and your husband's attorney make their opening statements, a speech to the judge explaining why they are there and how they plan to prove their case. Their comments must relate to the evidence they will introduce during the trial. The remarks should not be exaggerated or unsubstantiated but should provide an accurate preview to the court of what is to come.

The plaintiff's lawyer will present evidence to support the complaint and the defendant's lawyer will draw on different evidence to refute those points. Each side is allowed rebuttal testimony to address new issues brought up by the other side.

You will be expected to testify. The rules of evidence require that you can only testify about facts of which you have firsthand knowledge. That means you can only comment on what you have perceived: what you have heard, seen, or experienced yourself. For instance, you can't say your ex-husband left the kids alone if you didn't observe it. It doesn't matter what the children told you. They would need to testify to that fact.

While you are on the witness stand, your lawyer will ask you about significant events in your marriage or your children's lives that are important to the trial issues. These could be "Tell us about your child's fifth birthday party," or "describe your son's last parent-teacher conference." This is called the direct examination, the questions your attorney will ask you. The rules of court prohibit your lawyer from asking "leading" questions (questions that suggest the answer) during direct examination. He will ask you a question such as, "Describe a typical day in the life of you and your child," and you must answer it. You may tell how you get breakfast for the children every morning, pack their lunches, and drive them to school or day care, and after work, pick them up, shuttle them to after-school activities, make dinner, bathe them, and get them ready for bed. What you are trying to do is show that you are the primary caretaker or that at least you play a large role in their day-to-day life.

You should be well-prepared by your lawyer, so that his questions and your answers proceed smoothly and efficiently, and so that your answers provide the evidence he needs to prove his point. After your attorney has finished the direct examination, your husband's attorney is allowed to cross-examine you. Don't expect him to be Mr. Nice Guy. He isn't bound by the rule against leading questions, and he may ask a series of narrow, out-of-context questions suggesting answers that will challenge your version of the facts. For instance, your ex-husband's lawyer might question you: "Isn't it true that you spent three nights having dinner with your boss in the last month?" You might have to answer "Yes," even if the dinners were legitimate business meetings. (Your lawyer should clarify this on recross-examination, but it still might have caused some damage by an unconvinced judge.)

Your husband's lawyer will try to make you uncomfortable, to get you to slip up and contradict your testimony, to point out to the court the weaknesses in your argument. The lawyer's tone may be sarcastic, hostile, and downright unkind. On cross-examination, this behavior is allowed. The opposing counsel is trying to make you out to be the less suitable parent and even to discredit you. While suitability and fitness may have never been an issue before, it becomes an issue when you want custody.

As with a deposition, when you are cross-examined, try to be as brief and direct as possible. Your job on cross-examination is to protect the truth as you already have testified and to do it in a way that will enhance, not diminish, your credibility with the judge.

You may wonder why your lawyer is not objecting more. If you think she should be, ask her during the recess why she hasn't. There may be good, strategic reasons for her approach. In order to make that judgment, you will have to understand the legal proceedings, and if you don't, she should explain them to you. The bottom line is, you are the client, and you have a right to know why she is doing or not doing certain things at your trial.

No matter how well your lawyer has prepared you, realize that he or she may deviate from the script because of testimony and evidence brought up by your husband's attorney or because of questions from the judge. If your lawyer is good, she will know how to read the courtroom, while at the same time, keep you informed about why she is ad libbing. It could be that she has discovered weaknesses in your case or in your husband's case, or she may detect some predisposition of the judge that was not apparent before.

Don't expect court to be a cathartic experience. It is not a place where you want or will be able to vent about your husband. Much of what transpires is a dull recitation of facts. You will be confined to answering questions. You can't just "tell your story."

The cross-examination process is brutal, but there are ways to be proactive. For example, if your husband's attorney asks why you did something or asks you another open-ended question, you may be able to get in the points you want to make that you might not have been able to, under the rules of direct testimony. As soon as the lawyer from the other side figures out that you are telling more than he wants you to, he may object, but at least you will have been able to slip in a few comments that may lend insight into your situation. For instance, if his lawyer asks, "Isn't it true their father decided to take the children to the psychologist and pay for it?" you may be able to say, "Yes, after our eight-year-old walked in when he and his girlfriend were having sex, he decided they needed to talk with a professional." This is called "opening up the door."

Some judges ask a lot of questions; others feel more comfortable having the lawyers do that. Make sure you are prepared in advance. Some attorneys urge their clients to memorize a short speech on the points they want to make. Know what you want to say in response to likely questions. Always answer the question the judge asks. A witness can quickly alienate a judge by avoiding the specific question asked or by making speeches that are not responsive to the question. There are no more important questions than those asked by the judge. These are the issues and facts he or she wants to know about.

WITNESSES

Besides calling you to the stand, your lawyer may also introduce witnesses who can provide information to help your custody case. These people must be reliable and credible. Go through a list of your friends and others who know you and your child well. One Mid-Atlantic judge said that for her, the most important testimony in a custody matter is hearing nonfamily members, such as teachers, athletic coaches, the parents of the child's friends, choirmasters, Girl Scout leaders, or care givers, say that a parent is doing a good job. Independent or impartial witnesses are the most convincing witnesses. These are people who don't have a stake in the outcome of the case. Your close friends or relatives who want to see you win may not be as independent or as convincing witnesses as a teacher. Any statements your son may have made to impartial witnesses that can show that he is happy living with you could be very persuasive.

Your lawyer will decide which people to call as witnesses after conferring with you. She will interview them to determine if what they have to say will be credible and help your side. Good witnesses have firsthand knowledge of the facts and are articulate. As one Southern judge put it, "I want to know who is the parent who is there in the middle of the night, who keeps in contact with the school, who communicates with the teachers, who is there when the child falls down and cuts his knee, who attends PTA meetings." (A pediatrician's notes proving you have been the one to bring in your child for visits may be helpful, particularly if your husband claims he takes the children to all of their doctors' appointments.) These are the types of questions for which you will need to provide evidence to prove you are the "better" or at least as good a parent. Your job is to identify for your lawyer who the third party witnesses are who can answer these questions well. Remember, all witnesses are subject to cross-examination by your husband's attorney, so they need to be prepared for the courtroom by your lawyer just as you were. Don't let your lawyer call any witness to the stand unless he has interviewed the person and prepared her testimony in advance. More is not necessarily better. It is preferable to have four witnesses who can provide different perspectives and insights into your superior parenting ability rather than fourteen who barely know you but want to do you a favor.

One important function of independent witnesses is to address the hot button issue of "deliberate alienation by a parent." Many judges say this is often a critical factor in a mother's losing custody. The legal system promotes the proper role of both parents and may penalize a parent who attempts to subvert that goal by alienating a child from the other parent. *It is your job to make sure the judge understands that you want your children to have a good relationship with their father and you will do everything to foster that relationship.* Therefore, think of calling independent witnesses who have seen interactions between you and your child to prove this point. For example, if your child's school has a Father's Day and your child's teacher overhears you telling your daughter that you think it would be wonderful for her to go to her father's house after school and out to dinner to make the day even more special, that teacher might make an excellent witness. Don't forget the chess game. If custody is an issue, then genuine efforts to encourage your child's relationship with her father within earshot of the teacher or other independent witnesses can be a good strategy. You are the one who must build your case through positive actions. If you keep a detailed diary of comments and actions like this, you may be able to reconstruct evidence when you need it.

Besides bringing in outside witnesses to testify, have your child's school records on hand showing that he is excelling in school (but only if he is). On the other hand, if he is doing poorly and living with his father, you could try to prove his grades are a result of his unhappy custody arrangement. Your lawyer will have to prove that your version of the facts is the "correct" one. If your husband claims one thing and you can establish he is wrong by supplying contrary evidence, you will be in the stronger position.

Expert Witnesses

Other witnesses may include a custody evaluator, a guardian ad litem, a social services investigator, and sometimes a private investigator. At the beginning of custody litigation, a judge will often ask the court to appoint one or more of these experts. They are very important to your case because a judge will give tremendous credence to their reports and will often rely on their custody recommendation. Some judges consistently defer to their decisions. You want to impress them with your parenting skills, and that doesn't mean telling the experts what a lousy father or husband you have. Let them figure that out themselves.

Overburdened judges are increasingly relying on outside mental health professionals to make custody recommendations.

The Custody Evaluator

This expert is a mental health professional, often a child psychiatrist or psychologist, and sometimes a social worker. If you can, try to get a custody evaluator who is board certified in pediatric psychiatry. A private custody evaluator can cost from $1,500 to $10,000. Ask your lawyer what a court-appointed evaluator in your jurisdiction charges.

Checkmate: What Evaluators Look For

1. The spouse who is willing to share the children with the other parent
2. The parent who is mature, caring, nurturing, and even-tempered
3. The parent who might feel terrible about the divorce, but wants what is best for the child and puts the kids' needs first
4. A situation which is natural, meaning the child has not been coached by the parent about what to say or how to act
5. The parent who is competent, who can get the daily job done, and who the judge can feel good about choosing

Your attorney, if she is experienced, will know which custody evaluators are more likely to rule for you in your situation and will veto a judge's selection of someone who could harm your position. If your lawyer is not familiar with an evaluator on the judge's list, she will usually be allowed to do a little research. Your lawyer should choose someone who has an active practice and is familiar with real-world custody issues, rather than a professional witness who pays all the rent by testifying in court. Your lawyer may also recommend that you use an impartial evaluator who will only take a case if he is permitted to evaluate both the father and the mother.

Expect a custody evaluation to include separate interviews with you, your husband, and your children; interactions between your child and each parent with the evaluator present; IQ, achievement, and personality tests for both spouses; and interviews with others (teachers, coaches, pediatricians, neighbors, and possibly your therapist and the children's therapist) who might have insight into your parent-child relationship.

Be careful if your lawyer finds fault with the custody evaluator provided by the court and asks you to hire your own expert witness. Someone you pay may not be taken as seriously as an evaluator appointed by the court. It is also likely that if you hire an expert, your husband will, too, and that means you and the children will have to be grilled twice. However, if you get an experienced outside evaluator to review the report, he may be able to poke holes in the tests administered by the court-appointed evaluator. Your evaluator may also be able to document other inaccuracies in your case.

At the very least, the independent custody evaluator can advise you on your meetings with the court-appointed evaluator. He will be able to explain what to expect, do some role-playing, shore up what he thinks could be weaknesses in your case, and administer tests similar to what the evaluator will give you. Custody advisers who design court strategy for parents are also a booming business, particularly in large cities.

Getting Ready for the Evaluator

When it's your turn to talk to the evaluator, have a well-thought-out child care schedule arranged so you can discuss it. It will show you are responsible and don't intend to leave young children unsupervised.

Speak up about any concessions you have made at work or with volunteer or recreational activities so the expert will see that you put your children first.

Much as you may dread it, the evaluator is going to ask your children questions about you and your husband. Give them the same advice you did for testifying in court—that is, to be honest and speak freely. Coaching them will backfire. Your "help" will also be obvious to a seasoned evaluator.

When it comes time for the expert to "view" you relating naturally to your child (Who can act natural with someone observing you and grading you in the biggest parental test you'll ever have?), try not to perform. Rather than contrive a special project, do mundane "mom" activities, like helping with homework, hanging out together, or making a meal.

The evaluator will present a written custody opinion to the court. It could be for exclusive custody, shared parenting, or other legal arrangements. The evaluator could also decide one of you is unfit. If it's a close call, and one parent seems only marginally better than the other, the evaluator might award custody to that parent with liberal visitation to the other.

Guardians Ad Litem

These are court-appointed professionals for children who may be therapists or attorneys. Sometimes in a contested case, a judge may appoint a guardian ad litem, or G.A.L., as they are known, to look after a child's interests. One or both of the lawyers may request that a G.A.L. be appointed, or a judge may make the recommendation if neither parent is effectively representing the child—that is, when the parents' behavior is so outrageous that the child's interests are not being met— or when they feel they need additional information to make a custody decision. Their role is as an independent and objective observer who is an advocate for the child. They usually interview both parents, the children, and others familiar with the youngsters: their teachers; coaches; and family friends—anyone who plays an important part in the child's life. They might review children's medical and psychological records.

By observing your child separately with each parent, the G.A.L. is trying to find out how your son or daughter feels about each parent.

The G.A.L. will also ask you to recite a typical day with your child and may ask you hypothetical questions, such as how you would handle a temper tantrum. The G.A.L. might ask your five-year-old what life is like in Mommy and Daddy's house. Depending on the child's age, the G.A.L. may also ask your child where he would like to live. That answer will be given some weight, but it will just be one of a number of factors.

G.A.L.'s make a recommendation to the judge as to which parent they feel is the more suitable custodian. They want to make sure there is as much stability as possible for the children, while at the same time giving them the opportunity to have a close relationship with both parents. Since this professional makes a recommendation, it is important to impress a G.A.L. You do this by establishing credibility and being able to point out your ex-spouse's failures without appearing vindictive or angry. Be careful here: If you bad-mouth your husband, the G.A.L. may believe you are also telling the children bad things about their father. Knowing how destructive that can be for children, a G.A.L. might hold this against you and recommend the father.

A good lawyer will know which G.A.L. is most sympathetic in which situation—if you work or are gay, for instance. Think of it this way: Says one attorney from the East Coast who explains why it is critical to find the right G.A.L., "If a judge knows a G.A.L. has been before the court hundreds of times and spent dozens of hours with parents, teachers, the kid's friends, done the right interviews and psychological testing and has a recommendation that is well thought out and factual, and is faced with two lawyers arguing for three days and an objective mental health professional who has done his work, it's very hard to get a judge to go against that G.A.L."

If both parents can afford it, they will share the costs of the G.A.L., or the party who has more money will be ordered to pay. In cases where neither parent has money, the courts may incur the expense. Typically, a G.A.L. costs $115 to $175 an hour, and an average case may take twenty-five to thirty hours. The minimum is usually $3,000.

An Independent Investigator

A judge may order a social worker or an independent mental health evaluator to give the court an opinion independent from the custody evaluator or guardian ad litem of the parents' parenting skills and the home environment. This occurs when there are so many "hired guns" that a judge needs a separate opinion, or as one jurist termed it, "his own eyes and ears." Ask your lawyer if this might be done in your case.

Forensic Psychiatrists

If either you or your husband's mental fitness is an issue or there is a question of substance abuse, the judge or the parent who wants to prove there is a problem may also request a psychiatric examination with a forensic psychiatrist for the parent in question. The expert will determine not only whether one of the parents has an emotional problem but how and if it will impact his or her ability to take care of the children. If, for example, you are functioning well but are depressed because of the divorce and the custody battle and have seen a therapist, it may not be used against you. However, if you are addicted to liquor or drugs, are severely depressed, or have a mental illness that prevents you from fulfilling your parental duties, the forensic psychiatrist will be able to make an evaluation and report to the court. This expert will research the spouse's past employment, medical, and psychological records.

There is another modern use for forensic psychiatrists. Mothers are calling upon these experts to investigate whether their spouses have a secret, double life involving other women, and addictions such as sex and gambling. If you suspect your husband is not leveling with you and that his possible fantasy lifestyle will impact his parenting ability, consider a forensic psychiatrist. They commonly charge $200 to $350 an hour.

Private Investigators

The days of having a private eye lurk behind peepholes to dig up the dirt on an extramarital affair are history. But detectives can still be useful in contested custody cases when you think you can prove your husband is not acting in your child's best interests. The kinds of behavior that might merit a private investigator are:

1. Your spouse is abusing alcohol or drugs when he is with the children, or even when he's not, and it is impairing his judgment and compromising his parenting skills. If he is drinking or taking

illegal drugs and driving the kids and a detective can prove it, you have a major edge.

2. He is sleeping with a succession of women when the children are under his roof.
3. He may be on duty but not paying attention to the kids or spending real time with them.
4. He disciplines them too harshly with physical punishment.
5. The environment is unclean and unhealthy for the children.

Ask your attorney for a reference. Many matrimonial lawyers work regularly with investigators and know who is good and what to ask them to help your case. Make sure the detective you hire has an excellent reputation and looks presentable to a court. Detectives typically charge from $40 to $150 an hour, depending on where you live and the caliber of the firm.

OTHER EVIDENCE

Judges rarely get to see the children and parents interact. Many jurists like to have evidence that shows that a child is happy or wants to maintain the current custody arrangement. Therapists may get children to express their feelings about the divorce and custody issue through drawings. Show your lawyer any pictures or stories your children may have created that could be interpreted as a plus for you. These could be drawings with smiles and happy faces or "I love Mommy." Some lawyers ask a parent to look at a child's diary to see what he is thinking; some experts feel this is a violation of privacy.

Your lawyer may try to introduce a videotape of you with your children in a wonderful family moment. In some jurisdictions they are allowed to be entered into evidence, but not in others. Some judges may decide they don't want to waste their time with it because it may not be reliable. In other words, a parent might have staged the close moment for the courtroom. Other jurists are interested in anything that will help them make a custody decision and may look at the tapes and decide later what is and isn't relevant and reliable. As a general rule, most judges will permit pictures into evidence. Your lawyer will have to explain to a judge why she should look at them and why they are relevant to your case. For example, if you claim your husband is an alcoholic and drinks in the presence of your children and you have pictures or tapes showing him surrounded by beer cans and your daughters, you might be able to prove your point. You will need to have your lawyer decide if photos or videos will be effective. She should know the judge and the content. A judge may get angry if pictures are introduced merely to be provocative.

Many mothers believe that when they go to court they will get justice and everything will be fair. In a matter of seconds you will see that your husband and his lawyer are not there to be nice to you and fair. Your husband's attorney will use any legal means to try to show you are not a good mother. Any past indiscretion, no matter how small, will be mentioned and possibly exaggerated. For instance, if you have ever suffered from depression, your husband may use it as an example of your inability to cope with your children. Leaving your ten-year-old alone for an hour so you can get a haircut might be distorted into an argument that you care more about yourself and how you look than your child's safety. Of course, your attorney will turn around and try to do the same thing to your husband.

You are unlikely to find out if you've won custody on the spot. It usually takes several weeks or even months before the judge enters a ruling. She may want more time to review the evidence.

APPEALING THE CUSTODY DECISION

If you are unhappy with the verdict and want to appeal it, it must be based on evidence at the trial. You are not allowed to bring up new issues or problems unless they were unknown at the time of the original trial. (If there are new issues, see chapter 8.) The only way to appeal successfully is if you can prove an error of law was made by the judge or an outrageous outcome not based on the facts.

To appeal a verdict, you must file a Notice of Appeal, which is usually entered within thirty days after the judge's ruling. Your lawyer would submit the necessary documents from the trial. Usually, a panel of three judges will look at the evidence submitted during the trial to determine if any errors of law were made by the judge. It is uncommon to win an appeal, so your best shot is to make your case at the trial. An appeal can cost thousands of dollars. There is also an enormous emotional price for you and your children.

HOW TO LOOK, ACT, AND DRESS IN COURT

It's not enough to level with your lawyer and the court or even to be prepared. Just like chess, you have to know how to play the courtroom game. There are certain written rules that your lawyer will review with you before going to court. However, there are other, unwritten factors that are just as important to know. These include what to wear to court, how to conduct yourself, and what to say—or not say.

What Is Appropriate Attire?

Judges want to be shown the respect that their black robes demand. Often, a judge will hear a case for a few hours or a few days. This certainly can't give him a complete or necessarily accurate picture of your life and often leaves the judge to look for intangibles. That is why appearance really counts.

The first thing a judge will notice is your appearance, so dress conservatively. As one East Coast judge advised, "Dress like a mother." What does that mean? Don't wear a short skirt or too much makeup. "Women who wear skirts three-quarters up their thigh lose their credibility, and that applies to both litigants and lawyers," said one female Florida judge. A jurist may interpret that to mean you are more focused on your clothes than anything else. You are supposed to be saying, "I can take care of my kids. I can teach them appropriate behavior." That attitude should be reflected in the way both you and your children look in court. "If a mother comes into court looking ridiculously sexy, it will affect me," said one Wisconsin judge, who did not mean the impression would be favorable.

Dress the way you would for an afternoon business meeting. Don't look flashy. Try a simple pants suit or dress, a nice skirt and blouse, or a skirt and blazer. Keep the colors dark or muted. By the same token, if you lead an elegant lifestyle and want to continue that lifestyle, be sure to dress well. Still, leave huge pieces of jewelry at home. If the judge is female, one Northeast matrimonial attorney tells her female clients not to wear makeup "because you don't want her to be in competition with the judge. Also, be careful, because judges probably make $90,000 to $100,000 a year, so if they're sitting up there and you're all decked out and you say, 'I'm sorry, I can't live on $20,000 a week, not including child support,' it's not going to go over very big."

Make sure you (and your children if they are going to testify) look presentable. Judges like to feel that the custodial parent can give the child a sense of stability and well-being, and that includes paying attention to when their hair needs to be cut and their clothes washed and ironed. (Teenagers may not cooperate, but many judges are parents and know that adolescents are independent-minded.) Judges want to see that parents teach their children good habits of hygiene and appearance. As one jurist stated, "Judges want to know your children come first."

One judge said that she is turned off by mothers who claim they have no money to live but bring their children to court wearing pricey clothing and toting high-end toys. She said it makes her question the mother's value system. "If you claim you have no money to feed your children and you come to court wearing expensive clothing and carrying a designer handbag, your credibility is at issue. It might make me think that material items mean more to you than feeding your children."

What to Say

The next important rule is to watch your language. You will be judged not only by what you say but the way you say it. Stay away from slang and swearing. "People say things in a courtroom today that they wouldn't have said fifteen years ago in a tavern, and I find it a real turnoff," said one judge. It's critical to present a positive image about your parenting attitude. You want to convey to a judge that you are a wonderful mother who feels that her child deserves to have a great relationship with *both* parents. Use phrases like "our child" or "our children." If you make statements such as "He doesn't know how to act with *my* child," you may lose points with a judge. Don't treat children as if they are your property or a prize to be won—*your* prize. One judge said that she likes it when a mother speaks favorably about her in-laws and makes such comments as "I want our children to be able to see their father and their grandparents and to continue the loving relationship that they have with them." You also want to show the court that you plan to keep your ex-husband involved in your children's lives. You might want to say to the judge, "I always make sure to mail notices about parent-teacher conferences, school activities, and extra-curricular events to their father." By helping to maintain important relationships in your child's life, you will add credibility to your position that you want what is best for your child. One Southern judge said he can't stand the parent who thinks the child doesn't need the other parent. Of course, if your ex-husband has been physically abusive to your child, a judge probably wouldn't expect or even want you to have this inclusive attitude toward him, but would certainly encourage a relationship with loving grandparents.

How to Act

A court appearance is similar to a theatrical performance. When you see actors, you examine their facial expressions. The judge will be examining you in the same way. Make sure your behavior is appropriate. Don't laugh in court, particularly when your husband speaks. (Of course, if the judge or one of the attorneys makes a joke and everyone laughs, it's safe to join in.) Judges want you to take the courtroom seriously.

Your state of mind and your attitude are usually conveyed by body language. Unconsciously, people make faces when they don't like what they hear. Be careful to veil your feelings and try to convey an amicable attitude. If you say you want your daughter to continue to have a wonderful relationship with her father and then you scowl when it's his turn to speak, your words will lose their impact. Your demeanor, or the way you look when you make these statements, are just as critical as the statements themselves. Obviously, you don't want to appear stonelike and without emotion, or a judge may think you are severely depressed and the less fit parent. The best tack to take is to behave sensibly.

Negative gestures that show you don't like your child's father may backfire on you. Judges want to know that you consider your ex-husband as your child's other parent, not the person who ruined your life. Your attitude about your husband is important to the court. As one judge suggested, "Never show your anger in court because it could just as easily be directed at your child." If you bring your son to court with unkempt hair and start screaming that you would like him to get his hair cut but *his* father won't give you the money, a judge may decide you are excessively bitter and may not be a cooperative parent. Remember, judges take cooperation into consideration when weighing a custody decision.

Even though you may have excellent reasons for being angry, the courtroom is not the place to display it. A therapist's office, a friend's house, or a support groups meeting room are places where you should vent your anger. Judges in a custody case want to know that you can rise above these feelings so that you can have a decent relationship with your ex-husband. It's particularly important for you as a woman not to show overt hostility. In fact, your husband and his attorney hope that you appear angry and may even try to provoke that response in front of a judge. They will be trying to expose your flaws, and if you seem neurotic, unstable, or petty, and your husband appears rational, easygoing, and cooperative, they may succeed.

Expect your husband to make false accusations and think how you will handle them. Don't react visibly. If you want your lawyer to contest the claim, whisper to him or her or write a note. One judge advises mothers to "be calm." Admittedly, that advice is hard to follow in a custody battle. Simply walking into a courtroom may provoke physiological reactions, such as elevated blood pressure. One strategy you might try: Prior to your trial, visit an empty courtroom in the building where your case will be heard. Sit down. Look around. You may even want to try the witness seat. If you are familiar with the setup before time, it might relieve a little of the anxiety. Or you could visit a court where the judge who will be presiding over your case is sitting.

You need to thoroughly understand the legal process before your case begins. That includes the procedures that are followed, the key players, and how to behave. This should make the process more palatable and will increase your chances of winning.

11

Speaking of the Other House

What you say to your children about custody and what goes on at their father's house will depend on your situation—your children's ages, how frequently they switch homes, and whether or not you and your husband live close to each other, to name a few factors. There are no quick fixes, but there are techniques you can try that should make it easier for you all to get through this.

Remember, you may not be able to change your husband or his behavior, but you can control your own and help your children deal more effectively with their emotions and the fallout of divorce.

HOW TO TALK TO THE CHILDREN ABOUT CUSTODY

Typically, parents are overwrought about divorce and focus on their own needs and pain. It is easy to "forget" your children. Yet it is a time when the kids are equally devastated and need to be updated regularly on details of the custody process. The biggest questions they are going to have are where they will live, who will take care of them, if they will get to see both you and their dad regularly, and what role they will play in the proceedings. You have to give them some answers and re-assurance, even if your plans are not finalized.

It will be easier for you if you can separate how you feel about their father from what your children feel about him. One way to do this is to think about what they are experiencing and need, rather than what you think of the situation. You may believe your husband is not as good a parent as he should be, but the reality is that your child is going to have a separate relationship with his father. And he should (unless, of course, there is child abuse or another significant reason why they shouldn't see each other). You not only want your child to feel free to have a solid relationship with his father, you want to encourage it because it is important for your child.

Divorce is likely to be a lonely experience for your children. They will now have two homes but may feel displaced, as if they have none. To mitigate this, one mental health professional talks to children about "your house with Mommy" and "your house with Daddy."

ALL AGES

Just as it would have been best if you and your husband broke the news about the divorce together, you need to talk to your children as a couple about the custody process. If you can't get your husband to sit down with you to do this, there are still ways to have a positive conversation. You are going to need to stay calm so your children can focus on what you are saying and not be distracted by your feelings. You are not an automaton, and it will definitely be hard. You will want to repeat what you told them when you discussed the divorce with them. Reassure them that they aren't to blame for either the divorce or the custody situation and that both you and their father want what is best for them and will try to make sure that happens. Tell them how much you love them and that your love won't change even when their living arrangements do.

Children need stability, structure, and predictability. They need to be reassured that their parents will never divorce them, that their relationship with the family is permanent. Let them know that both you and your husband plan to stay active in their lives and continue to have a close relationship with them. If you are certain that your marriage is over, tell the children that Mom and Dad won't be getting back together so you don't raise false hopes for them.

The first thing to do is tell them about all the things in their life that will stay the same. These may be their neighborhood, their relationship with both sides of the family, school, town, or the play date with Joey every Friday after hockey. Be as specific as you can. Suggest that they keep a list of telephone numbers (your house and office, your husband's, their grandparents', and friends') by the telephone in both houses so they can call the people who are important to them, including you and their dad, whenever they want.

Only tell them about what you and their father have agreed on. It's possible the arrangements for next month have not even been negotiated yet. If they have, you want to provide it at your next conversation. The younger the child, the more important it is to keep the time period short and concrete. Describing the plan for Christmas vacation in September or even November may be confusing for them.

Let them know you will keep them informed and encourage them to ask questions and confide their worries so you can try to help them. If you and your husband sound united, they might feel less compelled to take sides—a situation that may still be difficult to avoid.

Make sure you tell them the truth as you know it and not pretend it will be a quick custody proceeding if it won't. You will need to prepare them for the custody process. Explain to younger children that when couples disagree, they sometimes turn to other people to come up with a custody arrangement. Tell them there may be people who want to talk to them to learn what they are feeling. For instance, if they must speak with a guardian ad litem (a court-appointed advocate for your child), you might say, "Dad and I don't always agree on everything and we decided to talk to someone who knows a lot about kids and parents getting divorced who will help make decisions on what is best for you. She wants to talk to you about how things are going." Children need to know that the agreement may not be what they want so they don't harbor unrealistic fantasies, but however it turns out, you and your ex-husband will always take care of them. Try to relate this information in as relaxed a voice as possible so they are not distracted by your misery or bitterness.

Let your children know that all that is required of them is that they be honest. By addressing this, they will be encouraged to be candid and will feel less torn about speaking with outsiders. Make sure you don't tell them what to say. In other words, no coaching. Giving them permission to say what they want and be who they are will empower them and help them feel less caught between you and your husband. (Coaching can also be obvious to someone appointed by the court to make a custody recommendation. It will not reflect well on you because you are supposed to be concerned about what your child wants, not what you want.) Sometimes, children are afraid to speak candidly during a custody battle. They may feel powerless and insecure. The court may seem intimidating, and they may be aware of their own role as a pawn in the fight. Children often worry that if they say what they really want, there will be dire consequences for the parent they feel is more vulnerable.

If you decide to go to court, you will need to prepare your children if they are going to testify. They should know why they are going (because the grown-ups can't agree and a judge is there to help them come up with a plan) and what to expect (the judge, lawyers, or others may ask them questions and they must answer truthfully). Your children should be familiar with the setup ahead of time (the witness seat they will sit in near the judge, who is near a court reporter), as well as the terms they might hear, such as *bailiff, parties* (not the kind they have for a birthday), *lawyers, testify,* and *guardians ad litem.* It may be possible to visit the courtroom ahead of time. Some courts give tours to children. Call your local courthouse to inquire. Youngsters get anxious about going to court (as do adults), but should be a little less nervous if they have some familiarity with it.

In a contested custody dispute, the court will evaluate your child's age and maturity and decide whether or not she would make a good witness. *If you can, keep your child out of the courtroom.* Having a child testify against a parent can only be traumatic and may have long-term psychological implications. Usually, when children are called as witnesses, the judge will ask an attorney to represent their interests in court.

CHILDREN AGE EIGHT AND YOUNGER

While all children need to have a sense of continuity, it's particularly important for toddlers and preschoolers. Children younger than age five may think that if you are out of sight, they are out of your mind. Youngsters this age sometimes believe that if something is not visible— like you—it doesn't exist. You want them to realize that even if they are with their father, you are still thinking of them. Therefore, it can scare them if they aren't with a parent and they may believe that parent has abandoned them. One thing you can do is pack a bunch of "love notes" you have written and have your child read one each day she is away. Or you could mail them to her so she receives one daily with a photograph of the two of you together. When the children are with you, encourage your ex-husband to do the same. If the children say prayers, ask your spouse to have them mention you, and make sure that is reciprocated at your house.

Some other ideas: Draw pictures and make maps of the route to your husband's house. Or create a calendar that will give the children a sense of the time and activities they will have at each parent's. For instance, with children three to six years old, you can use blocks of color to delineate what they might do during one day. "Wake up" might be red and "school" might be green. Events that take longer would be bigger blocks. The object is to give children something concrete to hold on to so they feel they have a sense of control. Talk to children six and older about what they can expect at your house. Start by describing the routine over the coming week. Include lessons, play dates, car pools, sports, and times with you and your husband. The older the child, the more weeks you can add. An eight-year-old, for instance, could understand a two- to three-week span.

The problem of maintaining a sense of continuity gets harder when you and your husband don't live near each other and the children are away for long periods of time during the summer and school vacations. Try to be in daily contact with your child regardless of her age. Divorce changes the relationship from contact on a daily basis to one that occurs only when your child stays with you. You want to maintain that daily connection as much as possible. If you have a computer and modem or a fax, you could fax notes or E-mail them, and your child could E-mail you back. If you can, a brief phone call to check in, see how her day went, and tell her that you love her would foster a sense of continuity and caring. Consider having a regular contact time. (That may be addressed in your parenting plan or custody agreement; see page 128.) If the sound of your voice, or the sound of your husband's, sets off one of you, think about getting your child a separate telephone line so she can talk directly with her father. Or, instead of a separate line, you might be able to get a phone feature that has a special ring for different family members. Check with your telephone company.

You don't want to call more than once a day, or you could be conveying your uneasiness to your child about being with her dad. Don't undermine her visits by telling her, "I'm sure you'll be all right with your father." She may also think you are lonely and overly dependent on her and may have a hard time bonding with him. Let your child know you will be fine without her and you will spend time with her when she returns. If she's worried about you, she may leave for her father's feeling she is abandoning you. You want her to know you are happy that she's happy, and if she is doing something special with her father, such as taking a trip or attending a special movie, that you are excited for her.

Not only do you need to prepare your children for long absences from you, but get yourself ready, especially if your husband lives far away. It's normal to feel lonely, even lost, without your children. In a long-distance arrangement, it's particularly important for you to have a life independent from them.

AGE EIGHT AND OLDER

They will want to call the custody shots. Make sure you listen to what they have to say about where they want to live, but be clear that they will not be the ones making the decision nor will you or their father. They should know that there are other factors that also go into determining custody, but that you, your husband, a mediator, or the court, will take their opinion seriously. Judges will often speak with older children, typically twelve years and up, and ask them with whom they would prefer to live. The judge will consider their answer as one of the factors in making the decision. If your children are going to have to state a preference, tell them you know they love both parents. You might consider telling the children that custody is fluid and may change as they get older. The message is that they have not given up on the other parent, and this arrangement may not be permanent.

After living with you for a while, older children might decide they want to move in with your husband, or move back and forth. That may work if you and your husband have a good relationship and are willing to be flexible and informal, but it certainly doesn't work for everyone.

BEING ON THE SAME PAGE

Another issue to be sensitive to is weekend activities. Your children may be signed up for sports, Sunday school, or art classes, but the parent in charge that weekend might not want to drive them or have them participate. It's a mistake to enroll your son on a swim team that practices every Saturday, for instance, if your husband has your child every other weekend and wants to take him skiing instead. *You need to negotiate what activities you both feel are important so your child can be supported.* Some parents get back at each other by enrolling the child in a class and insisting the weekend parent take him there without having an agreement about the class. It's the child who will suffer as a result of your power struggle.

MAKING TRANSITION TIME EASIER FOR YOU AND YOUR CHILDREN

Children of all ages need time to adjust after making the switch from one house to the other. Many youngsters need preparation or quiet time to make the transition—to gather their clothes, toys, books, and special blankets that travel with them, and to get ready emotionally. The kids will pick up on your tone, so make sure you sound enthusiastic about their upcoming time with their father. When the children come home, greet your ex-partner pleasantly. Practice in the mirror, grit your teeth, but do it.

It's normal for youngsters to be irritable and have difficulty when they first get back. They may not seem excited to see you because they may have had a tough time leaving their father. Transitions bring up a child's wish that his parents could live together and have a good marriage; moving between Mom and Dad brings home the fact that they don't.

If your child acts unhappy when she returns, don't assume it means something happened to prompt such melancholy behavior. You can't rule out a real issue, but realize that your child may feel compelled to carry on in this way. Youngsters are in a hard position. They may have had fun with their father but complain or act glum because they think you want them to. They think if they admit to having fun with your ex-husband, it will make you miserable and they will be acting disloyal. They could be trying to protect you from feeling left out, especially if you have been hurt by the breakup. This can translate into nervous, angry, or obnoxious behavior when they return from the other house.

You have to give your children permission to enjoy their time with their father. This may mean having to listen to some of the details of their visit that you don't want to hear. When new girlfriends or extravagant purchases are involved, it can make you mad and jealous. As difficult as it may be, try not to shut off communication about subjects relating to your husband that are painful to you. Your children need to be able to talk to you, and that includes issues relating to their father. How do you, then, find a way for your child to share her experiences with her father in a way that Dad does not feel like a forbidden subject? If the breakup is new and raw, this may not be possible. Of course, how much fun you can listen to depends on where you are in the custody process, your relationship with your ex-husband, and your own stage of dating. Over time, as you adjust to your situation and your anger abates, it should become easier to hear about your ex-husband.

Explain to your child that it's hard for you to talk about Daddy right now but that will not always be the situation. Reassure her that you want her to be able to talk to you about her father or anything else and that you will tell her if you don't feel comfortable discussing the subject. Let her know she doesn't have to worry about bringing up something that will bother you because you will tell her if it does. That way, she'll know when to save the topic for another time or speak to someone else about it. But you don't want her to have to tiptoe around an important part of her life because that can erode your relationship with her. Remember, you are doing it for you and her, not for your ex-husband, and to help to continue building your mother/child rapport.

You might not want to know the details of your husband's new life, but some mothers have the opposite issue. They view visits away as an opportunity to check up on their ex-husband. Don't pump the children for information about him. Be careful what you ask. Children feel safer when they aren't expected to make judgments about either parent. It's also in your best interest not to groom a minispy. You'll want to feel that your own privacy is protected when your ex-husband asks questions about you. If the children are older, you can set some guidelines for your questions with them. You shouldn't be asking your child about your ex-husband's love life, his financial situation, or what he's saying about you. Your child must feel that the boundaries of each household are established and respected. Let your son know that while you are available to listen to him, you don't expect him to be a go-between or a reporter.

If you and your ex-husband are on bad terms, consider cutting down the number of transitions to minimize the trauma to your child. (This may rule out joint physical custody.) Every transition may worry your child that another fight will occur. Your son or daughter may view these exchanges as potentially dangerous and become extra vigilant, trying to protect you from getting upset or harassed. Some parents make arrangements to drop off and pick up their children at a neutral place, like a friend's house. You could arrive a few minutes early and leave the children with your friend. Your ex-spouse could retrieve them ten minutes later so you don't have to see each other. When there has been domestic violence, the court will often require your ex-husband to make alternative transportation arrangements and order supervised visitation. You could hire someone to transport your child between the two of you. (If he has more money than you, the court might order him to pay for this arrangement.) You might also consider using a visitation center, where parents who have court-ordered supervision visit their children, as your drop-off location.

If your child comes back to you Sunday evening, make sure it's early enough so you can finish the transition well before bedtime. You might want to time the return right before a favorite television program begins. Television may be the perfect short-term balm that will allow your child time to unwind, but if you aren't thrilled with the idea, rent a video for him, have him read a book or read to him, or let him do a puzzle or engage in another form of quiet play.

Some parents arrange transition time around the school day. Instead of going to the other parent on Sunday evening, you could take your children to school on Monday morning and their father could pick them up at the end of the day. That way, you can say good-bye Monday morning, which happens to be a natural time for all children to leave their parents. With this arrangement, you have to make sure that your child doesn't forget important items that he must have at his father's house. (A checklist of belongings that need to be brought back and forth could help solve this.)

Some children find switching at school cumbersome and dislike having to take their clothes and sports equipment for the weekend to the other parent's. Or they may not have the clothing or other items they need at your place. If your child is old enough, let him choose between a Sunday evening or Monday morning transition.

An aside: You have to decide whether you are comfortable having your ex-husband come into your house, and if so, what parts of your home, when he returns your child. You may have strong feelings against inviting him in, but your child may insist. In that case, you will need to tell your child what the rules are: He will meet his father outside, for instance, or in the front hall, the kitchen, or the living room. Have the children ready to leave when your ex-husband arrives so the pickup period is brief. Remember that the friendlier you are with your ex-husband, the more comfortable it should be for your children. (Youngsters whose parents are hostile to each other may play sick or act out to get the parents to interact, even if it is at their own expense.) At the same time, setting boundaries is important and privacy may preclude this. It's easier to set clear rules and expectations from the beginning.

For your child's sake, restrain yourself from getting into a fight or criticizing your ex-husband in your children's presence or within earshot. Don't debate troubling adult issues in front of them. Take issue with each other when the children are not around. Otherwise, it may become increasingly difficult to get them to change households. Also, when your child returns, don't badger him about homework or chores immediately. It will only intensify a stressful situation.

Look for opportunities to say positive things about their father to your children. You can always find something (he's punctual, he sings well, he's handy at cars, he's good at business). Your children will appreciate it.

TIPS FOR MAKING THE MOVE

There are ways to make it easier for your children to move between your place and your ex-husband's. Make a calendar and mark your husband's time with one color (if you're a traditionalist, baby blue) and your time (passionate pink) in another. A third colored marker (lemon yellow) could indicate time for them to get ready for the transition between houses. Or you and your husband could keep identical calendars and consult them with the children, so they know when the next transition is to take place. Very young children may not understand the concept of time and this is a visual way to explain it.

They will probably keep toys at both places, but they may still want to have a bag with special clothes, toys, books, or even a custody schedule that they can tote back and forth. Ask them if there are things they would like to have at both houses.

Rituals are important for children. The ritual of packing a beloved bag they can take with them can provide a sense of control over at least part of their situation, as well as the belief that certain things—even something as little as the ritual bag—in their world are unchangeable. If they take their favorite book, they will know they can read the same bedtime story at both houses. Your children may worry they will leave their blanket or stuffed animal at the other house. Keep as many duplicates as you can afford and help them collect these items. Again, a checklist that would travel back and forth between parents could benefit everyone. It could include what the child brought to school that day, i.e., the Miss Piggy lunch box, the Bart Simpson sweater, and which backpack.

Suggestion: If they want to hold on to telephone numbers—yours, your ex-husband's, their grandparents', friends'—you can buy a special belt, like a jogger's pouch, a necklace with a pouch, or pockets on a string (used by travelers on vacation and available at luggage stores).

CHILL-OUT TIME

Expect that the transitions will be hard for your children and be sensitive. (It may also be wrenching for you.) Whenever possible, allow down time, or time to relax and readjust to the new house. When your children come back from being with their father, try not to schedule events immediately. By letting them chill out, they will get a chance to readjust. So if your four-year-old gets back from his father's on Sunday at 5 P.M., you may want to rethink a dinner out with another family at 5:30. Instead, consider rescheduling it for a weekend when your child is with you. You should ask older children whether a dinner date with another family will work for them or if you should decline. When they first return, most teenagers need to be given the space to do what comforts them, perhaps closing (slamming) the door of their room, calling their friends, and playing their CDs.

WHEN YOUR CHILD HAS MISBEHAVED AT ONE HOUSE

Your husband reports that your son talked back to him and has been punished. He can have no friends over the rest of the week. But now he's with you. It doesn't seem fair that you should suffer because of a punishment imposed at your husband's house. One way to handle this is to make a rule early on that any punishment meted out in one house must be carried out in that house. Therefore, when your son returns to his father's, he won't be allowed any friends. It's best if you and your husband keep each other informed of these punishments. Perhaps similar misbehavior is happening at your house and then you could work on a unified approach to the problem, or at least be aware of an issue that could surface with you.

If you feel your husband's way of disciplining is too punitive or too laid back, discuss it with him directly, but don't denigrate his discipline style to your children. It will undermine efforts to change negative behavior and instead refocus the problem into a power struggle between you and your husband.

If your ex-husband lets your ten-year-old go to bed at 9 P.M. instead of 8 P.M., and it's within a reasonable range (not 11 P.M. on a school night, for example), you might say to your child, "You know the rules are different here than at Dad's. When you are here, you follow the rules here; when you are at school, you follow the rules there, and when you are at your father's, you follow his rules. If you get a little confused, I'll understand and we'll work on this together." Or you might try,

"That's different than the way I do it, and it's okay to be different as long as you feel reasonably comfortable. But if you don't, you'll need to talk to Dad and me about it."

You have to decide which issues are between you and your child and what is rightfully between your child and your husband. For example, if your eleven-year-old daughter complains that she doesn't get to have enough friends over when she's at her father's, encourage her to advocate for herself and bring up the issue with him. If she feels she can't broach the subject, you might want to bring it up with your husband. But it's a good idea to have children who are age eight and older talk to their fathers about these issues independently of you. It will also help them learn how to negotiate, and that is a life skill. You can help them learn how to speak up, overcome their reticence, and take action. This might include role-playing with them about how to ask their father questions and express what they want, as well as problem-solving and planning strategies. After you have done this, you will have to stand back and let go—not exactly an easy assignment for most mothers.

BUT WE CAN AT DAD'S HOUSE . . .

Inevitably, the rules will be different at your ex-husband's house than yours. After you examine them and decide your rules are reasonable, you will need to stick to them. This is a promise: Your child will do some comparison shopping and play the more liberal parent (later bedtime, more junk food, less censored TV) against the stricter one. In most cases, you will take the fall and be the bad gal. This is going to be a popularity contest you will not win.

When you separate, things will probably not be the same way at your husband's house. While you won't have much control over that, realize it's okay for things to be done differently at each place. Children are resilient. What's important is for your child to feel comfortable in both houses—and he won't if you disparage the way your husband does things.

If you do communicate well with your ex-husband, you might want to come up with a plan with relatively similar rules, but they don't need to be identical. You may, however, want to pick two or three issues that you feel should be uniform at both houses. For young children, these may be making sure your husband's house is also child-proofed, choosing baby-sitters in a similar way, and agreeing on how old your son or daughter needs to be before being left alone. With older children, it could be curfews, entertaining the opposite sex when an adult is not home, and telephone rules. Being united on major issues will benefit your kids and lessen the chances of manipulating one parent at the expense of the other.

WHAT TO DO ABOUT MR. GENEROUS

Isn't it ironic? Your ex-husband may count his pennies with you but give lavish gifts to your children. How could you not be resentful, especially if you are struggling financially? But his motives may not be the love bribes you think they are.

Analyze why your ex-spouse gives these gifts. It may be that he sees your daughter for a limited period of time and feels the loss of that relationship (not to mention his marriage or house). While you may view the endless Barbie buys as nauseating attempts to buy her love, he may be trying to create a welcoming atmosphere for your daughter, but not know how to do it any other way.

If you have a decent relationship with him, bring up the subject diplomatically. Perhaps you could talk to him about gifts he could give the children that would be helpful to all of you: a new basketball, a lovely snowsuit, or a computer. If you feel you can't bring up the subject with him, don't waste your time. Rather, save the vitriol for a friend or therapist.

Of course it's hard to do when your blood is boiling, but consider a new take on the Disneyland dad. Say your husband buys a puppy to make his home attractive to your children, but you aren't allowed one in your apartment or you can't afford one. Or he takes the children on fabulous trips when you can't even pay for a getaway to the next state. Try to reframe these events. Instead of thinking, "He's an insensitive creep for trying to show me up again," see it as "Now my kids have these wonderful experiences." You can tell yourself that it takes the pressure off of you to find a way to give them a dog or expose them to other places. "Don't play into the game; he has more," said the Ohio mother of a son, fifteen, and a thirteen-year-old daughter. "So what if he's generous? Most kids don't care about something that is expensive versus something that isn't. In my experience, kids understand a hell of a lot." This mother left her husband and his money and moved when the children were six and four. "I can't tell you the number of people who ask, 'Isn't it hard that he takes them everywhere and you can't?' They say, 'How do you do it?' What I've found is that what's important for kids is where their friends are and if you can supply an environment with friends, they'll want to be with you. You don't have to assume the money difference is going to be a problem."

What do you do about duplicate items at each house? This is an economic issue. If you can afford two of everything, that will certainly make it easier for everyone. But most people can't. Figure out what is feasible. Large items, such as a computers, Nintendos, and CD systems are hard to transport. Sometimes your child may have to do without at one of the houses. If it's your house, try to accept the situation. It won't be easy for you, but you have little choice, and it will make it easier for the kids.

WHAT SHOULD I KEEP AT EACH HOUSE?

It depends on such factors as how much money each of you has, how far apart you live, how organized your children are, and how long the kids spend at each house. (How often do you want to do laundry?) Obviously, the more duplicates, the fewer the logistical problems. It also eliminates accusations of "I bought that and that belongs in my house." Both houses should contain enough so that your children don't feel like a visitor or hotel guest in either place.

You will have to decide what your priorities are. If having a computer at each house is important to you, then pay for that and do without something else, such as two entertainment games or two sound systems. (You could buy a portable CD player and your child will just have to remember that along with the in-line skates.)

What Each House Should Have

- A toothbrush and your child's favorite brand of toothpaste
- A comb and brush and blow-dryer, if she uses one
- Her favorite brand of shampoo and conditioner
- One or two pairs of pajamas
- Underwear and socks for four days to one week
- One pair of jeans, a few T-shirts, two sweaters, and a few other well-used pieces of clothing
- Whatever is in the medicine cabinet at the other house: aspirin, Band-Aids, thermometer, cough syrup, antibiotic ointment, insect spray, sunscreen, poison ivy ointment, cream for a sunburn or rash, tweezers, a sterile needle, your child's medications
- Separate toys, although your children may decide to bring a couple of their favorite toys or stuffed animals back and forth
- Their baby blanket (You can cut it and leave part of it at each house.)
- Snack and grocery food they like
- Dictionary, thesaurus, school supplies, such as notebooks, pens, erasers
- books (Have your child pick out books that she wants to keep at each house.)
- sports equipment (Depending on your child's hobbies, you might want to have a basketball, football, or tennis racket.)

What you probably can't duplicate: schoolbooks and the book bag (because youngsters usually get attached).

WAYS TO COMMUNICATE WHEN YOU CAN'T TALK TO YOUR EX-SPOUSE

When your children are younger, you will have to communicate regularly to share information. The kids will get sick sometimes and not be able to switch houses, you will come down with the flu, one of you might have a scheduling conflict, or your son could have a long-term school assignment he needs to work on at both places.

If you are constantly fighting with your ex-spouse, having as little face-to-face interaction as possible is prudent. That is a short-term solution, however. *Your ultimate goal should be to improve your relationship so you can communicate about issues relating to your child.* (In a case of domestic violence, it may not be possible to have direct contact or cooperation with your husband. Many experts advocate complete separation between parents in these circumstances.)

If frequent phoning back and forth leads to shouting or sarcasm, you could leave messages for each other on your answering machines when you knew the other wasn't in, or on voice mail at work. If both of you have a modem, send messages by E-mail, which tends to depersonalize the communication. You might be more comfortable writing notes than talking, so you could fax a message to your ex-husband's home or office. Of course, you'll need some kind of system to know he has gotten the message and so he knows you have received yours.

A huge mistake is making the children tote messages back and forth between bitter parents. It can only make them feel trapped in the middle, and it is very destructive for them. Tell your ex-husband whatever it is yourself, and ask him to do the same.

Try to communicate decently with your ex-husband. It may take years, but regardless of how old your children are, there will be times when you'll have to see, if not speak with, your spouse. (Imagine your daughter planning her wedding and having to worry that her parents won't talk to each other on her big day or even sit on the same side of the church for the ceremony.) There's another reason to get along: If your husband is feeling good about your relationship, and he has more money, he is more likely to help you with unanticipated costs that aren't part of the child support or alimony agreement.

YOUR HUSBAND ONLY WANTS TO DO WHAT HE WANTS TO DO

Your children may return from their father's complaining they are bored because he doesn't engage in activities they like. This frequently occurs when the mother has done most of the caretaking and the father might not know how to play with or be with the children. You have to rectify this situation quickly so your children will want to spend time with him.

In your husband's defense, he shouldn't be required to entertain the children every second. They must learn that everyone, including their father, needs some time for himself. But they should also know that they have a right to have some of the time they spend with him be doing activities they like.

Your job is to help your child figure out what kind of activities appeal to her so she can be clear with her father. If she's older than seven, encourage her to take up the issue with your husband. Help her role-play what she could say. It could be, "I'd really love to play a game, so I brought one over we could play together." If your husband is a decent person, he will respond to your child's suggestion. Or you could say to him, "I know it's hard because you haven't been in this position, and I wonder if you might like me to give you some suggestions about what you and Sabrina could do together." If he's responsive, propose they stay home and relax one day and the other day Sabrina could pick the activity. Recommend he divide the day so that each of them gets a chance to do what he wants part of the time. If your child is old enough, see if he will confer with her during one of his midweek calls so they can make plans. Suggest he get together with a family from the neighborhood or your children's school. If your husband doesn't want your help, tell him that Sabrina has been complaining she is bored and you want her to want to be with him. Be careful about how you deliver this information. If you say it in a sympathetic tone, he might take it that way; otherwise, he might view it as an accusation. Send some toys, books, and board games to his house that the children could do with him. There's a chance you won't be able to change him, but it's equally possible his parenting will improve.

CHILDREN DON'T WANT TO BE WITH THEIR FATHER

Your child may not want to spend time with his father, but the courts are requiring it. Try to figure out why this is the case. Is his girlfriend or her children unkind to him? Does your husband ignore him? Is it simply a case of a self-involved teenager who would rather be with his friends, or is there something about the custody arrangement that isn't working for your child? Is he tired of going back and forth between the two of you during the week? Is it because you unconsciously turned him against his father? Could your child think you want him to protest to show loyalty to you?

Ask why he doesn't want to be with his father. You might say, "You've been objecting for some time; what kind of visitation would you like?" It shows respect for your child's feelings, even if you can't necessarily provide the arrangement he seeks. If your son is showing severe stress about visits with your ex-husband, take him to a therapist. You could also contact your attorney, who may be able to get a guardian ad litem or an independent attorney for your child to prove he is really suffering from the custody or visitation arrangement. However, he would have to be experiencing serious anxiety and not simply acting out in an isolated, temperamental, or tired moment.

If you decide that the problem rests with your child, not your husband, be empathetic but firm. You might say, "I hear how you feel. I'm sad you feel that way and wish it weren't this way, but this is one of the things that sometimes happens when mothers and fathers get divorced and fathers want to be with their kids, too." Be aware of how you talk about your husband to your child, and if it is negative, try to change.

YOUR HUSBAND CHOOSES NOT TO BE WITH YOUR CHILD

According to one national study, close to 50 percent of children living with their mothers had not seen their fathers for one year or more. If your ex-husband has dropped out of your child's life for reasons that have little to do with you or her, you may not be able to fix the problem. But could it be that you've made him feel like a visitor with his own child and don't welcome him when he comes to pick up or drop off your child? Have you turned your daughter against him in subtle ways? Might he feel insecure about his relationship with her and worry that she will reject him or not want to be with him so he gives up before he gets hurt? Do you need to talk to her and say, "This divorce is really hard for Dad, too. How can we make him feel better?" If there is anything you can do to make the experience more positive for your ex-husband so that he will want to be a participatory father, then do it for your child's sake, and let him know you are trying to improve the situation.

Having a father not take an interest in a child is a painful problem, but it must be addressed. Reassure your child that she is a wonderful, lovable person, and say you don't understand why Dad doesn't come more often, and that it has nothing to do with how wonderful she is. You could also say, "I know you miss him and feel sad and hurt and I'm very, very sorry and I want you to be able to talk to me or someone else." Not having a father take an interest can be devastating to a child; there is loss and rage to work out, and it can affect your child's behavior. She can get aggressive, not simply sad. If possible, talk to your ex-husband about your child's feelings and the impact of his behavior on her. You may not be able to speak with him (or even know where he is), and even if you do, he may not be responsive, but you have to try.

Handling your ex-husband and your children well will help every-one in the family. Whether you live together or not, you and your ex-spouse are still parenting partners.

12

Hot-Button Issues

Once you divorce, there will be issues that did not get addressed in the custody agreement or parenting plan because neither of you anticipated them or you wanted to avoid them. Nevertheless, they can be emotional trigger points that can cause bad feeling and strife—and problems for your children. Knowing what some of these may be and how to handle them can mitigate the tension.

THE GIRLFRIEND IN HIS BED

Almost inevitably, your ex-husband will begin dating, if he hasn't already. What do you do if his girlfriend (or his boyfriend) spends the night and so do your children? You may be deeply opposed, but legally, you have little leverage. In many states, the law acknowledges both parents are grown-ups and there is little they can do to police sleepovers unless the situation is harmful to the children.

If he has a steady girlfriend, you may just have to put up with their nighttime arrangement and hope you can instill your own values in your children. It may be a different story if your husband has a succession of women sleep over when the children are around. You might be able to argue in court that he lacks judgment. If the children complain, that may be grounds for proving he has created an unfit environment for them.

If you have a civil relationship with your ex-spouse, explain why you believe his behavior is not helpful to the children. If you think you can be more effective and calm if you write down your thoughts rather than confront him directly, that could work, too. Don't accuse him; simply couch it in terms of your son's or daughter's welfare. Remind him there are many nights when the children are with you that he can spend with his girlfriend. If you decide you don't want his girlfriend spending the night, that will mean your boyfriend won't be able to sleep over, either. Are you prepared for that, even if the relationship becomes serious? In other words, *don't fight against something that you may want for yourself.*

There's a legal reason why you don't want *your* boyfriend to sleep over when the children are around, particularly if permanent custody has not yet been determined or your husband is seeking sole custody. They aren't supposed to, but some judges penalize mothers for having a sexual relationship and dismiss it for men with the reasoning that "boys will be boys." Confirmed one Midwestern female judge, "If a mother has someone sleep over, even if it's a steady boyfriend, then you are saying it's okay for girls to have a series of men. However, it *is* okay for guys to have a series of women. It's an inverse prejudice. It's a guy thing."

In some jurisdictions, it's common practice to include a clause in the custody order stating that no unrelated member of the opposite sex may sleep over or live in the house if custody is pending or there is a custody dispute. "A parent should know better than to have someone sleeping over," said one Chicago jurist. "That is not a question of morals. It causes confusion for kids and a sense of betrayal. If the mother is still married and that person is there, that can cause confusion. It is an overload on a child. The parent is putting himself first. Here's a child for whom the rug has been pulled out from under him. The spouse without a mate can't understand, so how can a child? I don't look favorably on these people." Said one Rhode Island judge, "I would take away custody if a parent continued to ignore a court order with respect to overnights."

Courts don't like to get involved in a person's private life. However, if the private life is harming a child's moral development, a judge may step in and decree when sleep-overs may take place. But you better have hard evidence that demonstrates your child is adversely affected by her father's behavior. If, at a hearing, your husband has teachers, neighbors, and coaches testify that your child is perfectly well-adjusted and doing fine in school and outside activities, you won't have made your point successfully.

NUDITY

In some cultures, nudity is a nonissue, but not in ours. Your husband may be uninhibited and feel comfortable walking around naked when he has the children. You will need to speak with him if this is a problem for you. You could say, "This makes me really uncomfortable, and I'd appreciate it if you would cover yourself." Children as young as age five do notice and can become overstimulated, frightened, or confused. Often a parent will shower with a child of the opposite sex. Experts say it's not a good idea for fathers to shower with little girls whose faces are at their genital level. At the same time, you don't want the children to think there is something dirty about the body. If your husband is getting out of the shower and your daughter walks in, he could casually get a towel rather than grab for it. You don't want him to parade around the house naked.

Keep in mind that the court is looking out for the best interests of the child. A judge will want to know if being nude in front of the children is appropriate for the youngster's age. Expert testimony could be helpful in court. If your child is seeing a therapist, you may want to ask her whether the behavior is acceptable. Said one Chicago judge on the subject, "A new boyfriend or mate walking in front of the children without a towel is terrible—nearly child abuse. It prematurely sexualizes the child. The child may be stimulated or ashamed or humiliated. That is the kind of disregard that would permeate the character, and I would not stand for it."

SMOKING, DRUGS, DRINKING, GAMBLING, AND OTHER ADDICTIONS

Unless your husband has a drug or substance abuse problem, you can't forbid him to have a beer when he's with the children unless it interferes with his ability to parent. If that is the case—he drives the children after he has had a couple of drinks, for example—and you think he is endangering them, consult a lawyer. Judges take alcohol abuse seriously. "If a person has a drinking problem," explains one judge, "then he can't be emotionally available to the children. Forget about the problems with severe abuse, such as falling down and passing out. If a custodial parent who is a drinker sleeps late, is hung over, or feels out of sorts, he can't give his children what they need. These could be grounds for losing custody."

If it is the noncustodial parent who drinks, a judge may order supervised visitation, but it would take unusual circumstances to curtail visitation. "Kids want to see their father either way," said one judge. A drunken father is sometimes better than no father. The better view is that Dad has a problem rather than Dad doesn't want them. A judge will usually want to hear from an impartial witness to attest to a drinking problem, and if abuse can be proven, may order visitation with no driving. "Prove to me that the behavior is a danger," another judge from Illinois said is her rule on drinking and custody. "Don't let people label anyone. Behavior determines my response. I would be concerned if a parent is drinking alcohol and became intoxicated and distracted from parenting, driving, or passed out. What a judge decides to do is subjective. I'd want to know when they are drinking, the age of the child—can he or she pick up the telephone and call for help if Dad passed out?—and how much time the visit is. I might order shorter, supervised visits with a third party, perhaps a family member, monitoring the pickups and drop-offs. I'd make sure the rules were clearly spelled out." Some judges make the addicted parent undergo periodic drug and alcohol testing.

If your daughter has asthma or another respiratory problem and your husband is a smoker, you might be able to prove he is harming her. You could try to obtain a restraining order preventing him from smoking in the house when the children are there. You must show that the child is exposed to smoke and that this exposure is not outweighed by other factors, such as a warm and loving relationship and strong bonding. "If a doctor testifies for a child with asthma, the parent who smokes may lose custody," said one Rhode Island judge. Typically, you will need to get expert testimony to establish the nature of the illness and its link to smoking. Not approving of his habits (or his friends) is not a legal issue. Your only recourse then is to explain why you think it's not good for your children. You might want to see if your husband will consider smoking outside of his house, but don't count on it. Cases are very fact-specific and decisions may vary from jurisdiction to jurisdiction and judge to judge. Five states now use smoking as a factor in deciding custody cases.

Stifle your impulse to say anything negative about the situation to the children. In other words, don't bad-mouth him. If your children bring it up, then you and your husband can decide together how best to handle the situation.

Drugs are a different issue because they are illegal. "I'd say you've got to lose visitation, but not forever," said one judge. But another disagreed, highlighting the fact that judges differ in their opinions. "You don't cut off visitation or custody because the behavior is illegal. You have to collect information. When are they smoking marijuana? What if they both abuse it? Or cocaine? Again, you don't want to cut off all contact with a parent." Judges weigh the parent's behavior and its effect on the children against the harm caused by excluding the parent from the child's life.

Substance abuse, alcohol, gambling, or continually squandering money (home shopping addictions, for example) are serious charges in a family court. Judges don't like to give children to parents who can't take care of themselves, let alone their offspring, and worry rightfully that the conduct could emotionally and physically endanger the children.

What if you're the one who is drinking, smoking, or gambling, and your husband disapproves? It depends on the degree and the circumstances. Are the children around? Will you see them under the influence? Are we talking one glass of wine with dinner or a couple of bottles every day? Are you using child support money to gamble? Smoking marijuana on occasion when the children aren't around isn't likely to jeopardize your chances of winning custody unless you are caught, even though it's illegal, but having a serious addiction will.

If you have a problem, get help. Don't dwell on your custody status; you are unlikely to win, anyway, if you are hooked on drugs, liquor, or money. Admit it: How could these habits be good for the kids? Enroll in a program and a support group where you can come clean. You will have to show the judge the steps you are taking to rehabilitate yourself. In order to demonstrate that you are a responsible parent, have a third party do the driving during this rehabilitation period.

Whatever the addiction, get into therapy and join a support group. If your problem is spending money, cut up your credit cards, cancel the cable TV, and find a financial consultant to put you on a budget. Document all your efforts for a judge. From a legal standpoint, the sooner you address these issues, the better. Remember, if your ex-husband is awarded custody because of your addictions, the longer he has the children, the less likely the courts will be to change the arrangement.

RELIGION

This tends to be an inflammatory issue and one that can change after divorce. You may have decided when you were married to raise your children in your husband's faith, but now you also want to expose them to yours. Let's say your husband is Jewish and you are Protestant. You can try to negotiate with him about having your children attend church as well as temple. If he becomes intractable and emphatic, you can either decide not to have them go to church when they are with you, or tell him, "This is important to me."

Let him know you are not reneging on your agreement, that they will still attend Hebrew school, but you also want them to be familiar with your heritage so when they get older they can decide for themselves.

Courts like to be impartial when dealing with the issue of a child's religious upbringing. If the parents are of different religious faiths, the courts won't decide the custody question on this issue. If there is a preexisting agreement, in some states it will be enforced as a private contract. If there is no contract and the visiting parent refuses to take your child to religious school, you have no recourse. "There are judicial decisions and parental decisions. This is a parental decision. It's terribly dangerous to take away the decision-making from the parent," one judge maintained. Check with your lawyer to see whether or not the court in your state would enforce this kind of agreement.

The court will deny custody to a parent if a certain religion is harmful to the child, or if the practice of that religion would in any way interfere with a parent's ability to take care of the child. That could be a religion that justified corporal punishment. If there is a danger to the child as a result of a parent's religious views, the courts may deny that parent custody. If the parent is always away from the house to attend religious meetings, a judge may also rule against the parent because of her absence.

Courts will not rule in favor of one religion over another. If the custodial parent is qualified in all other ways, the court will not get involved in a dispute over religion. Remember, though, that courts don't want a child to be in a hostile atmosphere or in a situation of conflict. If you prove to be an obstructive parent and prohibit an older child from practicing his religion, you may lose custody. If pushed, the court will make a decision on nonreligious grounds and allow the parent who becomes the legal custodian to choose the child's religion.

BRINGING THE CHILDREN BACK DIRTY OR LATE, OR SHOWING UP FOR VISITATION EARLY OR LATE

These are harassment tactics some fathers use. You will want to document these problems with dates and times so that if you decide to go to court, you will have concrete evidence. If it is a constant problem, consult your attorney. Judges don't like to handle "nuisance" problems and whining, but if there have been an accumulation of infractions, consider going to court on a contempt hearing if the custody order includes a pickup or return time. The hearing is a legal proceeding where your husband will be questioned about whether he is adhering to the custody order. A judge can reprimand him or make him comply with the decree. "I want to know what the cause of the lateness is," said one judge who is frequently confronted with this issue. "I use an enforcement proceeding as an educational opportunity to say there is a margin of error for everybody. Transportation is not always predictable, for example. But if it's simply a person's state of mind, I will come down harder. I will tell them that they are not only putting out their ex-spouse, but they are also not keeping the faith with their child. I let them know that to purge the contempt charge they must arrive on time and if they are more than fifteen minutes late, I will fine them. I tell them what is appropriate and inappropriate, and if it's inappropriate, bring your checkbook!" Other judges will deduct the amount of time a parent is late in picking up or returning a child from the next visitation. If your husband is one-half hour late in bringing back your son, for instance, the judge would knock off thirty minutes with him next time.

Your case will have more merit if the violations are blatant and you can show they are adversely affecting your child. If your husband continually returns the children one hour late on a school night or never bathes them, you could argue that he is not interested in their welfare, and these could be grounds for a violation of the order.

CREATING AN UNSAFE ENVIRONMENT FOR YOUR CHILDREN AND NOT PAYING ATTENTION TO THEM

There is lead paint in your ex-spouse's apartment, inadequate heat, a broken fence leading out to a busy street—in other words, substandard living conditions. Urge him to get them fixed immediately, and if he doesn't, take legal action. If you are the one with the lead paint and other health hazards and your husband has safe living quarters, you will have a hard time getting and keeping custody. Clean up your act! Listen to what he has to say, and if it makes sense, do something about it.

Get down on the floor and look around. Pretend you are a small child. Are there any health hazards? Any open windows without grates? Any lead paint chips or open electrical sockets? Take the perspective of an outside inspector. What do you see that might endanger your child's safety and well-being? Assume that if you and your husband don't work out this problem amicably, he might start court action. Keep your place neat, and assume an investigator might visit unannounced.

Legally, you need to understand that an unsafe environment can mean not attending to a child's emotional or medical needs. If your child requires counseling or special attention such as speech lessons, occupational or physical therapy, or even routine medical care and the parent doesn't attend to it, he or she could lose custody.

From a custody standpoint, if your child starts skipping or flunking school, gets into heavy drugs, drinking, or sex, runs away, threatens suicide, or is violent, a parent should worry. Obviously, you and your husband must seek help for your child. If your child lives with you, see if the therapist can document other reasons for his conduct than the custody arrangement.

If you suspect your child may have a problem, whether it is developmental, psychological, or medical, speak with the school, your pediatrician, or specialists. You have to take impeccable care of your child and show the court that you are doing so. Err on the safe side; it can't hurt to bring up a concern even if you aren't sure. It could get problems remediated more quickly, and if your worries are unfounded, it will demonstrate your love and concern.

YOUR HUSBAND IS NOT SENDING REGULAR CHILD SUPPORT PAYMENTS

This is a problem. However, by law you are not allowed to withhold the children because your husband is not sending child support. That is an issue for your attorney and the courts—but not your children. They need both parents. Don't discuss with your children any financial problems you and your husband are having. It is not appropriate and may make them feel emotionally torn and anxious.

DO WE ATTEND THE SAME EVENT SEPARATELY OR TOGETHER?

The best course is to try to discuss this issue with your husband before you get into one of these awkward situations. If you can, speak with him about whether you should attend alone or bring your new "friend" along, and vice versa. You want to have a unified front for your child and definitely don't want to discuss anything controversial or emotional at these times.

Ideally, it's best for your child if you could muster the maturity to sit with your ex-spouse at an ice hockey game, school event, or day camp performance. It's less embarrassing for your child if you seem to be together. If that will only provoke a problem, sit separately, but do attend and don't bicker. If you think your child would be better served if you didn't attend, think again. He will notice if one of you is not there. (He will also notice if you are both not on your best behavior.)

School conferences will be another area to cover with your husband. If your relationship is volatile, schedule separate conferences with the teacher. They are used to this issue. If you decide to attend together, make sure your children understand that this is school business, not a reconciliation.

THE CAMP DILEMMA

What do you do about visiting weekend at camp? There is no right answer on this issue. What you are all most comfortable with is going to be your best choice. Whether you attend together or separately or bring a significant other along will depend on your family dynamics. Remember that visiting day can be an emotional and vulnerable time for children, especially if they are young. (Even older children who might look as if they don't need you or care if you come will probably want you there, even if they don't admit it.) Camp should be a respite from the problems at home, not a reminder. If you absolutely can't get along with your husband (or he with you), think about being there at different times. You don't want to end up at camp bickering and not being able to decide which activities to attend.

If you don't get along with your ex-spouse, spending a full day together won't be beneficial to your child. In fact, your child might feel relieved if you don't come together if he knows he has two warring parents he will have to worry about and "manage." You might want to ask your child's pediatrician or therapist for a second opinion. Many camps offer separate weekends or days for divorced parents.

If your ex-husband insists on bringing his long-time or new girlfriend or wife and it is too much for you to handle, separate visiting days would probably be a smart idea. It may be tense enough already; your child doesn't need the added burden of your problem with the situation. You could always tell your child that "Dad will be coming separately or with Judy, and I will come a different weekend. That way we can spend time together and, in fact, you will have even more time with us."

Mental health experts and camp directors say visiting weekend is no time to introduce a new girlfriend or boyfriend. The place to begin a relationship between your child and your new lover is at home in a more controlled environment where each has time to get to know the other. Making the debut on visiting day has the potential for a strong negative reaction from your child. Tell your former spouse that even if this is a serious relationship, the other person may be a source of angst to your child. If your ex-husband absolutely insists he is going to bring his girlfriend and you think it will be harmful for your child, think about not being there.

The questions you and your ex-husband should be asking when you consider whether to attend together and/or to bring a new partner are: "Am I doing this for my child or am I doing it for myself? Am I being selfish?" The focus should be directed to your child, and if you bring someone else or are concentrating on your relationship with each other, you can be distracted and your attention will be divided. If the other man or woman has a close relationship with your child and you have no problem with the arrangement, then don't make one.

Decide what is palatable to you and if you could tolerate a joint visiting day. (In this case, joint would mean either you and your former husband, or you, your husband and his girlfriend or wife, or you and your boyfriend/husband and your ex-husband, or each of you with a new partner.) If you think you could handle any of these arrangements, ask your child what he wants. If he says he wants you to attend together, try to accommodate him. That doesn't mean you have to drive or fly to camp together or stay at the same hotel.

HAVING YOUR CHILD TRAVEL ALONE

One of you may feel uncomfortable having your child fly or take the bus by herself to see the other parent. What do you do? First, find out what "alone" means. The airlines, for instance, will escort children who are over the age of five and put them on connecting flights. There is usually a fee for this. The airline staff will watch them, but it is not a baby-sitting service.

Just because the airline says it is okay for young children to travel alone doesn't necessarily mean it's right in your situation. You have to assess the maturity of your child and decide whether it will work for him. If you think he would fare well, then decide what your comfort level is, or your husband's, if he is the one to oppose the plan. In that case, you will have to figure out what your other travel choices are. It might be that you could get a family friend to fly with your child or meet halfway rather than put her on the bus or train. If you leave the decision to a judge, you will get a ruling based on the judge's comfort level rather than yours and your husband's. You don't want arguments about the travel arrangements because that could put more pressure on your child and make the visits back and forth a time of anxiety rather than pleasure.

WHAT CAN YOU DO ABOUT THESE STICKING POINTS?

The answer is to learn to negotiate effectively with your husband. Conflict is normal in any relationship, but particularly when there is divorce and children. How you manage and resolve this conflict will affect your ability to get what you want from your husband rather than viewing these disagreements as power struggles. You may be spared some of the rancor if you know some conflict resolution techniques.

Before you begin, remember your focus. Negotiating is not about getting more or getting even, but rather coming to a resolution that is best for your children. Instead of repeating old, negative patterns and discussing past slights and incidents, think about the future and what you want to accomplish.

No matter what you feel about your husband, you want to stay on the best terms possible because that is what will be best for your children. You may also get more from your husband, emotionally and financially, if he is not bitter and at war with you.

Conflict resolution skills can also help you outside your marriage— with your children, colleagues at the office, and friends. In simplistic terms, what you want to do is be able to talk out your problems, understand the underlying reasons for the conflict, and put it in a larger context. This means deciding how important the problem is to you and your husband and thinking about whether there are other underlying issues that may be affecting your judgment. Is the conflict between you and your husband really about who has the children next weekend, or is it an opportunity for one of you to stick it to the other?

You want to learn how to move from your position (what you are demanding) to your needs and interests, so that you can examine why you want what you say you want. Sometimes, when you analyze those needs, you realize you really want something else or don't want it at all and can come up with a creative solution where you are both satisfied.

Think Before You Speak

Sometimes you can't agree. When you are angry or feel falsely accused or personally attacked, you might respond without thinking. That is likely to exacerbate the tension and not produce the results you want. There are some techniques that can help you defuse your anger and answer in a way that will benefit the negotiations. These might include:

· Mentally detaching yourself from the situation. Realize that other people may agree with you, even if your spouse doesn't. You could also think about how an outsider, like a neutral third party, might view the issue. Analyze the problem.

· In your mind, describe your husband's behavior. You might say, "He is trying to manipulate me" or "He is playing games with me" or "He is consciously trying to get me to lash out." Tell yourself you are not going to allow him to control your behavior.

· Keep thinking about your goal, which is to resolve the issue to your liking. Don't let your spouse intimidate or coerce you into making concessions that won't benefit you.

· Understand your negotiating style. Are you confrontational? Passive? Accommodating? Compromising? An avoider? If you know your style and its advantages and disadvantages, you can work on becoming more effective. While you're at it, analyze your husband's style and decide how you can use it to your advantage.

In discussing sensitive and potentially volatile subjects, whether it is your husband's sex life or your daughter's dislike of his girlfriend, you want to ask yourself:

· What do I really want?

· What are my underlying interests?

· What is important to me? Is this issue and the possible ill will it could cause *really* worth it?

· What do I want to happen and how do I propose getting it to happen?

· What can I offer my husband that he might want? (You might suggest he have the children an extra hour on Sundays once the days get longer or that you will do all the driving to and from activities, even if you aren't planning to stay at the event and he is, so that he won't have to take off more time from work.)

· What is important to him about this issue, and why would he object? How can I counter those objections?

· What options would meet both of our needs?

Other Strategies

Think positively. That means approaching negotiations with the belief that something will work out. Another winning tactic: When you're speaking about a thorny issue with your husband, approach it from what he *will* do rather than what he *won't* do. For instance, you could tell him he needs to return the children on time so you can bathe them and get them to bed at a reasonable hour, not that he can't return them late so they have to go to bed dirty.

There should be a few ground rules for your discussions. These would be: no yelling, no interrupting, and no criticizing each other's character. In *Getting to Yes: Negotiating Agreements without Giving In*, coauthors Roger Fisher and William Ury introduce the idea of separating the people from the problem. What they mean is thinking of negotiating in terms of working with your husband to attack the problem rather than each other. Explain why something your husband is doing upsets you and may not benefit the children. If either of you can't follow these rules, take a time-out. That may mean delaying your discussion. You will ultimately have more success if you adhere to civility and constraint. The location you choose for the meetings can be important. You may want privacy (away from the children), but also a public venue, like a deli or a restaurant, where you will be forced to keep your voice low and behave calmly.

Find a time when it is convenient for both of you to meet, when you will not be rushed. If you have a laundry list of items to discuss, focus on the most important first, and consider making a separate meeting time for the rest.

When you are unsure of your position on an issue, tell your husband you will consider his proposal, but don't feel you have to make a decision on the spot. If you and he have not resolved an issue and have run out of time, decide if there is anything either of you can do before the next meeting. This might include looking at your calendar to see if you can switch your weekend with the children and if there is any future date that he wants, so that you are not always asking for a favor.

Articulate the Problem and Define It Carefully

You could say, "It looks like we both want the kids next Saturday. The agreement says they are with me that day and I have already planned for a day trip out of town. But I will cut short the trip and bring them back so you can take them in the evening to the new movie that is opening and Sam has been dying to see." By putting the issue into words—that you both want the children the same day—you will have helped your husband recognize the problem and you will have clarified it for yourself.

The way you word the problem is also critical. Rather than use the accusatory *you,* try an *I* statement. Instead of saying, "You obviously don't care about Wendy and Josh, or you wouldn't have brought them home so filthy," you could rephrase it. It could be, "I get upset when Wendy and Josh come back with dirty clothes because I have to wash them and it takes time away from the kids." Instead of hurling barbs, you have told him how you feel and given him a good reason: your children.

How Does It Feel?

Showing empathy and insight is the key to a successful outcome. You have to understand your husband's position and what is at stake for him. In order to have an effective exchange, you must be patient and empathetic. It may be a cliché, but what you want to do is walk in his shoes. Of course he will need to do the same. Says Roger Fisher, cofounder of the Program on Negotiation at Harvard Law School, "Instead of pointing fingers at the other person and saying, 'You are wrong,' say, 'You and I seem to disagree. Let me make sure I understand your point of view.' You learn something: The other person feels heard, less frustrated, and more respected." Your husband may not necessarily get what he wants, but at least he will feel understood.

Why is it so important to acknowledge what your husband has said? You want him to know that *you* know what his concerns are. What it does is increase your power to persuade, because if he feels you are listening to him, he is more likely to listen to you. You have a better chance of changing your husband's mind after you have listened to his position. It is also possible that you will change your own view after what he has told you.

Phrases such as "What I hear you saying . . ." or "Am I right in thinking that . . ." show you have empathy, which is an important negotiating tool. As Fisher notes in *Getting to Yes*, "It is not enough to study them like beetles under a microscope; you need to know what it feels like to be a beetle."

Often you may think you know what your husband's needs are, but you may be wrong. Repeating it to him—"What you seem to be saying is . . ."—ensures that you really do understand his point of view and it gives you points, too, for compassion.

In a workshop on negotiation and divorce he teaches every January at Harvard Law School, attorney Robert Mnooken, who is coauthor of *Dividing the Child: Social and Legal Dilemmas of Custody*, talks about the importance of being both empathetic and assertive. He claims that if you want to negotiate successfully with your husband, you must have the ability to demonstrate that you understand his perspective, even if you don't agree with it. At the same time, he feels you must assert yourself and voice your own needs and perceptions. It's possible to be empathetic but not be able to hold onto your own interests, or to be assertive but be a bad listener. Those combinations don't work well for negotiating.

Tell Him Your Position

You have listened to your ex-husband and convinced him that he has been heard. Now let him understand how you see the issue. Tell him how you feel. Don't forget the "I" statements. Give him the information and let it do the damage, rather than stating it yourself. For example, you might say, "I have a problem when you return the children without most of the things they took with them. They get angry and frustrated because the things are at your house and they want them or need them. It reminds them of how difficult it is to be in two houses. I sometimes have to go out and buy them what they left all over again or else they blame me for it. It's expensive and ruins my time with the children because they are upset."

Reframe the Problem

Rather than countering your husband's demand with a demand of your own, try reframing the issue. Instead of thinking the problem is that your husband is lazy, thoughtless, or vindictive, you could reframe it as an issue of efficiency or management. You could have the children go to his place armed with a list of what they need to bring back with them. If they are old enough, the kids could take some responsibility for their gear.

Brainstorming and Collaborative Problem-Solving

You might ask your husband what he thinks would solve the problem, but come prepared to offer your own solutions, like the one above. If he says, "They're too young," or "It shouldn't be their problem," ask him for another option. Say, "Can you think of some way it could work?" Try to come up with options that would benefit you both. If you were really civil with each other, you could acknowledge your different styles and goals and try to find a way to address both of your needs.

Rehash the Situation

Evaluate how the arrangement is working by asking your ex-husband. Modify the arrangement, if necessary. It could be really powerful to compliment your husband for what he does well. Feeling that you are always critical will make him defensive.

WHAT IF YOU CAN'T STOP ARGUING OR RESOLVE THE ISSUE?

If you are deadlocked, you have several options. First, decide what the problem is. If you aren't making progress because of grudges you are holding, make sure you see a therapist who can help you with that anger. If it's more your ex-husband's issue, ask him to get help. But perhaps neither of you is causing the impasse. Maybe you just see the situation differently. If it's not an issue of safety and doesn't need to be resolved immediately, you may decide to have a cool-down period and tackle the subject in the near future. If that is not feasible or beneficial, consider having a third party step in. That could be a mediator, therapist, member of the clergy, or an attorney. An outsider may help you break the stalemate or force either or both of you to behave more reasonably.

There are also negotiation courses for laymen, as well as books and tapes at the library or local bookstore.

Understanding how the courts view certain situations, from sexual abuse to paternity to same-sex partners, will give you a sense of how you and your ex-husband could fare.

Domestic Violence

THE CUSTODY CONNECTION

Men who batter their wives are twice as likely to seek custody as men who aren't violent, and when they do, they win custody as often as their wives, estimates a member of the American Psychological Association's Presidential Task Force on Violence and the Family. Historically, family courts have not taken domestic violence into consideration unless the children were also being beaten. That is changing. In some states, spousal violence must be considered when determining custody because it is considered a form of psychological abuse of the child. Be aware that if you do leave your husband, it may enrage him and he may decide to assert his authority either through violence and/or a custody contest. Of course, that doesn't mean you shouldn't leave him. There may be violence no matter what you do.

Nationally, 40 percent of all female murder victims are killed by either a boyfriend or a husband. A study that looked at every woman age sixteen and over killed in New York City from 1990 through 1994 found that nearly half were murdered by current or former husbands or boyfriends in their homes; one-third were still married but not living with their partners when they were slain. The potential for abuse is high during disputed custody contests—second only to after a woman tells her husband she is leaving him.

Partner abuse is not confined to severe physical violence. It includes slaps, shoves, threats, name-calling, rape, and other degrading behavior. It may also entail withholding money, false imprisonment, stalking, and harassment.

As recently as a decade ago, law enforcement officials told battered women they would not touch marital violence because it was "a family matter." Today, abused women are usually taken seriously by police, judges, and lawyers, in part because of high-profile trials like O. J. Simpson's.

A proliferation of domestic violence legislation has given police broader powers of arrest, permission to seek protective orders by telephone when necessary, and more admissible evidence, even when the victim refuses to press charges. In 1994, Congress passed the Violence Against Women Act as part of the federal crime law, which offers grants to states that pass tougher domestic violence laws. Stalking laws are being enacted across the country, and police are increasingly recognizing out-of-state restraining orders.

DOMESTIC VIOLENCE AND THE LAW

Many states take evidence of spousal abuse into consideration when weighing custody decisions. The latest legal argument is that exposing youngsters to domestic violence is a form of child abuse. (You could file an action against the batterer for violating your civil rights, and if you win, you could receive money.) There are judges, however, who dismiss this conduct. While abusive behavior is supposed to be considered in custody matters, the courts also believe it is best for a child to have as much access to both parents as possible. And it is that conviction that makes it dangerous for mothers because they are frequently forced to see their abuser.

Massachusetts, which in 1978 was the first state to institute domestic restraining orders, recently passed legislation pending that states it may not be in a child's best interests to live with a parent convicted of domestic abuse. The bill restricts the custody or visitation rights of accused abusers and provides that if the court finds one parent has been abusive (but not convicted of abuse), there is a rebuttable presumption that he should not receive custody. That means the abusive parent is allowed to provide evidence to convince the court that the child should belong with him, but the burden of proof is substantial.

Check your state statute on domestic violence to see if it covers other family members (aunts, uncles, cousins) or someone with whom you are living. Some states require that the victim must be physically abused, while others have looser interpretations, such as stalking at a place of work, harassing telephone calls, or making threats of violence. A federal law enacted in 1994 called the Civil Rights Remedies for Gender-Motivated Violence Act allows the victim to sue for monetary damages if the batterer "commits a crime of violence motivated by gender."

Penalties for domestic violence differ depending on the state, but they can include the issuance of a restraining order against you or your husband or lengthy jail time. Visitation may also be suspended pending verification of a domestic violence allegation.

If you are a battered mother, you need to realize that your story of abuse may carry equal weight to your husband's denial. That is why you must document your injuries so that there is concrete evidence that these physical or emotional assaults did occur. Photograph all injuries, visit your doctor or an emergency room, call the police, and keep a diary of all incidents and dates. You also need to get an advocate. There are many ways to find one, including specialized domestic violence units in local courts or police departments, social service agencies, the bar association, medical centers, or the National Domestic Violence Hotline (800-799-SAFE).

Make sure you take your children with you if you leave the marital home. From a legal standpoint, the courts could interpret your leaving them with their father as proof that he really is competent and that you are overstating your fear of him. If he does harm them while you are gone, you can also be penalized. Warning: An abused woman who can barely protect herself and does not stop or prevent her husband from battering her child may leave herself open to attack, and even prosecution, for failing to protect her child. It's also possible that her parental rights could be terminated.

THE IMPACT ON CUSTODY

There has been a recent surge of legislation dealing with family violence and custody. Forty-four states, including the District of Columbia, have enacted custody statutes that have provisions on this subject. These provisions include rebuttable presumptions against the sole or joint custodial parent; laws that cover any perpetrator, regardless of the custody status; and the inclusion of domestic violence as a factor to be considered under the best-interest standard.

Many judges and psychologists believe it is in the best interests of the child to have contact with both a mother and a father, even when domestic abuse has occurred. Judges will try not to deny a parent visitation unless it is absolutely necessary, and then only for as short a time as possible. It's a balancing act for a judge to have the child maintain contact with the parent and still be safe. Ten state child custody statutes include a public policy statement that recommends that parents foster a loving and open relationship with the other parent. Eighteen states include this friendly parent provision as a favor to be weighed when a judge makes a custody determination. Some feel these provisions punish the victims of abuse. Battered women are often viewed as being uncooperative when it comes to visitation when they are really trying to protect themselves and their children.

Judges may order supervised visitation or make the parent enter therapy to help stop the abuse. However, jurists unschooled in domestic violence frequently allow visitation without providing protective measures. One judge from the Southwest said he weighs the severity of the charges, or the level of violence and what effect it has had on the children. Another judge looks at the frequency. Is it ongoing? Is it atypical? In that case, the judge may put safety measures, such as supervised visitation, into effect for a short period of time, and then order less restrictive visitation once the parent stops the abusive behavior. If your battering husband has a turnaround, expect that a judge may grant him unsupervised visitation. One judge said she always asks herself, "Does the violence affect the batterer's ability to parent?" She wants to determine the root of the violence, what the real problem is. Judges, then, try to find out what the issues are so they can set up a schedule that takes the circumstances into account. The point is not to be punitive but protective and to let a batterer ordered to have supervised visitation understand that the judge is not stripping him of his parental role nor trying to interfere with his relationship with his child. The abusive parent may feel anger and resentment toward you for causing these restrictions.

LAWYERS AND GUARDIANS AD LITEM

It is critical to have specialists who understand the dynamics of domestic violence and can explain them to the court. Don't assume a therapist or judge will grasp these dynamics automatically. That's why you need to hire an attorney knowledgeable about marital abuse who has had experience with these kinds of cases. Referrals may be found by asking your local police, your state or local coalition against domestic violence, a community organization or social service agency, your doctor, hospitals, schools, a mental health department, a shelter for battered women, a state or local crisis hot line, or your state or area bar association. Many legal services attorneys are better versed in domestic violence than your typical corporate lawyer. However, in many states, there isn't enough funding for legal services attorneys to take these cases. Unless an indigent mother is able to find a lawyer who will handle her case pro bono, she may have to represent herself in court. If the state's attorney or district attorney's office can help, these women may decide to settle their cases out of court rather than face their abuser.

One reason it is so important to retain a lawyer with an expertise in this field is because battering men often appear more competent than women in custody disputes. Abused mothers may act unstable, high-strung, angry, or without emotion. As a consequence of being terrorized and controlled, they may scare easily, have trouble maintaining self-control, lose their temper frequently, and appear unreasonable to outsiders. A judge may think a woman who moves to another state precipitously is impulsive and selfish, rather than believing that she is a terrified mother trying to protect her child and herself. As one judge who has heard many custody cases where domestic violence has been a factor advises, "Your lawyer must understand the process of abuse a victim goes through. If a woman appears angry in court, an attorney with domestic abuse experience can help explain to the judge that what may appear to be anger is really the effects of years of abuse. The lawyer should also be able to show the effect the abuse has on the child, as virtually every child has been exposed to the parent's abuse."

A battering father, on the other hand, can present himself as the more appealing parent. He may seem rational, calm, even cooperative, and have other qualities that courts often value, like more money than his ex-wife and a two-parent home. Men typically earn more than women—many mothers stopped working to raise their children—and men tend to remarry sooner than their battered wives. Judges may think the children have more stability with this arrangement.

To further compound the problem, many lawyers are unfamiliar with domestic violence laws. Since the 1970s, fault has ceased to be of importance in divorce law. The focus has shifted from who caused the failure of the marriage and how that affects the division of assets, to the division of assets alone. Some lawyers fail to realize that misconduct may be significant. They don't ask questions about a spouse's behavior that might make a difference in the custody decision. Often, battered mothers won't voluntarily reveal they have been abused, believing it is their fault, and their lawyer may not ask the questions that would elicit the information.

Some lawyers incorrectly believe that abuse is an issue that only should be brought up in a protection-from-abuse hearing rather than considered for its impact on custody. Attorneys may fail to introduce relevant evidence such as protection orders, prior convictions, medical records, photographs of injuries, and any documents that might contain threats. Lawyers may recommend mediation in cases where they are not aware of a history of violence.

Many professionals with little experience in this field blame mothers for the abuse, believing they could have stopped their husbands or at least left when the abuse first began. Increasingly, however, law enforcement and court officials have begun to understand battered woman's syndrome, a psychological condition in which abused women stay with their violent partners, forgive them repeatedly, and blame themselves for the beatings. They may be ashamed of their situation, still love their abuser, and believe he will change. Or they may be terrified of what he will do if they try to leave. They may also feel they have no place to go.

If this is your situation, consider getting a guardian ad litem or an attorney for your child. In some states, that is the same person. (A guardian ad litem is usually someone with a mental health background who will look out for your child's interests and may make a custody recommendation to the court.) If for some reason, the G.A.L. is hostile to you and doesn't believe your allegations, hire an outside expert who is a psychologist and specializes in abuse who will advocate on your behalf or replace the guardian ad litem. G.A.L.'s have the power to influence the judge, so if you don't believe yours will rule in your favor, you could have a problem.

SUPERVISED VISITATION

The courts may order supervised visitation in cases of domestic violence, but not necessarily and usually in extreme cases only. Some judges believe this arrangement makes it hard for children to establish a good relationship with a father if he can't see them under normal circumstances.

Supervised visitation works in a variety of ways. These include:

- **One-on-one supervision,** where an outside person is present during the visit. This is ordered when there is a concern for the child's safety. This type of visitation can occur at a visitation center, either at the courthouse or another designated place. When there is less risk, supervision may be ordered in a larger group with other parents in similar situations.

- **Exchange supervision** means the transfer of the child from one parent to the other at the beginning and end of each visit is monitored by a third party. This situation is helpful if violence tends to occur during the transfer or if the switch is traumatic for the child.

- **Off-site supervision** or monitoring of visitation occurs at a location not specifically designated by the courts, such as a playground. Drop-offs and pickups take place in a neutral location like family court or a police station. This arrangement is sometimes used as a transition between supervised visits in a specific facility and unsupervised visitation.

Some programs, like the Domestic Abuse Intervention Project in Duluth, Minnesota, offer monitored, on-site visits and exchanges. Those who participate are referred by the court or child protective services. Fathers (or mothers) receive counseling on parenting and learn about the effects of domestic violence on children.

Call your local court to find out if you are a candidate for supervised visitation. If you aren't and you fear further abuse, particularly during the exchange, choose another neutral location. It could be a friend's house, a store in your neighborhood, or a well-populated mall that might have police patrolling. If it's going to be your home or his, and you are concerned about a confrontation, ask him to wait outside and have the children go out to him, if they are old enough. That way you won't have to interact with each other.

RECONSIDER MEDIATION AND JOINT CUSTODY

If you are in an abusive arrangement and want to gain custody, be especially careful about mediation and joint custody. Mediation is often not recommended in cases of domestic violence because you may be frightened of your husband and concede to him out of fear rather than fairness. Some states exempt battered women from mediation in jurisdictions that mandate it in contested custody disputes. If your state does not, insist that you have separate meetings with the mediator. If you have a restraining order in effect, joint meetings are out of the question, as they would not only endanger you, but would also be in violation of a court order.

Joint custody may also be disadvantageous to battered women. The premise of joint custody is continued contact and communication between parents. With this arrangement, you won't be able to escape interacting with your husband, and this could be dangerous for you and your children.

THE IMPACT ON CHILDREN

Recent studies suggest that in households where there is domestic violence, up to 90 percent of youngsters have seen their fathers beat their mothers, and one study reports that 75 percent of battering husbands also abuse their children. The rate of being battered is seven times higher for a child living in a home with marital violence than a nonabusive home.

Just one episode of violence between parents has been known to produce post-traumatic stress disorder in children. They also can experience other problems, including withdrawal, aggression, anxiety, depression, delinquent behavior, and poor social skills. Reports indicate that daughters are more often the target of battering husbands than sons; they are 6.5 times more likely to be sexually abused by their fathers than girls in nonviolent families. So, *if you think domestic violence is just a problem between you and your husband, you may be wrong. Your child may also be in danger.*

Did you know that *you and your child are at least at equal risk of being physically hurt after you separate from your husband than as you were when living in the same house, and that the most dangerous time is shortly after you leave the relationship?* The chances also increase if your husband has a gun, abuses liquor or drugs, has stalked you, or threatened violence or suicide. If you are the one to initiate the divorce, the likelihood of being battered increases further. When there's a custody dispute, the situation is even more volatile and can prompt violence. Hospital records show that more battered women seek help for injuries after they are separated. One study reported that 75 percent of all emergency room visits by abused women occurred after the couple no longer lived together.

WHY ARE MEN ABUSIVE?

Many men act domineering and violent to try to force their wives to reconcile. Sometimes fathers genuinely want to have custody; others use a battle for custody as a way to have power over an ex-spouse. The mental anguish for you as a mother can be overwhelming. You may have stayed in an abusive situation because you were ashamed, still love your husband, or believed he will change. You might even rationalize an attack by thinking of it as a one-time situation that got out of control. But then you finally decide to leave him so you can protect your children. If your husband seeks custody, it can make you feel powerless and terrified. It can be devastating to think you could be subjecting your children to more misery and possible danger if he does win.

MAKING AN ACTION PLAN FOR YOU

If your husband is abusive, your first course of action is to call the police and obtain a *restraining order* against him from the court. This restraining or protective order can include a provision that forces him to leave the house and to stay away from you. If you are in fear of your husband, the court will usually grant you a restraining order. The order isn't difficult to procure, but you must prove that abuse did or could occur depending on the state. To document it, go to a doctor or hospital for treatment, photograph the injuries, and make sure you file a police report. In particularly nasty custody disputes, some women have been known to ask for a restraining order to be vindictive, not because they are afraid of their husbands. This tactic can cause you to lose custody.

During business hours, you can get a protective order from the trial court in your town or city. After work hours, you must go to the police department. An on-call judge will review the information and decide whether to issue the protective order. Once you receive the order, a hearing will be scheduled anywhere from the next morning to ten days, depending on where you live. Both you and your husband should attend. As the victim, you may be assigned a victim's advocate by the court, who will accompany you to the hearing and offer moral, legal, and practical advice. A victim's advocate will take you through the steps and help with the paperwork. If the judge finds a need for the restraining order, he may extend it for one year or more in some states. A restraining order is only in effect after it has been served. In many states, the abuser will be arrested if he violates the order, but you have to notify the police if he's in violation.

The most dangerous time for a battered woman (besides after she has left her abuser) is the first twenty-four hours after a restraining order has been issued. If the police have the resources to do it, ask them to drive by your house a couple of times a day. Some police departments offer cellular phones to battered women. Have the court or your attorney attach the full faith and credit provision of the Violence against Women Act to your protective order because it should capture the attention of law enforcement officials quickly. Have a trusted friend or relative stay with you, if possible.

Said one police detective assigned to a domestic violence unit in a suburb outside of Boston, "People get upset when there is a restraining order against them. Part of the abuse is the control and now she's taking control and it's a blow to his ego. In a lot of cases the restraining order is a wake-up call, and the batterer is genuinely sorry and will seek help. In other cases, he is so angry that he's dangerous. And other guys will say, 'Okay, I'll stay away, I won't bother her.' " Assume that your husband's response to being served a restraining order will be unpredictable.

A SAFETY PLAN

At the same time that you take criminal action, make sure that you and the children are safe. You should create what is called a safety plan, as well as contact a domestic violence group that will direct you to legal counsel and a shelter, if necessary. The shelter has access to support groups. (Since battering men frequently isolate their partners, a support group can help you build new relationships, regain a sense of confidence and worth, and get you to understand you are not alone.) To find out about resources in your area, call directory assistance, your local police, the Department of Public Health in your state, or the national, twenty-four hour domestic violence hot line at 800-799-SAFE (7233).

A safety plan is implemented if you need to escape. It lists items you should take, as well as the names and telephone numbers of important people in your life. Having a plan will make you feel less powerless. Rehearse your plan with a friend to get feedback and to further prepare yourself.

Children who have witnessed marital abuse often fear the period when the exchange between parents takes place, thinking there might be more violence. To reduce the fear and give them a sense of empowerment, domestic violence experts suggest that children age eight and older help the battered parent form the safety plan. If you can, get a professional with knowledge of domestic violence to work with you and your child on the safety plan. In addition, if your husband is not legally permitted to visit, make sure your children and the baby-sitter know not to let him in the door.

As part of the plan, keep change for telephone calls with you at all times so you can phone the people on your list. Open your own bank account so you aren't dependent on your husband. Otherwise, he may deplete a joint account and you could be left without money.

The following steps are crucial to take if you think your husband could be abusive. These items should be kept hidden in your home or another safe place. The plan can include:

- An address book with the name and number of your doctor and dentist, as well as your child's, the school, the police, a domestic violence hot line, a shelter for battered women, a local or state coalition against domestic violence, your friends, your bank, and your insurance agent and company
- Important documents, such as your driver's license and registration, the deed to your house, a lease or rental agreement, passports for you and your child, green cards, work permits, Social Security cards, welfare identification, birth certificates, mortgage payment book, unpaid bills, insurance papers, bank books, medical and school records, divorce papers, and police papers, such as a restraining order
- Money (at least one month's living expenses, if possible) and credit cards
- Keys to the house, car, and office
- Medication and prescriptions for you and your child
- Jewelry, photographs, other small items that are meaningful to you
- Some of your children's favorite toys and blankets
- a change of clothes

OTHER SAFETY STRATEGIES

Even though it is hard to admit you have been abused and still harder to discuss it with outsiders, you will need to come to terms with your situation. Designate two people you can tell about the violence and have them call the police if they hear anything suspicious. If you have a restraining order against your husband, keep it on file at the police station. Many police departments record the protective order in a central computer so if you report an emergency, the officer answering the call will know the situation before reaching you. If there's a restraining order, appoint two neighbors to call police if they see your husband or his car near your home. Have one or more of your friends check on you daily. Consider exchanging cars with a friend or relative so your husband doesn't recognize your vehicle. Work out coded messages with neighbors, friends, and colleagues so that if they happen to call, you can alert them to your husband's presence. Confide in one or two coworkers and ask them to screen your calls. Keep your protective order at your office. Monitor your calls at home with a caller I.D. feature. You can buy an answering machine or voice mail, and program your phone to 911 or get an unlisted number. You can block your number by using the *67 feature or by calling your telephone company to find out what the equivalent is in your area. A new computer program called MOSAIC@-20, available to police departments and prosecutors, predicts if an abuser is likely to murder his partner. Authorities used it after the killing of Nicole Brown Simpson. It asks abused women questions, matches the answers with cases that have led to murder, and predicts the probability of homicide. This technology is expected to be accessible through the Internet soon.

Since a batterer sometimes traces his partner's new address through mutual friends or acquaintances, don't reveal your whereabouts to many people. Make sure the ones who know don't tell your husband. Motor vehicle records often list addresses, so request that yours be kept confidential.

Inform your children's regular and after-school teachers, principal, or day care provider about your situation and give them a list of people who are allowed to pick up your child, and a photograph of your husband. Make sure the school informs all substitute teachers. Your husband would not legally be allowed to take your child from school if you had sole custody and he had no visitation or supervised visitation. If you have joint custody, leave a copy of your custody agreement with the school. If you have a restraining order, keep a copy at school so your ex-husband can't pretend he has permission to take the children.

Write down four places you could go if you needed to escape. One should be a shelter for battered women. Once your relationship is over, change your locks, add dead bolts, secure your windows, and consider installing a security system with a panic button, a smoke detector, and an outside lighting system. Don't move to an apartment on the first floor.

Think about joining a support group such as Parents without Partners or Parents Anonymous (check the Yellow Pages) and/or about getting individual or group therapy. Many abused women become depressed and may have symptoms of post-traumatic stress disorder. These psychological consequences can interfere with your ability to take care of your children's needs, and then you are truly in danger of losing custody. Many women who are battered also turn to alcohol as a way of coping with their situation. If you feel that you have a problem with drinking, Alcoholics Anonymous can be helpful and supportive. Above all, take care of yourself and get the help you need to cope with your difficult situation.

Special Considerations

Just as people are all different, the situations in which they find themselves also vary. If any of these circumstances apply to you, it's important to know the issues and their possible impact on custody.

CHILD AND SEXUAL ABUSE

If you are convinced your husband is sexually or physically abusing your child, you must take action. This can start with a visit to a hospital emergency room or a call to your pediatrician or a report to the protective service agency in your community. If she is old enough, encourage your daughter to confide in her physician. Doctors are obligated by law to report suspicious or actual signs of abuse to the state. You should also make your own call to the state agency responsible for child abuse.

The state will investigate the case and make a finding. If there are grounds for abuse, your child will be removed from her father, and he will be prohibited from seeing her or given supervised visitation pending the outcome of an investigation or trial. A danger is that those in the protective and justice systems may not believe your child has been sexually abused. In such circumstances, the court may decide you don't have your child's best interests in mind and award custody to the father and you could face criminal penalties.

After the state determines that evidence for abuse does exist, the criminal arm of the state, usually the district attorney's office, may prosecute your husband. At any point in this process, a guardian ad litem may be appointed by the court. This is an independent third party, usually a lawyer or mental health professional, who conducts an independent assessment of the situation to make recommendations to the court about what is in the best interests of the child. Often, the court will order a psychological evaluation for your husband, or he may request one if he is fighting the charge.

If he is convicted at a trial, the penalties range from mandatory counseling to jail time. This conviction will have an impact on custody. Most judges prohibit visitation, and at the least, order supervised visitation with convicted abusers. If your husband has been a sole or joint physical custodian, he will probably lose that privilege and if you are deemed fit, you will be awarded sole custody. Remember, your husband could try to modify the custody order at a later date.

You will want to get a therapist for your child because whatever the outcome of the case, your son or daughter will be affected by the proceedings and the allegations, as well as the abuse itself.

GRANDPARENTS AS CUSTODIANS

According to the 1995 U.S. Census Bureau, close to four million children live in households headed by grandparents. Parents may lose their children to their parents in a custody contest or relinquish custody because of drugs, alcohol abuse, or economic factors. Because of AIDS, mental illness, incarceration, and other unanticipated circumstances, many mothers and fathers are unable to care for their children.

The laws on grandparents vary from state to state. Consult a lawyer to find out what the rules are in your jurisdiction. When grandparents take care of a grandchild for a considerable length of time and both parents agree with the grandparents' request, the courts usually grant custody to the grandparent. In some states, grandparents are permitted to go to court to request that they be appointed the legal guardian. Usually, a grandparent seeking custody must explain to the court that both the natural mother and father have died or prove they are unfit parents. Proving they are unfit is difficult and requires showing there is a serious problem with the parents and their parenting.

All fifty states have laws that give grandparents the right to visit with their grandchildren if their parents are divorced or separated, the natural parents are not fit custodians, or have died.

Some grandparents raise their grandchildren without asking for legal acknowledgment. This situation can be problematic. Children may need legal permission from a custodian or guardian to obtain medical help. A pediatrician may refuse to inoculate a child or test for lead poisoning without consent from a guardian. Sometimes a school will not permit grandparents to enroll a child in the district where they live unless they have a letter or a custody order proving they are the child's legal guardian or custodian.

Grandparents may end up being custodians for a certain period of time. If the grandparents continue to care for the children, they may find themselves becoming the psychological parents. This term refers to an adult who forms a strong emotional bond with the child and takes care of the child a significant amount of time. Psychological parents can request visitation. Some states allow grandparents who have become psychological parents to file for, and in some instances retain, custody of grandchildren. This can become a problem if there is tension between the grandparents and the parents, especially if the seniors disapprove of the way their children are raising their offspring.

Grandmothers or grandfathers who need child support money may have a problem. They can go to the federal government, such as Health and Human Services, to try and get financial aid. But if they request monetary help such as kinship care, which provides foster care money for family members who care for relatives' children, the agency must take the children into its custody. It could then place the children with the grandparents as foster parents. Grandparents are obviously reluctant to do this in case the government gives the children to someone else.

Education and support groups for grandparents have formed across the country. They advise grandparents about their legal rights, offer programs geared to their situation, and consult about job and housing opportunities.

UNMARRIED PARENTS AND PATERNITY

The number of unmarried women grappling with custody in the courts has increased dramatically. Judges have begun to see a significant number of cases where unmarried women are denying fathers the right to see their children. One sure way to lose custody is not to respect the other party's visitation or placement rights. Therefore, if you are considering establishing paternity, think hard about whether you are comfortable having your child's father as your coparent.

Paternity is a thorny issue. You may have no idea who the father is and may not care. You may know but decide not to tell your partner that you are pregnant. When your child reaches school age, she may want to know who her father is and have a relationship with him. Whatever your situation, you should know your rights, as well as those of your child's father.

There is an economic incentive to establishing paternity. You will be entitled to child support until your child reaches the age of eighteen, depending on your circumstances and state guidelines. Your son or daughter may receive medical coverage if the child's father has a policy through work or is able to pay for the insurance. In addition, your child becomes the legal heir to his father. Financial reasons aside, if your partner is decent, your child will be able to develop an important relationship with his other parent.

Just as fathers have certain economic responsibilities, they also have legal rights. One is that they will get to see their child. This concept is often difficult for a mother intent on not sharing her child.

How do you establish paternity? A man who is not married to a woman can acknowledge paternity of the child. He can sign his name on the child's birth certificate or a written and signed document that can be filed with the court. Or you can file an action with the court to establish paternity. If the father denies his role, the court can order a blood test to prove it.

Should I Establish Paternity?

Realize that once paternity is established, the father has an absolute right to partial physical custody of the child. Courts will not restrict visitation, even if the father at first denies paternity. A father would have to be proven unfit or some type of threat, like a substance abuser or a molester, in order to lose the right to be with his child.

Many unwed mothers don't tell the father they have had a baby because they don't want to share visitation. If the father does become an integral part of your child's life, you will have contact with him whether you want to or not.

RACE

The law is clear that race should have no bearing on custody. In 1984, the United States Supreme Court ruled that it was unconstitutional to consider race when a noncustodial parent petitions the court for a change of custody. The case was brought in Florida. A white couple had divorced and the mother had been awarded custody. She married an African-American and moved to a predominately black neighborhood. The father sued for custody, citing changed circumstances, namely that his son was now living with an African-American man in a black neighborhood.

The Florida court granted the modification, but the U.S. Supreme Court reversed the decision. It noted that social stigma, particularly one involving race, can't be the basis for a custody decision.

Although it is not supposed to happen, a judge may hold strong views on mixed marriages and vote his or her bias. This, however, could not be done outright, and the judge would have to pin his decision on other faults of a parent in order to deny custody.

If race is an issue in your situation, see if your lawyer knows if the judge assigned to hear your case is biased. If so, consider settling the case out of court or have your attorney continue the case in the hope that you can get a different judge.

SEXUAL ORIENTATION

Sexual orientation is another area where judges are expected to be neutral and not let their personal opinions rule their decisions. But, like the issue of race, there is always the possibility that a judge may feel it is in the child's best interests to place him with a heterosexual parent, regardless of what kind of parent the lesbian mother is. Again, the judge would have to deny custody and visitation for a different reason.

If either you or your husband is gay, you may have a number of questions. These might be: What is the best way to tell my children? When do I or my ex-husband or we tell them? If I'm the one who is gay, should I introduce my children to my new partner? Will my kids feel weird about inviting their friends to my house?

How, when, and if you introduce your same-sex companion to your children depends on various circumstances, such as the ages of your children, your relationship with them, the attitude of your former spouse and his relatives, and whether your children already know you are gay. You also have to decide whether it strategically makes sense for you to disclose your sexual orientation if you are in the throes of a contentious custody battle.

Whether or not you share this information will be an individual decision that depends upon your personal circumstances. How your husband reacts to your homosexuality may influence what you tell the children. If he is enlightened, you may be able to conduct your social life without fear of reprisal. But in a custody battle, where your ex-husband will look for ways to prove he is the superior parent, you may need to be discreet (see chapter 4). Although you may feel it is hypocritical to hide your sexual preference, realize that if you want custody, you are opening yourself up to attack on all levels. If you choose to fight and are candid about your sexuality, you have a chance of losing if the judge is biased.

It may be that telling your children, your husband, or your family will put you at a legal disadvantage. "In an ideal world, I don't think secrecy makes sense, but we don't live in an ideal world," said one lesbian mother who is a psychologist. "If you are in a situation where you risk losing your job or custody, it's not such a good idea to burden a child with a secret or risk that the secret could come out."

If you decide you want your children to know, assume that they will share the information with others, and don't get mad if they do. It's best to have an ongoing conversation with them about your homosexuality and the issue of homophobia *before* you introduce them to your partner. Be prepared to cope with your children's discomfort about the subject and have ways to help them deal with it in their own lives. A consultation with a mental health professional could be beneficial. Be supportive of your children's feelings. They may not be uncomfortable at all, but you need to anticipate in case they are and be prepared to address it.

The information you disclose must be appropriate to your children's age and ability to understand so that your talk will make sense to them. To a three-year-old you might say, "Jim and Sarah live together because they love each other and so do Joanne and Mary." Older children will be more sophisticated and will already know about lesbianism. You will want to find out what their understanding of homosexuality is and what they think about your sexual preference. You might say, "Some men love each other and some women love each other, and some people think that's a terrible thing." Then you can discuss homophobia. Don't tell them any more than what they ask, and don't force information on them if they are not ready to hear it, particularly during a custody contest. Make sure political correctness and politics don't blind your judgment. You don't want to force your life choices on your children. If you do, it could be argued that you are more interested in yourself than your kids.

If your children know you are a lesbian, they will assume the new special person in your life is your girlfriend. Introducing your gay partner should not be different from introducing a heterosexual partner. That is, don't have anyone new come around until your relationship with that person is stable. Otherwise, it could subject children to more instability at a time that is already uncertain for them. Psychologically, bringing people into and out of their lives is not a good idea. Legally, it's unwise because it could be argued you are not behaving in the best interests of your child.

No matter how warm and hospitable you are, some children may feel uncomfortable having their friends over to your house. Be sensitive and don't force the issue. Let them know their friends will always be welcome.

What do you do if you are a lesbian and want your child to be brought up with as little prejudice as possible? First, think about where you live. Is it a conservative community where there are few other couples or women like you, or is it more of a diverse, enlightened place? Many lesbian parents live in liberal areas near cities where people are more receptive to different lifestyles. According to the Lambda Legal Defense and Education Fund, a gay rights advocacy group, California, Ohio, New York, Connecticut, New Jersey, and the District of Columbia were the most accepting of gay men and lesbians as parents. The most intolerant were Florida, Massachusetts, Virginia, Tennessee, and

North Carolina, although there are, of course, cities and towns in these states that are accepting, like Provincetown and Northampton, Massachusetts. Lambda has four regional offices:

120 Wall Street, Suite 1500
New York, NY 10005-3904
212-809-8585

6030 Wilshire Boulevard, Suite 200
Los Angeles, CA 90036
213-937-2728

11 East Adams, Suite 1008
Chicago, IL 60603-6303
312-663-4413

1447 Peachtree Street, NE, Suite 1004
Atlanta, GA 30309-3027
404-897-1880

Consider joining a support group or having your children join one. Contact Gay and Lesbian Parents Coalition International (P.O. Box 50360, Washington, DC 20091), or Center Kids, part of the Family Project of the Lesbian and Gay Community Services Center (208 West 13th St., New York, NY 10011; 212-620-7310). They may be able to steer you to a group in your area.

If any of these special considerations apply to you, analyze whether they could impact your custody position. If you are not sure, pay for a legal consultation rather than paying later and risking losing your kids.

Blended Families

You, your ex-husband, your children, your new husband, your husband's former wife, their children, your children with your new husband, your ex-husband's new wife, her children, and their children—if you're not familiar with the term *blended family,* get used to it. The Stepfamily Association of America estimates that by the year 2000, blended families will be the most common type of family.

According to a professional journal, close to 75 percent of divorced people remarry, and many have children with their new spouses. Another periodical on family issues found that 80 percent of divorced men and 55 percent of divorced women tie the knot again within ten years. Today, 40 percent of all U.S. marriages are remarriages, with 7,000 stepfamilies forming every week. Yet statistically, 60 percent of all second marriages fail. One reason may be because of all the stressful, interconnected relationships.

You are not only marrying a new partner but marrying his children, and he is marrying yours. It's complicated. What if your stepchildren don't like you? What if you don't like them? What if your son thinks your husband's son is a loser and refuses to spend time with him? What if your daughter detests her father's girlfriend? What if your children are resentful and jealous of their half siblings or the baby you and your second husband have together?

If you know how to anticipate and address problems commonly experienced in stepfamilies, you have a good chance of not being a statistic. You will need patience, perseverance, and concrete strategies, but your new family can be close and loving. Step and half siblings can become friends and cherished relatives.

THE KIDS' POINT OF VIEW

With a new marriage, children gain grandparents, aunts, cousins, and family friends. There are more opportunities for role models, more people to love and know them. But don't expect your kids to see it that way. Starting over after a failed marriage may be exciting for you but depressing for them. A new marriage is confirmation that their mother and father aren't getting back together. You might have wanted to leave the marriage, but they probably wanted to keep it the way it was. This is a change that they didn't elect and over which they may feel little control.

Before the remarriage, you might have been miserable, but your children may have loved having you to themselves. Now there is this new man in the house, who is not their father, and often instant brothers and sisters—his children. Your kids may feel they are being replaced. Your daughter, the baby in your family or an only child, may find she's now the oldest. She may fear you will love your new husband and new children more or that her father will pay more attention to his new wife. Children can feel out of place, like a visitor in their own homes.

Although youngsters (and adults) typically find the first few years in a blended family difficult—remarriages typically fail within the first two years—children whose parents remarry usually turn out well. And so do their parents. Researchers say that second marriages that have weathered the five-year mark are often stronger than first marriages.

Eminent psychologists Mavis Hetherington and James Bray have studied children of divorce and remarriage. They found that 80 percent of these children did *not* have behavioral problems.

THE DECIDING FACTORS FOR CHILDREN

What causes problems for children, say mental health professionals, is not divorce or remarriage but the tension and conflict between the child's parents— you and your child's father. So, if you and your ex-husband can parent cooperatively, it is more likely that your new family will have a better chance of making it. By the same token, you want to encourage your new husband to have a good parenting relationship with his former wife. In other words, don't obstruct or undermine it. You can be jealous and resent their contact, but keep it to yourself. Interfering will be terrible for the children and can jeopardize your marriage. If your husband tries to block your communications with your ex-spouse, set him straight.

There are myriad factors that determine how well a child adjusts to a parent's remarriage: the age of the children, the relationship between their parents, and if your husband has his own children. Young children who have not formed opinions about you or the situation may be the most resilient and receptive to a blended family. Teenagers, particularly girls, can make a remarriage tense. In the Bray and Hetherington study, hormone-crazed adolescent girls tended to fight more with their stepmothers and flirt with their stepfathers.

You can't control the kinds of children your husband brings to the marriage, but you can control other factors: your children, your relationship with your ex-husband, how you treat his wife or girlfriend, how you handle his kids and guide him to deal with yours, and your behavior as a couple.

STEPPARENT STRATEGIES

Children universally hope their parents will reunite. To dispel this fantasy, you might say, "Dad and I both love you very much, but we are not getting back together." That will be a reality check and may make your children more open to either parent's new partner.

Before you remarry, make sure you aren't setting up your children for problems. If you think your soon-to-be husband's son might behave inappropriately toward your daughter, reconsider blending the families until you can be sure there won't be a problem—or find another place for the boy to live. By the same token, if your partner tends to have a bad temper or be overly demonstrative with your daughter, you must protect your children. If you have any reason to believe there might be a problem, discuss it with your husband-to-be and make sure he has a similar conversation with his children. It would be wise to seek counseling, too. It is your job to address these concerns and make sure the boundaries are clear—not only between your new husband and your children, but between the children of the two families.

Reassure your children that you love them, but let them know you also love your husband. When your kids try to test that love (they will), tell them if they put you in that position, you will support your husband. Inform them that you expect them to treat your husband with respect, and make sure he tells his children the same about you.

Tell your stepchildren that you are not trying to take their mother's place or disrupt their relationship with either her or their father. Show them by your actions. Don't bad-mouth her; make sure you speak about her respectfully. His children are more likely to think more of you if you treat their mother well. It should make the adjustment easier for them and therefore for you.

If you don't like your stepchild, think about why you feel this way. How would you feel if you were this child? Is there a reason she may be acting disagreeably? Does it even have to do with you? If you really can't stand your husband's child, fake it. That doesn't mean be a phony, but be kind and see if time will change your feelings. Be realistic: Don't expect an instant happy Hollywood family. *The Brady Bunch* is just a TV show. But don't "go after" your stepchild. It will produce terrible tension and fights between you and your husband and can affect your marriage.

You can't demand that your stepchildren love you or force yourself to love them. If love grows, that is great. What they are like and how you and they get along is, to some extent, determined by luck and chemistry. It's also normal to love your biological children more. Don't feel guilty, but try not to show it.

Develop a plan with your husband. What are the family rules? What are the consequences for breaking them? Discipline your own children and let him discipline his. That can be hard if you're the one home when the misbehavior occurs. Still, try not to put yourself in the position of being the heavy. Save the discipline for when your husband comes home. If you can, think of yourself as an aunt or a baby-sitter, not their mother. That doesn't mean you can't tell them when you don't like their behavior or that you expect better from them. If your stepchildren blurt out, "I don't have to listen to you, you're not my mother," tell them, "You're right, I'm not, but these are the rules of our home." If you don't like the way your husband disciplines his children, discuss it with him when they aren't around. It's important that you support each other in public. Once you have a more solid relationship with your stepchildren, you won't have to sidestep behavioral issues as much.

Devise a holiday schedule with your children in mind. They may not only have to put in an appearance at your house or your ex-husband's, with your parent's or his, but at his new partner's parents' house as well. Try to be flexible and listen to your children's wishes if they are reasonable.

Let the kids have a say, but not *the* say. They should be included in major issues that will impact them (summer vacations, having a baby with your new husband), but they shouldn't be allowed to make the final decision. You could say, "John and I are thinking of having a baby and you are a major part of the family," not, "Is it okay with you if we have another baby?" Don't ask permission.

Don't compete with your husband's ex-spouse. So what if she buys nice presents for your children or takes them on special trips? The kids will enjoy them, and it may be her way of feeling close to them. His children can have a good relationship with both of you. There is no contest, and if you make it one, you won't win. If your child or his children are the ones competing, sit them down and tell them there is room in your heart to love them all.

Don't be a doormat. If there is something that upsets you, tell his children and your husband, but do it calmly and not in the heat of the moment.

To make all family members feel important and a part of the group, let each one choose one family activity for the week or month, whether it's getting pizza on Thursday or a movie on Saturday. Work hard to make every child in the family feel loved and valued.

Make individual time for just you and your child, and encourage your husband to do the same with each of his children. Also have him spend time alone with your child and do the same with his. If it feels awkward, stick to an activity that doesn't require too much intimacy or intensity, like a trip to the library, shopping, or seeing a movie.

Make time with your husband away from the children.

Get counseling before there is a crisis. Couples often blame each other for normal difficulties in making the transition. Just because these problems are normal doesn't mean they aren't stressful. New husbands and wives sometimes blame the other mate's children for problems in their own relationship. Several sessions of family and/or individual therapy might be sufficient and may be covered by insurance. Think about getting into couples therapy so you can anticipate problems and work through issues and strategies. Find someone who specializes in stepfamilies, since these families have unique problems. Try the regular avenues for finding a good therapist: your pediatrician or internist or friends in a similar position. Or contact the American Association for Marriage and Family Therapy (1133 15th Street NW, Suite 300, Washington, DC 20005) or the Stepfamily Association of America (800-735-0329), which will give you a local referral. Interview the counselor and find out what experience he or she has had with couples and family therapy. Does the prospective therapist have many clients who are stepparents or are trained in working with blended families? Does he approach stepfamilies differently than first marriage families? It's wise to have an introductory meeting to see if you like the therapist's style and feel you could work together.

If your second (or third) marriage doesn't work out, allow your children to continue a relationship with your ex-husband and his children. Those bonds are important to maintain.

BLENDED FAMILIES AND THE LAW

The rights and responsibilities of stepparents vary from state to state. Usually, unless you have adopted your stepchildren, you have no legal rights to visitation or custody if your ex-husband says you can't see them. Some states, however, do give stepparents the legal right to seek visitation. Even if yours does not, if you develop a strong bond with your stepchild, you may be able to convince the court that as a psychological parent you are an important part of the child's life and it is in the child's best interests to continue the relationship. Check with a lawyer or guardian ad litem to see if it's an issue.

MONEY MATTERS

You or your ex-husband might have married someone with money. Even so, they are not legally required to support your children, their stepchildren. (Child support guidelines are based on the parents' incomes and not the new partner's income.)

It is common to feel resentful about money in a blended family. You may think your husband is paying too much child support to his ex-wife, that he is too generous with his kids and not generous enough with yours, that your ex-spouse is not giving you enough money for the children, even though his new wife is independently wealthy. It can also be hard to take if your husband pays out a big part of his salary to his ex-spouse, but your former husband doesn't send you the support checks you are owed.

You can talk to your husband or ex-husband about the situation, but if you don't get the results you want, he probably won't change. The support checks your husband writes may seem excessive, but they're not likely to be. Usually, they don't cover many incidental costs necessary for raising kids. If he does contribute more than he's required, it means he cares about his children. Of course, if you're barely getting by, then there's a problem, and it makes sense to discuss it and see if you can work it out.

If your spouse piles on the presents to his children (but not yours) or gives them an unusually large allowance, or your ex-husband plies them with gifts you can't afford, see if you can sensitize this money-burning creature. After a visit with Dad, if your son brings home toys and clothes and does a show-and-tell in front of his half or stepsiblings, you may want to take him aside and say, "It's wonderful that Dad buys you these things, but it's really hard for Jeremy and Alison, because they don't have them. I want you to enjoy what he gives you, but be sensitive and think about how they must feel."

Realize your husband may be splurging because he feels guilty about the situation. Suggest he find other ways to show the children that he loves them that don't require massive amounts of money, such as a picnic or a trip to a museum. If he's bent on buying them gifts, ask that he also get a small gift for your child. You might also want to tell your children that your husband is giving his children presents because he misses them, not because he doesn't like your kids.

DO SOME ESTATE PLANNING

Estate planning is always wise, but particularly with remarriage. Your husband may have terrific intentions to provide for your children if you die suddenly, but circumstances change. His children or new wife might try convincing him that their financial needs are more important than your children's after you are gone. To protect yourself and your children, do estate planning no matter how in love you are.

Smart estate planning gives you a way to make sure you and your spouse are financially secure and leaves your money to the children from your first marriage, while getting as many tax breaks as possible. A lawyer can draft estate planning documents, that can include a prenuptial agreement (a property settlement agreement drawn up before marriage), a will, and trusts. These documents typically cost $3,000 to $10,000 or more, and a planning service can run $5,000 to $10,000, depending on how large and complicated your estate is.

Your Will

If you don't have a will, the courts divide up your assets when you die; without this legal document, they might not be allocated the way you want. In most states, a spouse is entitled to 25 to 50 percent of your estate. If you want your children to inherit most of your assets, you have to state that in your will.

If you don't want one of your children to inherit any of your money, write in your will that you are not leaving anything to that child. Review your will every two to three years or when there are major changes in your life: a divorce, a baby, loss of a job, or a promotion.

Prenuptial Agreements

These make sense if you are worried that your new marriage could affect your children's inheritance. Prenuptial agreements allow a spouse to waive his rights to a specific share of your estate, which is determined on a percentage basis by the state in which you live. You could also waive those rights after you have remarried.

This is how two common trusts work for blended families: With a *credit shelter trust,* formed with $600,000, which is exempt from estate tax, the trust will provide income to the surviving spouse for life, but the principal goes to the children after the spouse dies. A *QUIP trust* is for people with estates larger than $600,000. Ask your lawyer about other kinds of trusts.

Think carefully before you choose a trustee. If possible, the person should be a professional in the financial field: a banker, an accountant, a money manager, a financial planner, a stockbroker, or a successful businessperson. It should be someone who knows how to invest money. You could make a relative or friend a cotrustee if you want the assurance that your money is being directed according to your instructions.

Before writing out a prenuptial agreement or setting up a trust, talk with your husband about what each of you wants to leave to your respective children. If your children are mature enough, consider a similar conversation with them. You don't want there to be any misunderstandings or hard feelings; even though a stepchild has no legal rights to an inheritance, you don't want him to challenge the will and tie up your estate.

To get a referral for a trust estate lawyer, ask your divorce attorney, a friend, or write the American College of Trust & Estate Counsel, 3415 S. Sepulveda Blvd., Los Angeles, CA 90034. They have a list of lawyers specializing in this field from your state who have had at least ten years of experience in estate planning.

Blended families are a lot of work, and learning how to navigate the transition and beyond takes skill and grit. Don't forget, however, to safeguard your assets so that you and your children are in the best financial position possible, no matter what happens.

What if You Don't Have Custody

"When you relinquish custody, there is always going to be that heartache for you and your children. It's like a longing, and it's something that can never be replaced. You can remain close, but it's just not the same. At times, I feel like the doting aunt or the good friend, not the mother."

"I'd walk around the house, and my children weren't there. I'd cry for hours at a time. I'd think, *What is it I've done so badly that I lost my children? What am I paying for?* For a while, I would go to sleep with pieces of my sons' blankets under my pillow."

"When I first lost custody I felt stripped of any identity I might have had. I was no longer a wife or mother. I thought society looked upon me as someone who must have done something terribly wrong. When your child is taken away, you also have a sense of loss and abandonment. That's exactly what I felt."

"I never thought I could live without my children. I fell apart. I didn't want to live. I felt like a brick. What I mean is, I felt nothing after a while except empty of feelings."

"For a woman to relinquish custody is the most unselfish thing she can do for her kids."

"When a man divorces, the neighbors bring him food and his buddies take him out for drinks. They don't do that for women, particularly noncustodial mothers. Instead, they stay away."

It can be agony to be a noncustodial mother in a society that still believes children belong with their mothers, and only an unloving mother lives without her children. Coping with the loss of the marriage and not having the children become double burdens.

Some of society's judgmental attitudes come from the fact that most people don't understand how or why a woman becomes a noncustodial mother. They don't realize that courts make gender-neutral rulings, and mothers no longer have the edge. Outsiders might not believe you can choose to be a noncustodial mother and still be a good parent. They think that if the children don't live with you, you must be:

- Uncaring and selfish
- Mentally ill or have something else the matter with you
- An alcoholic or a drug addict
- Oversexed and promiscuous
- Incompetent

Wrong. Today, a woman can be caring, selfless, emotionally healthy, alcohol- and drug-free, abstinent, and a competent parent. And she may still wind up being the visiting parent.

How could this happen? Your ex-husband may have more money to hire big-gun attorneys who know how to fight for custody and win, or your children may ask the court to live with their father. You may decide your ex-husband can provide a better life for your children because he's in a better position financially or emotionally, and you feel you have no other choice. You might not want a costly and bloody courtroom battle that is sure to damage the children as well as you. Or you ruin your chances because you behave in a way that alienates the courts. You might be physically afraid of your husband and what he might do to your children if you push for custody. Or he might have threatened to withhold child support and alimony if you try to keep the children. There are scores of reasons that can cause a mother to not have her children, and they have little to do with incompetence.

The irony is that society may judge you harshly for doing what in some cases is really a noble act: putting the interests of your children before your own, even when it's at your expense.

If your children don't live with you, you will still be able to have a strong and close relationship with them.

WHAT YOU MIGHT BE FEELING

On shame: Again, it goes back to societal beliefs that mothers should have the children, and what it implies if they don't. Three years after relinquishing custody, one mother said she still pretends she is the custodial parent. "Even today, I talk like the kids are at home. There's such a stigma associated with not having your children. Some people I did tell at the beginning automatically assumed I didn't have my kids because I wasn't good to them or was abusive. I couldn't deal with it. I couldn't say I don't have my children. I'm a little better now, but I still haven't come to grips with it. I always feel I have to justify not being the custodial parent."

On blame: "I know I did the best with the cards I was dealt, and what was best for my girls, but it doesn't stop me from saying, 'I must have caused this; why else wouldn't I have them?' And sometimes I secretly think, *All those people out there must be right; it is my fault.*"

On guilt: Even if you believe you did what was best for your children by relinquishing custody or you had no choice because the court ruled in your ex-husband's favor, it doesn't erase your feelings of guilt. Says one mother, whose son and daughter are now in their twenties, "When they are going through a tough time, the breakup of a relationship or not being able to work through a job situation, I ask myself, 'If I had been there while they were growing up, would it have made a difference? If I had given them the little part of the foundation their life needed to weather the situation as adults, would they be having an easier job today?' That feeling is always there. It's the not knowing. When I get together with other noncustodial mothers who have grown children, I either hear them ask this question or see it in their faces, or one of us will say, 'Do you think if you had been there, it would have made a difference?' "

Every noncustodial mother knows that without the children she will have a large amount of disposable time. This will give you freedom, but it can also make you feel guilty. You may be relieved not to have to undertake the tedious day-to-day parenting, particularly when your children are difficult (which they tend to be after their mothers and fathers split up). But you think a good mother is not supposed to have these thoughts. You may doubt your maternal instinct. This sense of relief is normal.

On low or no self-esteem: If you felt like a failure when your marriage was breaking up, not being awarded custody if you wanted it is bound to test your self-esteem. Between a battering from society and your own self-doubts, this is guaranteed to be a tough personal time. How can you feel good about yourself when you are told in all sorts of ways that you have dropped the ball?

If your custody arrangement is working, you may also be conflicted. It can make you feel you aren't needed—a rough thought when it has been drilled into you from birth that your biggest role is as a mother.

Adolescents, who tend to tax a mother's self-esteem in solid marriages, can be especially draining for noncustodial mothers. Teenagers trying to separate from you (and every other adult on the planet) may not want to spend the little time they have with you. And that may confirm to you the belief that you have failed as a mother.

On lack of control: Mothers like to be in control, to do things their way. Many think that their way is *the* only way. If you believe you are the parent who will do a better job of raising your child, not having them is going to be particularly hard on you. When your ex-husband is awarded custody of the children, it makes you feel less in control. If you tend to be stricter, it is going to be frustrating.

DISCUSSING THE SITUATION WITH YOUR CHILDREN

"I still remember when I came home from court and told my eight-year-old he couldn't live with me," said one woman who had collapsed in the courtroom when the judge awarded custody to her ex-husband. If you don't have custody, you will need to reassure your children that you wish you could be with them more, and that would have been your choice. Emphasize the positive. Let them know that even though they may be living with their father most of the time, that you still love them as much and will spend as much time as you possibly can with them. They should know that you want to be with them and that they will not be losing you emotionally. Say that you will miss them and that you will speak with them every day or very often.

You could explain that their father also wanted to be with them and that the judge decided they should live with him, if that's the case. (If you relinquished custody, you would eliminate the explanation about the judge.) If your child says, "It's not fair, I want to be with you," you might reply that you want to be with her, too, but that's not what the judge decided. Even if, in your view, the judge made a mistake awarding custody to your ex-husband, you will want to spare your child from seeing how distraught and angry you feel about the arrangement. Again, focus on the enduring quality of your relationship and your investment in your child. (Then return to court if it's merited.) Tell her it is perfectly normal for her to feel sad. It's also all right for her to see you sad, as long as she realizes you can function and she doesn't have to worry about you.

If you lose custody because of severe depression—a possible reason for not getting the children—you need to give your kids some explanation. Children as young as eight can be told, "Mommy is feeling terribly sad and it's making it hard for me to take care of myself and others. Nothing matters to me more than you, but I am feeling so sad it is making me sick. There are special doctors who help people with problems and I am going to one to get better." Tell them that if they ever have a problem to let you know, and they may want to talk to someone about it. Older children will understand the concept of depression. You can explain that you are having difficulty coping, and that you are receiving psychological help. Let them know that most people who get help overcome depression and you believe you will, too. Let them know you are trying to overcome this problem not only because it's important for you, but also because you want to be the best mother you can be. (Substitute whatever reason you don't have custody for depression.)

TURNING A TERRIBLE SITUATION AROUND

Many mothers who have settled into their noncustodial role say that, although they may not have chosen the arrangement, there have been benefits. Having the children less of the time has given them more of a chance to work on their own struggles and to forge careers. As one stay-at-home mother who went on to counsel teens in an outpatient substance abuse program puts it, "My time alone was healing. I could work on me without other distractions. I had no excuse not to get better. Looking back, I have to think not having the girls afforded me a better opportunity to grow and become a better mother. My relationship today with my grown daughters would never have been as good. We wouldn't have been as close, because I would have been a crazy person. I felt so damaged by the breakup of my marriage. Being the noncustodial parent gave me an opportunity to find out who I was, to get myself well, and to grow as a person rather than allow my ex-husband to control me."

Says another mother who now runs an adoption agency, "The freedom has been nice, although it's not one of the biggest things. It's clear in my mind that I would never have been able to achieve the career I achieved if I had custody. I would have struggled financially and emotionally, my kids would have been deprived materially, and I would have been emotionally drained and too distracted. Those character-building lessons gave me confidence to know I could literally do anything."

A school librarian believes that leaving her marriage was the first step toward getting professional help. She suffered from low self-esteem from childhood. "I blossomed over time. I progressed faster because I didn't have the children around and could reflect on myself. It became a nine-year odyssey of self-healing. The point is, you don't have to be stuck with your plight. You can come out on the other side. Once I did, I realized my ex-husband did get involved in the girls' day-to-day life, and it's been good for them to get to know their dad. I think that's great, because I had a terrible relationship with my father. This is not how I had hoped custody would unfold, but there have been some positive parts to it for all of us."

MORE ON NONCUSTODIAL MOTHERS

There is little research on this subject, but Geoffrey Greif and Mary Pabst, authors of *Mothers without Custody*, have conducted the most comprehensive study available. Between June 1983 and January 1987, they interviewed 517 noncustodial mothers. Ninety percent of them spent five overnights a month or less with their children. Most were white and middle class. Twenty-six percent had split custody and had at least one child living with them. Here is what Greif and Pabst found:

- The biggest reason mothers gave for not having the children was money (30 percent). They said their ex-husbands had more money to raise the children or had threatened not to pay alimony or child support if their wives had custody. The next causes were: The children asked to live with their father (21 percent), they could not control the children (11 percent), they were unstable (11 percent), and they lost custody in court (9 percent).

- Noncustodial mothers most comfortable with their arrangement had accepted their role. The situation that worked best for these mothers was when they had come to terms with the custody decision, had a cooperative relationship with their former husbands, an ex-spouse who liked being the primary caretaker, and well-adjusted children. Not surprisingly, mothers who had lost a courtroom custody contest felt more guilty than those where the children chose to live with their father and the mothers agreed.

- Some mothers wanted to go to court to win custody but decided not to because they couldn't afford to or felt it would be too traumatic for the children.

IN THEIR OWN WORDS

Maryanne

"To this day, I haven't figured out why I don't have the children. I looked at the court transcript, and all it said was the judge thought the children would be better off with my ex-husband. Never in a million years did I think a judge would take two young children from their mother. I thought custody was a sure thing. I was naive and wasn't worried about getting witnesses to testify about my character. I call March 5 my sentencing day. It is the day the judge gave my one- and four-year-old sons to my husband. My now eight-year-old still remembers when I came home from court and told him he couldn't live with me.

"I had told my husband I wanted a divorce. He moved out of our home and I stayed with the boys. I worked part-time as an architect. My grandmother lived with me, and she would watch my little one. I would drop off my four-year-old at day care at 8:30 A.M. and get to work by 9. Then I would pick him up at 3 P.M.

"During my separation, I began dating a guy. Right after I got divorced, we went to Vermont and got married. My new husband was being transferred temporarily to Vermont, and I told my ex-husband I wanted to take the boys. He went ballistic when he heard I wanted to move. He hated my guts because I had asked for the divorce and he asked the court to nullify the marriage and filed for sole custody. He also hired a private detective. I quit my job so I could be an at-home mom when I moved to Vermont. I was so sure I was going to win custody that I told my ex-husband that when I moved with the kids, I would meet him halfway one weekend a month and every three-day weekend.

"The judge was nasty to me and said I only got remarried so I could take my boys to Vermont. I walked out of the courtroom and started crying. I told my new husband I had lost the kids. He said that was ridiculous because I had only been in the courtroom briefly, but I had a very bad feeling about the outcome. On the witness stand, my ex-husband started bawling. He said he only lets the children watch religious movies, and I thought, *Oh my God, he's making it up, his lawyer must have prepped him!* My ex-husband went on about what a wonderful father he was. His mother and sister testified for him, even though he didn't get along with his sister and they didn't have much of a relationship. I swear on a stack of Bibles that his sister never set foot in our home. She said that when she visited, she saw him bathe the kids and cook meals for them.

"The detective got on the stand and called my new husband my 'paramour.' He said he had seen us doing ninety-five miles an hour in a tunnel on Memorial Day weekend. You can't do ninety-five miles an hour on a Friday night of Memorial Day weekend. He testified that the kids were in the backseat, and I was giving my boyfriend a blow job. I never even kissed my husband in front of the kids!

"My ex-husband got sole custody, and I collapsed in the courtroom and was on tranquilizers for some time. He got the house, and I had to pay child support even though I had resigned my position to move to Vermont and didn't have a job."

Maryanne's mistake: She remarried someone who was moving out of state, assuming she had the right to take the children with her and she would be awarded custody. She should have consulted a lawyer about her move. She did not bring witnesses to the hearing in support of her side of the story.

Anne

"When my children were eight and ten, my husband and I had already separated several times. When he assaulted me, I realized I had to get out of the marriage. The police suggested I leave the house. My husband said if I tried to take the kids, he'd kill them. I thought it was better to get out and then get the children back. I started proceedings for custody. I thought at a later date, the kids would be with me. In the interim, my ten-year-old son kept running away from his dad and calling me. I'd pick him up and take him back to his father. The third time my son called, I told his father he was going to stay with me, which he did.

"At a custody hearing, my ex-husband was told he had to give me our eight-year-old daughter. One day, I took her to my office and she asked to go to the drugstore. She didn't come back. Five hours later, I got a call from my ex-husband and he said she was with him. My daughter had planned the whole thing with her father. That summer, my son decided he wanted to be with his dad.

"I decided, *I'm not fighting anymore. These children are so screwed up, the best thing to do is give my ex-husband permanent custody and go on with my life.* During the divorce hearing, I relinquished custody. My feeling was I would have a better chance of reestablishing a relationship with the kids. My ex-husband had threatened to take our children away if I lost custody, so I decided if I gave him custody, he would stay in the area.

"I moved twenty-five miles away and was given every other weekend. I gave up all holidays and birthdays in order to have them Christmas Eve and morning until noon. I was totally devastated. I had read an article by a noncustodial mother in *Single Parenting* magazine put out by Parents without Partners. Up until that point, I thought I was the only person going through this. I called up the author, and she told me about Mothers Without Custody.

"I was not prepared for what I saw at the meeting. There were thirty women in this small apartment. I was crying and people were crying and I thought, *Oh my God, I have to get out of here.* It was too heart-wrenching, and I was dealing with my own pain. I thought I was never going back, but seven months later, a MWC leader called. In the meantime, I had gotten into counseling and resolved a lot of issues. I was in a much better place. I was able to listen to stories and offer encouragement and eventually became a local coordinator. I was fortunate that many of the people I surrounded myself with were noncustodial mothers. I believe that's what saved my sanity.

"I realize I needed to give up custody, that it was better to try to work it out this way than through the courts. To have subjected my children to the back-and-forth pulling would have been disastrous for them. I had meager surroundings and no money and was working three part-time jobs as an office manager, bookkeeper, and secretary.

"Some people may view it as a poor decision, but the alternative was court fights and teaching them things about life that I didn't want them to learn. They needed to see a healthy relationship between a husband and wife, and I thought, hopefully down the road, they would see one between my husband and a new woman or me and a new man.

"My relationship was hardest with my daughter. When she was a teenager, she reluctantly came to my house and always had to bring an entourage of girlfriends. I hung in there. For a while, she resented the fact that I made her come. At one point, I told her she didn't have to come if she didn't want to. The same thing happened with my teenage son, who wanted to do things with his friends. I decided not to push them and it worked. They sometimes didn't come, but when they did, it was because they wanted to.

"Over time, the quality of my relationship with the kids improved. When they saw me involved with MWC, they realized I was going to be okay and they could be okay. They'd hear me talk to other mothers in crisis and felt I was doing something positive with a negative situation."

Anne's mistake: She should have gotten a protective order from the courts, which could have included giving her custody, and taken the children with her when she left the house. She should have retained an attorney to explain the custody laws and not have given up so easily if custody is what she really wanted. Anne needed to get immediate counseling for herself and her children, which might have helped her cope better with the situation and fight for custody.

Laura

"When we first split up, my husband told me he wanted a divorce. He had a girlfriend and moved out of the house. I stayed with my eight- and six-year-old daughters, and I ended up getting involved with someone else. I was so emotionally distraught over the breakup and decided to let my husband move back into the house and I moved out. I sold my clothing store and found a new job an hour away. I moved with my boyfriend and thought I would make some money and get my head together. I was away for seven months, but I saw my kids every other weekend. In my mind, it was a temporary move and I would come back and be with the kids. I thought the children could stay in the same house and there'd be more stability for them.

"When I found out my husband was going to fight for custody, I moved back to the house on my attorney's advice. I had an inept attorney. It was the first custody case he had ever had. My children's court-appointed attorney was laughing and chatting away with my ex-husband's lawyer. We lived for three months under the same roof until the court told me I had to move out. In court I lost the girls.

"It took me seven years to regain custody. This time around, I had an experienced lawyer and the court-appointed attorney was a woman. My husband had remarried, and he and his wife were control freaks. I had to establish that my daughters' stepmother was emotionally abusing them. My new attorney showed how my ex-husband's wife's behavior was ruining my daughters' self-esteem. When she was fifteen, another of my girls told her dad she was either going to live with me or run away. I didn't have to go to trial because my ex-husband's attorney threatened to quit if he didn't accept the agreement. Luckily, throughout those years, I had been able to stay very close with my daughters."

Laura's mistake: Laura should never have moved out of the house and in with her boyfriend, leaving her children with her husband. She assumed she could return to the marital home and reestablish her position vis-à-vis custody. She hired a rookie lawyer who did not know how to stand up to her ex-husband's attorney or object to the relationship between him and the children's advocate. She underestimated the importance of hiring a seasoned attorney and assumed, like her lawyer, that she would win because she was the mother.

CUSTODY FOR NONCUSTODIAL MOTHERS

Not all noncustodial mothers want custody, but if you do, keep in mind that you will have to win your children back. You will have to be organized in your approach. Preparation is essential, and so is a competent lawyer. The judge will be faced with the question, "Why should I take the children out of their current living situation and give custody to their mother?" The only way to regain custody is to convince the judge that there has been some change in circumstances in your living situation or a turn for the worse in your husband's household or in the condition of your child. You have to prove it is in your children's best interest to live with you by demonstrating why they would be better off living with you than the person with whom they currently reside. Judges don't like to uproot children without good reason (see chapter 8).

Find a lawyer who is supportive of your position, and try to anticipate what may happen in court. Make sure you have a solid chance of gaining custody and that you understand the process. Besides consulting your attorney, speak with other noncustodial mothers who have tried to gain or regain custody.

You will need to revisit your first custody dispute. If you lost in court, what do you think prompted the judge's decision? What can you do this time around that will change your position and affect the outcome in your favor? If your husband was awarded custody because you have a drinking problem, for example, you will have to be rehabilitated.

You must plan your life to show the judge that you are better able to be the primary caretaker. That will include convincing the court that your living arrangements are better suited to your children's needs than your ex-husband's. This is where live-in boyfriends can be a problem, especially if your ex-husband has remarried. Judges like to give custody to a parent who has time for his children. Therefore, make sure your job is not perceived as interfering with your ability to take care of your children. You will have to tailor or eliminate your extracurricular activities to show that your needs come second to your children and that you will be available to them. Demonstrate that you have painstakingly thought out your plan for custody. Come to court armed with a list of baby-sitters you can call on if you work and your child is sick, whether it is a relative (preferred by the courts) or an experienced older woman. Show a willingness to include your ex-husband or other primary caretaker in your children's schedule. (For more advice on how to win custody, see chapter 4.)

WHEN THEY COME BACK

Prepare yourself and save your strength for the readjustment. Even though this is what you wanted, it is likely to be a tense time for both you and the children. Your full-time parental skills may be rusty. "I had to reteach myself how to parent, because I hadn't been in a real parental mode for all those years," said one mother, whose daughters came to live with her after spending eight years with their father. "It was stressful. They took all the emotional stuff from the other house. They were angry with everything—their father, the situation, me—and I had to deal with their emotions. They tested me to see how far they could go, how they could manipulate the rules. Eventually—it seemed forever!— I was able to establish boundaries for them and set goals for myself. We all went for counseling."

TIPS FROM THE TRENCHES: ADVICE FROM NONCUSTODIAL MOTHERS

· **If you are considering relinquishing custody, really think hard about what it will mean on a daily basis.** "I thought all the times

I would spend with the girls would make up for the absences," one noncustodial mother confides. "But I will never be as close to them as someone who is there all the time. It's possible to have a good relationship—I know, because I have one—but it is still altered." Before voluntarily relinquishing custody, consider all of the consequences and the effect on your life. Make an educated decision.

- **Find a support system.** That may be neighbors or friends or a group like Mothers Without Custody or Parents Without Partners (call local information for the number). You will need help dealing with society's notion that if you are not raising your children, you are not a whole woman. Groups like Mothers Without Custody can give you a sense of belonging and offer a nonjudgmental place to share your feelings. As one woman active in Mothers Without Custody put it, "I don't think anyone understands what a noncustodial mother feels. People can be empathetic and supportive, but they never really know." Another mother who attends Mothers Without Custody meetings regularly said they have given her some perspective on her own situation: "Someone's story is always worse than mine. At least my children love me dearly. Some of the women talk about not having much of a relationship with their kids or not knowing where they are. And I might not be able to stand my ex-husband, but he does love his children."

- **Get private and/or family therapy.** A skilled professional can make the soul searching and the changes less painful. Counseling can make you feel better when you are with your children so you will have the most positive experience possible. It may also help them adjust and keep open the lines of communication.

- **Try to work closely and communicate with your ex-husband around the issues of your children,** even if you are on lousy terms with him. It will make your situation more bearable and be easier for your children.

- **Find ways to stay involved in your children's lives.** When they're not with you, phone them regularly or send letters. Let them know you care. If you think your ex-spouse will give them the letters, you could send them through the mail. If not, see if your child's teacher or principal will deliver the loving notes. The point is to let your children know that even if you can't be with them, you are still think-ing of them. Children sometimes fear that if they don't see a parent regularly, that parent will forget them. The calls and notes help relieve that fear. If your ex-husband blocks communication, keep a record and copy of the letters and notes you tried to send. If your custody agreement provides regular contact with your child but your ex-husband won't permit it, go back to your lawyer to get the courts to enforce it. These copies will also be evidence for a professional. In addition, the children will have evidence that you tried to have an active relationship with them.

· **Wait it out.** If you have a positive, ongoing relationship with your children, they may try to move back with you when they are adoles-cents. Remember, the courts usually listen to the custody wishes of adolescents if they are reasonable. Even if it's not in the agreement, your strong-willed teenager may decide she doesn't want to live with her father anymore, and he has little choice but to honor her wishes.

· **Put your children's needs above your own.** Hopefully, living with their father will be beneficial for them, and you can use this time to get your life back together.

· **Accept the fact that someone other than you can also do a decent job of raising your children.** If your ex-husband is a capable parent (or, perish the thought, even more capable), you need to see that the situation can be beneficial for them, which is the goal anyway. According to Geoffrey Greif, a social worker who is an expert on noncustodial mothers, there is no evidence that children raised by their father are affected negatively. In fact, says Greif, "most of the research on custodial fathers says the kids do fine."

· **Don't bad-mouth your ex-husband to your children.** Save that for your friends. It definitely won't help your relationship with your children. Said one noncustodial mother, "I didn't say anything bad about their father, even though I hated his guts. It worked, because my daughters knew they could be open with me, that I wasn't going to make them feel bad about him and be critical." Another mother admits, "There were probably times my kids thought of me as a victim or a wimp because I didn't fight back by name-calling. I wanted them to feel my house was a safe place, and they wouldn't have, if I had bad-mouthed their father."

· **Think of the children's absences as an opportunity to concentrate on yourself.** Women tend to be caretakers and forget about themselves. Do whatever it takes to stay healthy: counseling, a support group, a new hobby, exercise, night classes, vocational training, or a book group. Let your children see that you can take a terrible situation and make it at least somewhat positive. Work on your pain, on building a career, on putting together a new, albeit, different life. This will make you a positive role model for your children.

One college student brought up by her father recently sent her mother a school paper she had written. The assignment was to pick a hero. The young woman chose her noncustodial mother, whom she described as working successfully through difficult issues.

· **Make the time you spend with your children special.** That doesn't mean constantly buying them goodies, but having fun, staying close, repeatedly telling them that you love them. It also doesn't mean telling them how much you miss them when they aren't with you and how hard it is for you. That will only make them feel guilty and torn.

· **Take advantage of not being the heavy.** If your ex-husband gets the job of being the day-to-day disciplinarian, you can focus on the sweet parts of your relationship with your children.

· **Keep a journal for your children.** One mother who has been writing in one every few months for three years uses hers "as a means for them to understand when they're much older what she went through.

It helps her say things she wishes she could say now." You may also choose to write in a journal as a way to vent your anger and emotions with the intention that you will never show it to your children.

· **Don't assume it will be easy to gain custody once you relinquish or lose it.**

· **Make sure your children keep in touch with the friends they've made when they're with you.** If your children live in another community or state and come to see you for the summer and vacations, encourage them to keep in contact with their friends during the year. Otherwise, at the end of the eighteen years that they have visited you and are no longer obligated to see you, they may feel less inclined to return because they have no friends there.

Being without your children can be excruciating, whether it's temporary or permanent. Nevertheless, you can still have a strong relationship with them and be a major influence in their lives.

The Parental Kidnapping Possibility

CARLA

"At first, I'd go crazy for days solid and had to be given tranquil-izers," said Carla, whose estranged husband stole their baby, Josh, five years ago after a weekend visitation. She has not seen him since. "I couldn't go into a mall for over a year because there are so many children there. A mother would leave her baby and walk into an-other aisle and I'd think, *I would never leave my child, and look what happened to me.* I'd only shop at minimarts really quick because I'd be crying and couldn't handle the shoppers with all their kids. Now I realize I have to keep living. Every night I pray that Josh is happy. Every week I talk to the police, the federal government, and miss-ing children's organizations."

WHAT ARE THE CHANCES IT COULD HAPPEN TO YOU?

Parental kidnapping is always a possibility with divorce. The hurt can reduce a parent to spiteful, downright mean behavior. What better way to settle the score, make a statement, and really show your ex-wife? What is the "thing" that matters most? The children, of course. Parents may be so angry they can't handle that anger anymore. Now they just want to get even. Revenge is by far the biggest motive in these abduc-tions, and you need to think about it. As one Florida man whose ex-wife asked for a divorce tells it, "She told me to go to hell, so I'm telling her the same."

With more than one million children affected by divorce each year, anywhere from five to ten million youngsters are at risk for family abductions (kidnapping by a parent, relative, or parent's boyfriend or girlfriend), estimates one government report. It may take years to locate a stolen child, and some parents never do. However, this same study found a 99 percent success rate for the searching parent. Commonly accepted statistics place the number of parental kidnappings in a range of 100,000 to more than 350,000 a year. The latest comprehensive study, conducted in 1988 by the U.S. Justice Department's Office of Juvenile Justice and Delinquency Protection, found 354,100 family abductions, or 3 to 7 percent of the five to ten million children who had recently experienced divorce. It makes sense that child stealings have increased even more as divorce itself has soared.

By law, *parental kidnapping*, or child snatching, as it is often called, is defined as a parent taking a child in violation of a court order. Custody orders should be rendered by a judge in the state with the longest and strongest ties to the child. However, some parents engage in custody-hopping, where a parent dissatisfied with the custody outcome in one state skips to another state with the child and requests a new ruling. A law, known as the Uniform Child Custody Jurisdiction Act, was enacted to discourage this behavior, but it is not foolproof (see page 299.)

In 1984, Congress passed the Missing Children's Assistance Act to establish a national resource center for child abduction. The National Center for Missing and Exploited Children (NCMEC) works with the Justice Department to find missing children (2101 Wilson Blvd., Suite 550, Arlington, VA 22201-3052; 800-843-5678).

THE PENALTIES

The legal punishment for parental kidnapping differs from state to state, but all states, as well as the District of Columbia and the Virgin Islands, have criminal parental kidnapping statutes, and most make the crime a felony when a child is taken out of state or is concealed from the other parent. If your child is abducted abroad, the treaty called the Hague Convention on International Child Abductions requires all countries that are signatories, including the United States, to return a child to the country from which he was kidnapped. Under the International Parental Kidnapping Crime Act of 1993, any parent who takes a child out of the United States with the intent to deprive the other parent of the child could face a fine or up to three years in prison, or both.

If you steal your child, you could lose custody for your actions, even if your ex-husband was abusive. Your best course of action is to go through the police and the courts and request an emergency hearing to obtain custody if you believe your child is in danger of being abducted.

BUT THE CHILD IS WITH A PARENT, HOW BAD COULD IT BE?

That is what the courts have been saying for years. And it's also why law enforcement officials have been slow to press charges, and judges have been reluctant to impose serious sentences. In 1982, there was only one state clearinghouse for information about missing children; today, almost all states have one. That attitude is changing as officials discover how poorly some of the children fare. A 1993 University of Maryland study estimated that 7 percent of the children stolen by a parent were sexually abused, and 24 percent were physically harmed.

Studies have shown that a parent with a violent history is more likely to kidnap his child and may become abusive. The University of Maryland study found that of 371 parents surveyed from five missing children's organizations, 54 percent said domestic violence existed in their relationship before the abduction.

Even if your husband has never been violent, he might still take out his frustration on your children. He may resent your son and daughter for having put *him* in this position, for making *him* a fugitive. He may regret having stolen them because it's a huge responsibility and now he feels he has lost his freedom. There is little time to make new friends or date. A kidnapping parent may not be prepared for the hardships on the run. It's a lot of work to uproot yourself, find a job, leave friends and family, and keep up the pretense.

Youngsters may have their names changed and their hair dyed to elude police. There are fathers who kidnap their children, give them to a relative or friend to raise, and leave the picture entirely. Some parents drag their children from state to state, not allowing them to attend school, or enrolling them in a blur of different schools. The victims have an impossible time forming friendships, something critical for healthy mental development. Children stolen as babies may not remember their custodial parent.

They may be told their searching parent is dead, will hurt them if she finds them, can't be reached or has moved, doesn't want them, or is a bad person so never mention her name. Stolen children may be traumatized a second time if there is a resnatch (where the other parent steals the child back). Sometimes, police with sirens shrieking will come to arrest the parent and retrieve the child. The searching parent may hire a detective who might have to grab the child and make a frightening getaway.

Stolen boys and girls suffer from insecurity, especially if they are moved around. Even the best parental kidnapping scenario—where children are settled in just one community—deny youngsters the love of grandparents, their left-behind parent, family friends, playmates, their familiar bed and surroundings, and their beloved pet. Imagine being kidnapped to a foreign country where people don't speak your language

Divorce itself is traumatic for children. Abducted children are still grappling with having their mothers and fathers split up. Now they have the added trauma of losing contact with one of their parents. Young children stolen when critical developmental bonds are being formed with the left-behind parent may suffer serious emotional problems.

JoAnn Behrman Lippert, a clinical psychologist in private practice in Reno, Nevada, treats parentally abducted children. She has worked on a federal grant that studied the effects of these kidnappings on children and helped develop a model to help mental health clinicians treat returned children. According to Lippert's research, the extent of children's psychological damage depends upon what they are told about the left-behind parent, how the kidnapping was carried out (during a routine visitation or violently), and the circumstances of their time away.

BECKY

As divorces go, Becky Comeaux believed hers was civil—so civil that even though the Louisiana courts had awarded her temporary custody of one-year-old Beau Arceneaux, her estranged husband Vaughn would sometimes baby-sit while she worked. "We were not having an ugly divorce. It was friendly," said Becky. One afternoon, she went to Vaughn's to pick up Beau. The baby and all the furniture were gone. Six weeks later, she traced them to her in-laws' home in Texas.

Becky and her sister drove the four hours to Texas and told her in-laws she was taking Beau. "They said no, and we grabbed him," remembers Becky. "I got into the driver's seat. They were on the passenger side, holding his legs, while my sister was holding on to his arms." Becky escaped with the child. Terrified Vaughn would kidnap Beau again, she and her son spent five weeks hiding out with friends. She went back to court to request supervised visitation, but the judge denied it. Soon after, Vaughn kidnapped Beau during another visitation.

Two years after the second abduction, Vaughn phoned Becky at work. "Drop the charges," he ordered. "I can't, only the FBI can do that," she told him. "If you don't drop the charges, you'll never see the baby again," he informed her. On the run, Vaughn changed his first and last name and Beau's last name. For thirteen years, they eluded police, moving to Canada before ending up in a run-down trailer park in Texas, not far from from his parents' upper-middle-class home.

According to newspaper accounts the trailer had no air conditioning, no locks, windows that had been boarded up, and rats. Vaughn was a college graduate who had been an oil driller in Louisiana. In Texas, he drove a cab and worked at a pizza parlor, leaving Beau alone for hours while he visited his girlfriend. If there wasn't money, he would do chores for neighbors to earn it. His clothes had holes, and he often wore shorts in cold weather.

Beau would ask about his mother. Vaughn would say she didn't want him and had run off with another man. The child befriended a woman from the trailer park. She let him talk on the Internet to her friends. He would repeatedly write, "I wish I had a mother. My mother doesn't want me." One of her friends thought something was wrong. "Do you think the boy could be kidnapped?" she typed to the neighbor.

It hadn't occurred to the woman. She contacted the National Center for Missing and Exploited Children, who called the FBI.

Just seven days before Christmas, Becky received a telephone call. "I think we've found Beau," an FBI agent told her. Becky was used to false leads; there had been more than fifty after she had appeared on a national TV program on missing children. Still, she drove to FBI headquarters. Beau had been found in Austin, Texas, just seven hours away. "We couldn't believe it was that close. We fell apart," recalls Becky. Faxed photos from Beau's school made Becky even more skeptical that he was her child. She had had an age progression done on Beau, a photographic simulation of what the one-year-old might look like as he grew up. When she compared the two, she decided it couldn't be Beau. But the agent told her to look at the boy's eyes. Becky's are big and deep blue, and so were the child's.

While the FBI worked on arresting Vaughn and recovering Beau, Becky went Christmas shopping. She had no idea what he looked like, so she bought him clothes and CDs she thought a teenager would like.

"We've got your son, and he wants to talk to you," the FBI agent from Austin told Becky on the telephone when she returned from the stores. "Hi, Mom," were the thirteen-year-old's first words. "Oh, Beau, I've missed you and looked for you for so long," Becky told him. She told him she was getting on a plane and that she loved him.

"I have no plans to see my father. I just want to be with my family and live life as normally as I can for my last years as a child," Beau said upon his return. "My dad told me there was a divorce but no custody battle, that my mom didn't want me and she left both of us. I believed him. It was all I ever knew. I didn't realize I had been kidnapped.

"When I found out, I felt cheated. I felt my life was a lie. Everything I was told was a lie. When I would ask my dad's side of the family if my mother really didn't want me, they said everything Dad said was true. It seemed unusual that I had no contact with my mom. It was lonely. I wondered what life would be like to have a mom and thought it was true, that I'd never see her again. It made me feel really left out. All my friends had happy families and we were dysfunctional."

CHARLIE

Meet "Charlie" aka "Bill" aka "Jim." His father kidnapped him and moved to five states in seven years to avoid detection. Charlie, eight, wasn't allowed to go to birthday parties or have play dates because his father thought he might slip and blurt out that he had been stolen. His teacher became suspicious after she saw him writing one name on his paper, erasing it, and replacing it with another. The principal asked why he kept erasing his name and changing it. Charlie broke down, admitted his father had abducted him, and confided his real name. That night, Charlie went home and told his father about his talk with the principal. An hour later, they were in another state. His father managed to get away that time, but he was eventually arrested.

WHEN SHOULD I BE MOST VIGILANT?

The answer is all the time. Of course your ex-husband may have no intention of stealing your child and most fathers don't. The best tactic is to be aware of research studies and information gleaned from mothers whose children have been kidnapped.

A Justice Department study called the *National Incidence Studies: Missing, Abducted, Runaway, and Throwaway Children in America* found just 3 percent of all children were stolen in the first six months after the breakup. Most kidnappings occurred when the parents were still together (41 percent) or two years or more after the relationship was over. Almost half the abductions took place two years or later.

The majority occurred during routine visitations. School and the other parent's home were mostly the locations of choice. Weekends were prime time for abductors because it gave them a couple of extra days to flee without getting the other parent or school officials suspicious.

You Are Most at Risk of Having Your Children Stolen When . . .

- You and your husband are still living together or three to four years after the marriage is over.

· During weekends or vacations or when school vacation ends, such as July, August, and January (Christmas vacation).

· Either you or your ex-spouse have changed circumstances: A boyfriend; a new wife, particularly if she's a homemaker; a job in a different community.

· You rebuff or antagonize your ex-husband by blocking visitation or telephone calls from the kids, badmouth him to the children, or act uncooperative. Parents steal when they feel slighted or rebuffed.

· Your husband threatens to kidnap your child. Caution: Fathers who never threaten to abduct may anyway.

· Your husband has a history of abuse and violence.

WHY THEY DO IT

Revenge
The University of Maryland study found that in 80 percent of the cases, anger was the prevailing motive for parental abductions.

"Who, Me?"
"How can you kidnap your own child?" one man asked incredulously as he was being booked on a kidnapping charge. An abductor may have an exaggerated, unrealistic fear that his child is in danger. Kidnappers often cite their ex-wife's new boyfriend, her shabby living quarters, or joblessness as reasons for taking the children.

A Bad Court Call
Occasionally, judges do make mistakes and give custody to an unfit parent, or award unsupervised visitation, even if the parent is dangerous and has a history of parental kidnapping. Note: Parents unhappy with their arrangement should consult a lawyer and go to court to argue their case rather than try to fix the system themselves.

Bargaining Chips

Fathers who don't want the relationship to end may threaten to kidnap or actually steal in an effort to keep the marriage together. They may call and say, "Come back to me, and only then can you see the kids." Sometimes an ex-husband will telephone with such requests as "Stop seeing another man" or "Sell the house and give me half" or "Tell the courts I don't have to pay child support anymore."

Child Support

Fathers who resent having to pay child support (especially if their ex-wife doesn't allow them easy access to their children) may feel entitled to the kids. If they have to pay for them, they reason, then they "belong" to them. As one disillusioned member of a men's rights group put it: "Let's face it. What's a parent going to do? He's either going to leave without the kids, not make his support payments and get thrown in jail, or pay them and not be allowed to see the children. Or he can steal them and go and lead a decent life."

TRYING TO PREVENT AN ABDUCTION

Barring a twenty-four-hour bodyguard, there is no way to thwart your husband from stealing your child. You can and should, however, take immediate legal action, which may discourage him or, at least, give you leverage with police and the courts if he goes ahead with his plan.

Below is what you need to know to be in the best position possible.

Checkmate

· **Hire a lawyer and get legal custody of your child, whether it is temporary or permanent.** Seek custody, even if you and your child's father never married. Why? While an unmarried mother has automatic custody rights in some states unless there is a contrary custody order, if the child is taken to a state that has different custody laws regarding unmarried mothers, having an order can expedite your child's return. States that don't award unmarried mothers automatic custody give fathers equal claim to the child.

· **Provide police with a copy of your custody order.** It allows law enforcement officials to begin an investigation without having to wait

for the custody decree. If the order doesn't include a visitation schedule, leave a copy of that, too.

· **Register your custody order with the court clerk in the county
where your ex-husband lives,** especially if he lives in another state
and takes your child back and forth. That order shows the court in
the new state that there is a preexisting custody decree in case your
ex-husband tries to gain custody or modify an existing decree in the
second state.

· **Think about getting counseling to work out differences with
your ex-husband.**

· **Take any threats about abduction seriously**. Ask the police or
your local prosecutor to speak with your ex-husband about the penalties for child abduction.

· **File a report with the local police stating the threats your husband has made.** That way, if he does kidnap, the police and the
judge will have it on record. Contact your lawyer after filing the report
to see if he or she can require supervised visitation.

· **Warn your children.** If they are old enough, teach them their telephone number and area code and how to make a long distance call.
Have them practice making collect calls and dialing 911. Tell them
to call you immediately if they are taken, or if they are told you don't
want them, or don't love them, or have died. Parental abductors
sometimes feed these lies to children before and during an abduction.
Let your child know you will always love her and drill her on escape
plans in a matter-of-fact way.

· **Have a good relationship with your child so he will confide in
you if he notices or is told something that seems odd.**

· **Keep up-to-date information on your child.** Take photographs
two to four times a year for preschool children, annually for older
youngsters. Videotape them from time to time. Keep current dental

and medical records. Note birthmarks and your child's weight and height. Include school records and the names and telephone numbers of your child's teachers and friends. Mark down your child's Social Security number, if she has one. (Every child older than age one is required by the government to have one if she is claimed as an exemption on her parent's tax returns.) Consider having your child fingerprinted. Most local police departments will do this free of charge. Keep all this information, with photocopies, in one folder that is easily accessible.

· **Leave your certified custody order at your child's school, day care center, camp, or with baby-sitters or after-school instructors.** Let them know you are afraid your ex-husband might abduct your child, and make sure all staff, including substitutes, have been informed. If your ex-husband is the noncustodial parent, insist on being called immediately if he makes unscheduled visits or requests to leave with your child. Tell the staff or sitter not to let him leave without your permission, and to call you if your child doesn't show up when he's supposed to. Tell the school when each parent is picking up, as well as other adults who are allowed to take your child home. The element of time is crucial. If your child does disappear, you will want to begin your search immediately. If your ex-husband takes your child, instruct the staff to call the police, even before reaching you. If you have left your custody order with them, they can begin their investigation right away.

· **Stay on good terms with your in-laws.** While they often aid abductors, they may sympathize with you and disapprove of their son's behavior. They may decide to tip you off to your child's location if they know.

· **Assemble information about your ex-husband.** Use a notebook or binder with detachable paper that you can pull out and photocopy in case the police and the FBI need it. Not only will a notebook save time, but how you present yourself to police is important and may determine how you are treated. You need to be viewed as efficient and thorough, rather than a "hysterical" mother. It can make the difference between real action and lip service. The notebook should contain a recent photograph of your ex-husband; his date of birth and Social Security number; his driver's license number, license plate number, car model, color, and year, and car loans or the name of the dealership where it was leased or purchased; the names and numbers of car and home insurers; credit card and passport numbers, and if he is foreign-born, his immigration status, visa, and work permit numbers; bank information, including mortgage and account numbers and the name of the lender, and bank card numbers; lines of credit or other loans; insurance policy and passport numbers; magazine subscriptions; addresses and telephone numbers of past and current employers, your ex-husband's parents, grandparents, siblings, and close relatives.

Provisions to Consider in Your Custody Order

· **The exact times your ex-husband will spend with your child.** Be specific so if there are flagrant breaches, you will have the necessary documentation for police to act. This will apply even if you and your ex-husband agree on joint custody. Include which major holidays your child will spend with each of you, and put it in writing if you want your child to spend your birthday with you. Parents typically wrangle over vacations, holidays, and other special times. If they are discussed and clarified right from the start, there is more time to get used to the idea. That may mitigate some of the friction and resentment, conditions that can lead to kidnapping.

· **A clause requiring your ex-husband to get the court's permission before moving out of state with your child.**

· **A stipulation prohibiting your ex-husband from leaving the state without the consent of a judge or you, the custodial parent.**

· **With a past kidnapping record or suspicion of an imminent snatch, a request for supervised visitation by an impartial third party or at a special center.** (Caution: The request might antagonize your former spouse.)

· **A bond your ex-husband would post and have to forfeit if he didn't return your child from a visitation.** The bond, a special insurance policy your child's father would have to buy, should only be used if he has abducted before or you believe he might. If your husband does bolt, the money will most likely go to you and could help fund your search. Warning: Bonds are not available everywhere. Make sure you will be able to collect the money if your ex-husband does take your child. (Some bonds are paid to the county, not you.) The amount of the bond should be large enough to discourage your ex-husband from stealing your child. If he has no money, consider collateral other than a cash bond, such as title to his car or any property he may own.

· If you have sole custody, **a provision barring school, day care center personnel, and baby-sitters from releasing your child to your noncustodial husband without your consent.**

Caveat: If you think your child is at risk, by all means include these provisions. Take necessary precautions but not excessive ones. Too many restrictions in a custody order might infuriate your ex-spouse and set him off. As in any "routine" divorce, you want to keep the peace by being reasonable, flexible enough (if your ex-husband changes visitation plans occasionally for a legitimate reason), and respectful of his need to have a relationship with his child. Your child is less likely to be kidnapped and will make the best adjustment possible under the circumstances.

What to Do if Your Child Is Abducted
You will need to work with your lawyer, police, and prosecutors, and make a search yourself.

· **File a missing person's report with your local police.** Most departments let you do this, even if you have joint custody, especially when the order stipulates specific times the child is with you and your ex-husband. Have the police enter information about your child into the National Crime Information Center's (NCIC) Missing Person File computer.

· **If you don't have custody, get it.** You will need a lawyer to do this. The order can be legally enforced in whatever state your child is found.

· **Ask police or a prosecutor about filing criminal charges against your ex-husband.** If he is charged with a felony, get your state to enter that felony warrant into the NCIC computer. If you think your husband has fled the state, ask your prosecutor to get the local U.S. Attorney to issue a federal Unlawful Flight to Avoid Prosecution (UFAP) warrant. That allows the FBI to join the search.

· **Call the hot line of the National Center for Missing and Exploited Children** (800-THE-LOST) to report your kidnapped child. Contact one or more missing children's organizations. Many of these groups have newsletters that offer strategies, support groups, and legal counsel on staff or by referral. They are likely to know which therapists specialize in this field and may help disseminate photographs and posters of your child to media organizations, conduct public record searches, and act as the go-between for you and the police. They may be able to advise you on what you can expect once you have your child back and suggest resources for the whole family.

· **See if the local media will run your story, along with a photo of your child and ex-husband.** NCMEC may also help you with publicity.

· **If your husband is in the military, contact the Worldwide Locator Service.** For the U.S. Army, 317-542-4211; Air Force, 210-652-5774; Navy, 703-614-3155; Marine Corps, 703-640-3942; Coast Guard, 202-267-1615 for enlisted personnel, and 202-267-1667 for officers. If your husband is retired from the military or civil service, contact the Office of Personnel Management at 202-602-2424. Check the Veterans Administration if you think he may be receiving benefits or medical care.

· **Ask a state court judge, police officer, prosecutor, FBI agent or U.S. Attorney about entering your husband's name into the**

Federal Parent Locator Service (FPLS). Run by the Office of Child Support Enforcement in the U.S. Department of Health and Human Services, it's a computerized national location network that hooks into six government agencies. Because it is updated only once a year, it works best for kidnappers who have been gone six months or more.

· **Obtain telephone records for calls made to and from your husband before the abduction.** You will need a subpoena or search warrant, which must be issued by a prosecutor or your lawyer. Find out about tapping your telephone and the telephones of your husband's friends and relatives.

· **Is your husband eligible for welfare and food stamps?** Contact the security or fraud divisions of the agencies that provide state benefits programs. Try yourself or ask your lawyer to help.

· **Consider hiring a private detective.**

YOU'VE LOCATED YOUR CHILD

Rather than a do-it-yourself recovery, retrieve your child legally. If you decide to steal your child back and you botch it, you could be charged with assault and battery, disturbing the peace, burglary, and any number of other offenses.

Here, then, are the legal options:

· **File your custody order with the family court in the state where your child has been taken.** You will probably need to go to that state. Bring photographs of your child and his birth certificate. Some jurisdictions allow you to take your child after you have filed your custody decree. Ask the police or your lawyer if you can do that. If so, bring along a police officer for protection. If you aren't sure if it's legal to reclaim your child, file a petition with the local court to enforce your custody order.

· **Bone up on the Uniform Child Custody Jurisdiction Act (UCCJA).** This is a law that says that state courts must recognize and enforce custody orders made in another state. It ensures only one state has jurisdiction over your child and that all custody litigation is decided in your child's home state—the state your child lived in for at least six months before the commencement of the proceeding, or when that's not possible, a state that has significant ties to your child. When the child is younger than six months old, the home state is the state in which he has lived since birth. Except under rare circumstances, all states must enforce and not modify the original custody order.

The UCCJA has loopholes. For example, it doesn't provide a way to verify if another state has already rendered a custody decision. Your ex-husband could always pretend there was no prior custody order. If he stays in the new state long enough and establishes a good life for himself and your child, the courts may not want to disrupt your child's life, despite what the UCCJA stipulates. While the UCCJA says that the home state has jurisdiction, your husband could argue the circumstances have changed, that since your child is settled in the new state, it should have jurisdiction because her ties to it are greater than to the original state. Changed circumstances are grounds to modify an existing custody order. The UCCJA is only applicable when parents have a custody order (many don't), and relies heavily upon the discretion of a trial judge, who may interpret the provisions of this law broadly.

The UCCJA also tells how to file a certified copy of your custody order in the state where you find your child.

· **Understand the Parental Kidnapping Prevention Act** (also known as the PKPA). It is a federal child-stealing statute designed to limit jurisdiction to just one state and to supplement the UCCJA and help states resolve interstate custody conflicts. Unlike the UCCJA, the PKPA stipulates that even if circumstances have changed, the state where custody was originally determined remains the exclusive forum as long as the child or the person contesting custody stays in that state. The PKPA also authorizes using the Federal Parent Locator Service for computer searches and allows the FBI to get involved in state felony child-stealing cases (those involving interstate or international flight).

· **Hire an attorney in the state where your child is now living who knows the judges or ask your original attorney if she can represent you in the new state.** Have your lawyer give you the name of an attorney in the other state. If your case is particularly complicated, consider hiring your original lawyer to be the cocounsel with the new attorney.

· **When petitioning for enforcement of the custody order, request that your husband pay your attorney's fees, as well as any expenses incurred in finding your child.**

· **If you are worried that your husband may try to flee with your child during this process, ask a judge for a pickup order requesting police to retrieve your child and take her to a relative, friend's, or even the county child protective services, until the enforcement hearing is held.**

· **If your husband files a counterclaim asking to change the custody order, have your lawyer file a motion to dismiss that counterclaim.**

IF YOU FEAR YOUR EX-HUSBAND MIGHT LEAVE THE COUNTRY WITH YOUR CHILD

BE EXTRA CAREFUL IF . . .

· Your ex-husband was born or raised in a different country and still has family or friends there.
· He has business or religious ties to another country or is fluent in a second language.
· Your child is a dual citizen of the United States and another country. Your ex-husband may believe your child is entitled to live in the other country.

PREVENTIVE TACTICS TO TAKE

· **Get your child a passport and keep it. That will force your ex-husband to obtain a phony passport, which he may find too difficult or risky to do.**

· **After receiving custody, include a provision barring your ex-husband (who must be the noncustodial parent) from leaving the country without your consent or a judge's.** If your ex-spouse defies the order, it will give you leverage with the State Department. Once they expire, the government will not renew the passports of Americans living abroad, which could prompt your husband to return to the United States or at least not hide in another country. The Passport Office will renew the passports if that provision is not written into the custody order. If you are the noncustodial parent and are afraid your ex-husband may steal your child, add a clause to your custody decree forbidding your kids to leave the jurisdiction. Send a certified copy of your custody decree highlighting the clause forbidding foreign travel to the Office of Citizenship Appeals and Legal Assistance, Department of State, Washington, DC 20520. If your child is already abroad and you have an idea where, send the denial requests to the nearest American embassy or consulate. You can still stop your child's passport from being processed without having this provision limiting travel in the custody decree. Send the government your custody order and ask that the passport not be issued without your permission. Unless informed otherwise, the State Department assumes a passport request has the backing of the other parent. If your ex-husband (who needs to be the noncustodial parent) obtains a passport before you contact the State Department, you may have to wait as long as four years when the passport expires for him to renew his or your child's. Passports that are issued are almost never revoked because of custody problems.

· Make sure you have a **requirement in your custody order stating that your ex-husband surrender his passport** to a judge, court clerk, mediator, police officer, attorney, or minister before a visitation with your child. You would only want this provision if you were concerned that your ex-husband might try to abscond abroad with your child. Remember, a criminal prosecution and even a conviction for parental kidnapping won't automatically terminate your ex-husband's visitation rights. Even if he has kidnapped in the past, your child may still have a loving relationship with him and want to see him.

· **Add a clause in your custody order requiring your noncustodial husband to post a cash bond before traveling abroad with your child.** If your ex-husband has little money, consider placing title to his property in escrow.

· **If your ex-spouse isn't a U.S. citizen, send a certified copy of your custody order to the embassy or consulate of your husband's country and ask officials to deny issuing a passport or visa for your child, or to notify you if your husband applies for either.** The country is not required to comply.

· **Be familiar with the Hague Convention.** It is a treaty that to date has been ratified by thirty-one countries, including the United States, and is designed to get children who have been kidnapped to a foreign country promptly returned to their own. It works in a similar way as the UCCJA. Both countries—the one where your child used to live, called the habitual residence, and the one where she has been taken—must have ratified the Convention in order for a searching parent to get help from this source. The habitual residence could be where the child was born, where the divorce is pending, or where there is a "substantial connection." It establishes judicial and administrative ways to get your child returned and to expedite visitation in another country. Call 800-843-5678 to find out which countries have ratified the treaty.

If the country to which your child has been taken is not a signatory to the Hague treaty, it could be a problem. Ask your lawyer about filing a proceeding for enforcement, which is a foreign judgment, assuming you know the location of your child.

GETTING YOUR CHILD BACK

- After obtaining custody, contact the Office of Citizens Consular Services (202-736-7000), as well as local police, the FBI, and the National Center for Missing and Exploited Children (800-843-5678).

- Get a federal UFAP warrant. If felony charges are filed against your ex-husband, you can ask your prosecutor to apply for this warrant. A foreign country may feel it has to comply with the criminal charges or else risk the wrath of the United States.

- Ask the U.S. Passport Service at the State Department to revoke your ex-husband's passport. You can do this if you have a UFAP warrant. This will make him an undocumented alien in another country and some governments will deport an undocumented alien. Without a warrant, a passport can be revoked if there is a criminal court order against your husband or if he is on probation or parole that prohibit him from leaving the United States. If he violates these conditions, he could be subject to the Fugitive Felon Act.

- Contact the Immigration and Naturalization Service (INS) at 425 I Street NW, Washington, DC 20536; 202-514-2000. If your kidnapping husband tries to get back into the United States, his name would appear at border checks and on computers hooked into the FBI's National Crime Information Center's Wanted Persons File. The INS could arrest him if a state or federal felony warrant has been entered into the NCIC. If your husband is foreign-born, ask the INS about revoking his visa or work permit.

- Consult Interpol, an international police agency, c/o U.S. Justice Department, Washington, DC 20530; 202-272-8383. They may help you locate your husband and tip off police and border agents in other countries if he decides to travel.

- Make sure the U.S. Customs Service has entered your husband's name into its computer (hooked up to the NCIC computer), which does random checks at borders and in airports of citizens returning from abroad.

· If you have an idea where your child is, have the U.S. Department of State (202-736-7000) conduct a Welfare and Whereabouts check. U.S. embassy officials in that foreign country will try to obtain information on your child's location and health.

· Take all the steps you would if your child were stolen within the country, i.e., contact missing children's agencies, check his credit cards and bank accounts, and think about filing a civil lawsuit against him and attaching his assets, as well as those of family and friends you believe have helped him pull off the abduction.

ONCE YOU HAVE LOCATED YOUR CHILD ABROAD

Just as in domestic cases, stealing back a child is dangerous. You could be arrested and jailed abroad or deported and barred from ever returning to that country. You have a few choices. First, speak with the State Department's Office of Citizens Consular Services (202-736-7000) to find out what works best in that country. Is court the best route there? What are their customs and policies? What can you expect?

Ask that office for a list of foreign attorneys and the number for the U.S. Embassy. Or try the International Academy of Matrimonial Lawyers (617-542-3881), the Family Law division of the International Bar Association (703-532-9300), the International Legal Defense Counsel (215-977-9982), or the bar association in the foreign country. The National Center for Missing and Exploited Children's legal department might also be able to help.

Questions to Ask a Foreign Lawyer Before Hiring Her

· How many child abduction or child custody cases have you handled?

306 · WHAT EVERY WOMAN SHOULD KNOW ABOUT DIVORCE

- Do you understand the principles of comity, where courts of different countries recognize one another's orders?
- Do you know about the UCCJA?

Doing everything you can to prevent an abduction and knowing how to proceed if it occurs will ensure your best chances for success.

Your New Single Life with Children

When you are separated or divorced, you will be starting over. It will be different than when you were younger or a couple. Take dating, for instance. In high school or college, you wondered when to introduce your boyfriend to your parents. Now, it's your children you have to worry about. Day-to-day life is also altered. Without your husband, there will be more chores for everyone else. Holidays and vacations, too, are affected when you are a single parent.

The changes are likely to be sad, but they don't have to be grim. With proper planning, you should be able to have new, healthy relationships, meaningful holidays and traditions, and fun family vacations. When you are ready, you will want to extend yourself and reach out to find new communities. These could be close female friends and their children, parents of your children's friends, a church or synagogue, clubs that interest you (the Appalachian Mountain Club for hikers, for example), and friendship groups that have potluck dinners. You will have to make an effort, but you can do it slowly and on your terms.

DATING

As lonely as you may be, don't rush into a new relationship. Being single gives you time to relax and settle into your new living situation. Life without your husband will be different—maybe better, maybe not. For one thing, you will get to do everything your way. If you want to read at dinner, not have a formal meal, watch TV, throw out the TV, or have a pajama party on the living room floor, you can do it.

You also need time to recover from the divorce. No matter how amicable, it is a major trauma in your life and you have to begin to heal. Take care of yourself, do things that will make you feel good and more in charge of your life: Take a yoga class, sign up for an accounting course, or join a museum group. Think about how you want to live your life. This may be easier to do without a man in the picture. If you have typically defined yourself in terms of your relationships to men, it may be especially important to be on your own for awhile. Get a life before you start sharing yours with someone else.

When you do think about dating, keep in mind that you can be a great mother *and* still have a life outside of your children. You are not being disloyal or selfish. It is important for you as a woman and as an adult, and it's equally important for your kids, to see that you have a full life. Responsible—not indiscriminate—dating can make you a happier person and a more mellow mother. You have to do what's best for you while making sure it does not hurt your children. Living your own life—not living through your children—will help you move on.

Dating, however, presents challenges for juggling and reconciling your romantic and parenting lives. Before you get serious, think about how you want your boyfriend to interact with your children. You may not want him to discipline your children or make any parental decisions. When you do have a discussion with your children about your new partner, let them know how you envision his role and ask them for their input. (You have to be willing to really hear it, though.)

When and How to Date

When do you know that you are ready to date? You might not know. Maybe you feel you should resolve more issues before you start a new relationship. It could be, however, that dating will actually help you "get over" your husband and move on with your life. When you do meet that new person, think of him as someone who will complement, not rescue, you.

There are a variety of ways to meet people. These include asking friends and colleagues if they know of anyone eligible and interesting. Take a course, join a volunteer or professional organization, or participate in group sports. There are clubs geared to singles, some specifically for single parents. Some parents take out personal ads in newspapers and magazines, subscribe to video introduction services, or cruise the Internet. These can be dangerous ways to date. Even if a match-making service claims it has screened its members, it will still be up to you to do your own research.

Telling Your Kids You Have a Love Life

Children need to know that just as they have friends, grown-ups need them, too. If your child is age ten or younger, you might want to explain that concept, and name your women friends. Then you can tell them it's just as important for adults to have male friends. Tell older children, "I need to have a fulfilling relationship in my life, someone I can be close to."

Don't expect your children to embrace the idea of your seeing someone other than their father. Often they are hostile to the idea. They want their parents to get back together, and seeing them with new partners makes that possibility more remote. "They might say they dislike your boyfriend, but that's really code for their own anger at the situation and their yearning for the parental reunification," notes one Northeast child psychologist, who is also a custody evaluator. You might say, "I hear that you don't like John. I wonder if part of it may be your wish that Dad and I could get back together in the way it used to be. I really understand that, but it's not going to happen and that's why it's important for me to find new friends."

If you are in an adversarial divorce, you might not want your child's father to know you are dating. The bottom line: If you don't want your children to tell your soon-to-be ex-husband you are dating, don't bring a new man home. Assume your children will tell their father, and don't be angry if they do. Don't make the children keep the secret. They have to be free to talk to their father.

If you do decide to go public, be careful what you tell them. Don't forget that they are your children, not your confidantes. Putting them in this role may seem to bring you closer, and it might feel flattering to them, but it's not appropriate.

When Do You Introduce Him (or Her)?

Child therapists say it is best to keep your new relationship separate from the children until that relationship is steady. If it's possible, meet someone for the first couple of dates away from your house. (That is also a good safety measure.) If the children must meet him and your relationship is tenuous or new, keep the encounter brief. Don't invite him over for dinner right away. Your children have already been hurt by the dissolution of your marriage. If you're not sure it will last, you don't want them to get close to your new partner and then have him disappear if your relationship doesn't work out. Of course, you can't always protect your children and a new and seemingly serious relationship may not lead to marriage, but be sensitive to your children, too.

If the relationship is getting serious, you will want your boyfriend to spend time with your children so you can see how he interacts with them. You don't want to make a commitment to someone who doesn't like children or your children. At least, it will give you a chance to think through the situation carefully if he clashes with one or more of your children. If you are really interested in this man, and he in you, it's okay for him to be part of your child's life as long as you are honest. You don't want youngsters to have unrealistic hopes and assume you will marry your boyfriend if you don't intend to. You need to prepare your children for the possibility that it will not work out. You could say, "I like John very much and know you like him, but I can't promise we will stay together. If it doesn't work out, it would be sad for me and I know it would also be sad for you, but I can't do more." This allows your children to keep their distance. Be aware that they might not want to make your partner a part of the family if they're not sure it will be a permanent relationship.

The more common scenario is that your kids won't like your new boyfriend. If your child persists in disliking your partner and he has been kind and caring in the interactions you have seen, tell your child, "I like John a lot, but you can come to your own conclusions. I'm interested to hear what you have to say." Let your daughter know she is not obligated to like your boyfriend, but that her approval of him is also not required for you to like him. You need to listen to her, be respectful of her opinion, and acknowledge her feelings. Even if she says she doesn't like him, you should thank her for being candid (you probably won't feel like it!) but tell her you view John differently. You might also ask your child what you can do to make the situation better for her. If she answers, "I don't want him around," you could say, "Fine,

I'll see him elsewhere for now" or "I'll try to spend less time with the two of you together." That may defuse any power struggle she may have tried to create or give her time to get used to the idea and also see you without him.

There are so many issues for children of divorce that are out of their control. You can't expect them to support your emotional needs. That is not their role. At the same time, they shouldn't be allowed to call all the shots. You are still the one in control and it is your life.

Tell your children what is acceptable and unacceptable behavior around your boyfriend and your husband's girlfriend. They must know they have to act respectful, even if they don't like them, just as they should be with any adult. If your children have something negative to say about your boyfriend, have them discuss it with you, and if it concerns your ex-husband's girlfriend, ask them to address it with their father, but let them know they aren't allowed to tell them, "I hate you, you're a jerk." You might say, "I know it's hard for you, and anytime you want to talk, I'll be here. I might not be able to solve the problem, but I'll listen and, if you need help, I'll get you help." Your children must be able to express their negative feelings about your partner or your ex-husband's girlfriend. Also think about a support group for children of divorce where they can vent about these issues and hear similar stories.

Should You Live with Your Boyfriend?

Legally, if you are seriously involved or engaged and this will become your children's new home, a judge may not mind. However, if this is a short-term relationship and just a place to stay or a pleasurable interlude, courts may think you are unsettled and selfish and may hold this against you in a custody battle.

If your boyfriend asks you and the kids to move in with him and they object, think seriously about not doing it. It is their home, and their needs and rights are important. You would be forcing a relationship they don't want *and* taking them away from what is familiar. You should seek counseling to review the relationship and try to understand why your children are opposed. Ideally, you should engage in family therapy before making a decision about the living arrangements, so your children can discuss this change and what it means to them. The last thing you should do is force a new person on your children without adequate preparation.

You have to know the man well and make sure he acts appropriately around the children. This is a big issue. Studies have shown that step-fathers tend to abuse children more than biological parents.

MOVING WITH YOUR CHILDREN

The economic impact of divorce on women can be devastating. In all likelihood, you will have to lower your standard of living and this may mean a move to smaller quarters. Now you have to sell the concept to the kids. You might say, "We're going to move to a smaller, more affordable house (or apartment). We can make it wonderful, warm, and cozy. I'm looking forward to your help." If it's accurate, tell them the new place is also closer to your work, which will give you more time to spend with them. The reality may be that you are furious because the divorce settlement doesn't allow you to retain the family home, but don't share that with the children.

It is helpful to discuss their feelings about the move. It's all right to say, "I feel sad, too, and wish it didn't have to be that way." Ask them what they will miss about the old house so their feelings can be ac-knowledged.

Have your children see the new place and their bedrooms before they move, and make those the first rooms to be completed. With younger children, you will want to re-create the environment they moved from. You might have the same set up as in their old bedroom, with the the stuffed animals lined up in order on the bed and the same comforter.

THE REDISTRIBUTION OF CHORES

The workload in the house is likely to increase without your hus-band. If you have worked part-time in the past, you may need to go back to work full-time. If you have been a stay-at-home parent, you'll probably seek at least part-time work. Doing everything yourself will only make you harried, frustrated, and overwhelmed, and it will not be helpful for your children. They need to see that you are still a family, and that means pitching in as productive family members. Tell them you are going to need more help and have them join you in deciding what their contributions will be. Even a young child can place spoons on the table and fold napkins.

HOLIDAYS

Begin thinking about how you will spend the holidays without your children. If you live near your former spouse, you will probably alternate major holidays. When it's your ex-husband's turn, give yourself enough time to make plans so you don't have to be alone. Think about beginning a new ritual. It could be joining other friends at your favorite restaurant whose children are also with their father, having friends over to your place, or taking an annual trip with a relative. If you can't find friends or family to join you, think about helping others: Sit with a lonely adult in a hospital; serve a meal at a shelter; or hook up with an organization or church that is doing community service.

If the children will be with you for the holiday, you will want to discuss the arrangements with them. They should be told that families change and that things will be different now that their parents will no longer celebrate the holidays together. You can say, "We both want to be able to spend time with you." After discussing the logistics with your husband (assuming you have a civil relationship), ask the children what they have in mind. Teenagers may want to spend some of the time with their friends. Try to figure out the schedule well in advance so they can be prepared for which parent they will see. Is it to spend Christmas Eve with Dad and Christmas Day with you? Splitting the holiday is one way of having each parent enjoy time with the children. Spell it out in kids' terms. Let them know they will get two chances to celebrate (and cash in) rather than one. If that's not possible, celebrate the holiday when you can. It doesn't have to be on the exact day of the holiday, just as kids whose birthdays fall during the week often delay having a party until the weekend. Who says you can't hold Christmas before the actual day with one parent and on the day with the other?

VACATIONS

Many single mothers find it awkward and scary to take a vacation with the children. Lack of adult companionship may make a vacation alone seem like the trip from hell. But it doesn't have to be isolating. If you can't find another family to join you on vacation, hotels, resorts, and cruise lines now offer trips geared to single parents, sometimes at a discount. Many have children's programs, which will give you time to socialize with other adults or have some breathing space for yourself.

Another way to travel with children and cut expenses is to join forces with a single mother who has children close in age to yours, or you could try a family camp, or arrange to break up your trip by meeting relatives or friends in the middle of the vacation stretch.

Divorce is an emotional time, particularly when custody is involved. Your relationship with your child changes once your partner no longer lives with you. At first, it can be strained and intense. Taking a trip together can help normalize that relationship. A vacation can also give you a chance to shed your "house" roles. For you, that may mean getting away from being the taskmaster and the disciplinarian. You become a person, not just a parent. In a different environment, your child also takes on other roles.

It's not just the shared experiences that can bring you closer. The process of planning the vacation can be mercifully distracting and create excitement for all of you. When you plan your trip, consider these suggestions.

- **Know yourself and your children.** Decide how your family travels best and the kinds of vacations you like. If you dislike driving long distances, take a train trip or drive partway and take a ferry the rest of the way. If your children enjoy long car rides and you don't mind driving, you might opt for a destination farther away. But rethink your plans if your son or daughter tends to get carsick or you are too impatient or distracted to make a car trip fun.

- **Research your vacation.** If your son adores dinosaurs, dig around and find out if there is a dinosaur museum on the way or a museum of natural history. Ask the kids what they'd like to see. By conferring with them, you involve them in some of the decision making, which will make them feel even more excited and invested than if you had planned the whole trip yourself.

· **Be organized.** There are volumes of books available on traveling with children. Ask a travel agent for destinations that are child-friendly or that have children's programs and deals. Consider traveling off season to places like the Caribbean in the summer or Europe in the winter, which can save you money. Try charter flights or airline wholesalers, such as World Travel Network (800-40-WORLD) or another company listed in the travel section of the newspaper. Call the airlines repeatedly for the best rates. Many change their rates three times a day, at 12:30 P.M., 5 P.M., and 8 P.M. You can buy an entertainment discount book that offers coupons and shaves as much as 50 percent off selected hotels, restaurants, and recreation. Discount books cost $28 to $48 and are available for at least 125 cities (call 800-374-4464 or 800-445-4137).

Try the Internet and connect to a search engine like Yahoo, Webcrawler, or Alta Vista. They offer categories, including travel. Search the words *single parents* and *children* and see what you find. Log on to see what kinds of activities and events take place at your vacation spot and buy or borrow a guidebook about the area. Hotels located in cities often give discount prices on the weekends or allow children to stay free and provide a children's program. Suite hotels, which typically have a bedroom, living room, and kitchen, may also be reasonable and give you space and privacy so you don't suffer from too much togetherness. Many hotels, especially during holidays and vacations, offer kids' camps. Always call the hotel directly—even if there is a toll-free number—more than once because rates vary. You might try booking your hotel through a consolidator, which typically offers deep discounts (i.e., Hotel Reservations Network 800-964-6835). If you are thinking of taking your child on a kid-oriented trip in the United States or Western Europe, consult Families Welcome!, an agency that finds houses, hotels, apartments, guided tours, child care, and children's programs for youngsters ages three to twelve; (92 North Main St., Ashland, OR 97520; 800-326-0724 E-mail: europalet.e~net). If you can't afford a resort for a full week but think you could pay for a couple of nights, find a bed-and-breakfast for the beginning of the trip and save the hotel, pool, and children's program for the end.

If you own a house in an inviting location, one option is to do a home exchange. You pay a fee, usually under $100, to an agency, which will get you in touch with homeowners in other parts of the country or world who want to swap houses (and often cars). Some organizations that specialize in home exchanges are:

Vacation Exchange Club
P.O. Box 650
Key West, FL 33041
800-638-3841
E-mail: homelink@conch.net
Internet: http://www. swapnow.com
($88 for two-year membership)

Home Exchange Network
P.O. Box 915253
Longwood, FL 32791
407-862-7211
E-mail: linda@ihen.com
Internet: http://www.ihen.com
($29.95/year)

Intervac
P.O. Box 590504
San Francisco, CA 94159
800-756-4663
E-mail: intervacus@aol.com
($78/year)

Trading Homes International
P.O. Box 787
Hermosa Beach, CA 90254
800-877-8723;
outside U.S., 310-798-3864

E-mail: Info@trading-homes.com
Internet: http://www.trading-homes.com
($65/year for publication or Internet listing; $95/year for both)

There are also agencies that cater to grandparents and children. A grandparent who is a custodian might find this appealing, as might a single parent who wants a break from her son but also wants him to spend a good time with a grandparent. Contact GrandTravel, 6900 Wisconsin Ave., Chevy Chase, MD 20815; 800-247-7651. Their E-mail is <grandtravl@aol.com>, and on the Internet, <http://www.grandtrvl.com>.

· **Don't overdo it.** The point is to take a break from being over-programmed but still make the trip great. Plan enough activities that are geared to your child's age and developmental level. Be sensible. If you are driving, arrive at your new location by late afternoon so you have time to relax and get a chance to explore the place.

Build in breaks to your day. Play catch or skate in a park, have a picnic on the beach. You don't want anyone to be exhausted and out of sorts. Break up the activity and think of everyone's needs. If you long to visit a museum you think may not appeal to your children, keep the trip brief and plan an activity right after that they will consider fun.

Sometimes it's hard to imagine that your situation will be significantly different or better than it is now. When there's a blizzard, you think it may never be balmy again. When you've got the flu, it's hard to believe you will feel great in a few days. Divorce is similar. You may not think you will be able to enjoy a trip alone with the kids or manage major holidays or a change of address. But divorced parents all over the world are able to handle painful situations like yours and cope well. Preparation will make the process go much more smoothly. You can do it, and you will.

Recommended Reading

RECOMMENDED READING FOR MOTHERS

Abrahms, Sally. *Children in the Crossfire*. New York: Atheneum, 1983.

Atkinson, Jeff, et al. *The American Bar Association Guide to Family Law: The Complete and Easy Guide to the Laws of Marriage, Parenthood, Separation, and Divorce*. New York: Random House, 1996.

Belli, Melvin, and Mel Krantzler, with Christopher Taylor. *Divorcing*. New York: St. Martin's, 1988.

Benkov, Laura. *Reinventing the Family*. New York: Crown, 1994.

Berry, Bradley Dawn. *The Divorce Sourcebook*. Los Angeles: Lowell House, 1995.

Blau, Melinda. *Families Apart: Ten Keys to Successful Co-Parenting*. New York: Perigee, 1993.

Bricklin, Barry. *The Custody Evaluation Handbook*. New York: Brunner/Mazel, 1995.

Buchanan, Christy, Eleanor Maccoby, and Sanford Dornbusch. *Adolescents After Divorce*. Cambridge, Mass.: Harvard University Press, 1996.

Cohen, Harriet Newman, and Ralph Gardner, Jr. *The Divorce Book*. New York: Avon, 1994.

Collins, Victoria F., and Ginita Wall. *Smart Ways to Save Money During and After Divorce*. Berkeley, Calif.: Nolo Press, 1994.

Cummings, E. Mark, and Patrick Davries. *The Impact of Family Dispute and Resolution*. New York: Guilford Press, 1994.

Emery, Robert. *Renegotiating Family Relationships: Divorce, Child Custody, and Evaluation*. New York: The Guilford Press, 1994.

Engel, Majorie, and Diana Gould. *The Divorce Decisions Handbook*. New York: McGraw-Hill, 1994.

Fisher, Roger, and William Ury. *Getting to Yes*. New York: Penguin Books, 1981.

Folberg, Jay, ed. *Joint Custody and Shared Parenting*. New York: The Guilford Press, 1991.

Friedman, Gary. *A Guide to Divorce Mediation*. New York: Workman Publishing, 1993.

Friedman, Gary. *How to Reach a Fair Legal Settlement at a Fraction of the Cost*. New York: Workman Publishing, 1993.

Gardner, Richard A. *The Parents Book About Divorce*. New York: Bantam, 1977.

Greif, Geoffrey, and Mary Pabst. *Mothers Without Custody*. New York: Free Press, 1988.

Hoff, Patricia. *Family Abduction: How to Prevent an Abduction and What to Do if Your Child Is Abducted*. Arlington, Va.: National Center for Missing and Exploited Children, 1994.

Horgan, Timothy J. *Winning Your Divorce: A Man's Survival Guide*. New York: Plume, 1994.

Kaganoff, Penny, and Susan Spano, ed. *Women on Divorce*. New York: Harcourt Brace, 1995.

Kalter, Neil. *Growing up with Divorce*. New York: Fawcett Columbine, 1990.

Klain, Eva, J. *Parental Kidnapping, Domestic Violence and Child Abuse*. Alexandria, Va.: American Prosecutors Research Institute, 1995.

Lansky, Vicki. *Vicki Lansky's Divorce Book for Parents*. Minnetonka, Minn.: Book Peddlers, 1996.

Leving, Jeffrey, with Kenneth Dachman. *Father's Rights: Hard-Hitting and Fair Advice for Every Father Involved in a Custody Dispute*. New York: Basic Books, 1997.

Lyster, Mimi E. *Child Custody: Building Agreements That Work*. Berkeley, Calif.: Nolo Press, 1995.

Maccoby, Eleanor, and Robert Mnooken. *Dividing the Child: Social and Legal Dilemmas of Custody*. Cambridge, Mass.: Harvard University Press, 1992.

Margulies, Sam. *Getting Divorced without Ruining Your Life*. New York: Simon & Schuster, 1992.

Marston, Stephanie. *The Divorced Parent*. New York: Pocket Books, 1994.

Martin, April. *The Lesbian and Gay Parenting Handbook*. New York: HarperCollins, 1993.

Nolo's Fast Facts: Child Custody and Visitation. Berkeley, Calif.: Nolo Press, 1995.

Palmer, Nancy S., and William D. Palmer, with Kay Marshall Strom. *The Family Puzzle*. Colorado Springs: Pinon, 1996.

Pekala, Beverly. *Don't Settle for Less*. New York: Main Street Books, 1994.

Phillips, Patricia, and George Mair. *Divorce: A Woman's Guide to Getting a Fair Share*. New York: Macmillan, 1995.

Portnoy, Sanford, and Joan Portnoy. *How to Take Great Trips with Your Kids*. Boston: Harvard Common Press, 1995.

Ricci, Isolina. *Mom's House, Dad's House*. New York: Collier, 1980.

Ross, Julie A., and Judy Corcoran. *Joint Custody with a Jerk*. New York: St. Martin's Press, 1996.

Shaw, Mary. *Helping Your Child Survive Divorce*. Secaucus, N.J.: Carol Publishing Group, 1997.

Spencer, Anne, and Robert Shapiro. *Helping Students Cope with Divorce: A Complete Group Education and Counseling Program for Grades 7–12*. King of Prussia, Pa.: The Center for Applied Research in Education, 1993.

Tasker, Fiona, and Susan Golombok. *Growing up in a Lesbian Family*. New York: The Guilford Press, 1997.

U.S. Commission on Child and Family Welfare. *Report to the President and Congress. Parenting Our Children: In the Best Interest of the Nation*. September 1996.

U.S. Department of Health and Human Services. *Evaluation of Child Support Guidelines. Vol. 1. Findings and Conclusions*. 1996.

U.S. Department of Justice. Office of Juvenile Justice and Delinquency Prevention. *Missing, Abducted, Runaway, and Thrownaway Children in America*. 1990.

Wallerstein, Judith S., and Sandra Blakeslee. *Second Chances*. Boston: Houghton Mifflin, 1989.

Wannamaker, Catherine. *Divorce: A Practical Guide*. Sarasota, Fla.: Equity Enterprises, 1996.

Warshak, Richard. *The Custody Revolution*. New York: Poseidon Press, 1992.

Weintraub, Pamela, and Terry Hillman, with Elayne J. Kesselman. *The Complete Idiot's Guide to Surviving Divorce*. New York: Alpha, 1996.

Winner, Karen. *Divorced from Justice*. New York: ReganBooks, 1996.

RECOMMENDED READING FOR CHILDREN

Ackerman, Marc. *Does Wednesday Mean Mom's House or Dad's? Parenting Together*. New York: John Wiley & Sons, 1996.

Brown, Laurene Krasny, and Marc Brown. *Dinosaurs Divorce: A Guide for Changing Families*. Boston: Little, Brown, and Co., 1986.

Cook, Jean Thor. *Room for a Stepdaddy*. Morton Grove, Ill.: Albert Whitman & Co., 1995.

Copen, Lynn M., Sheila Martin, and Linda Pucci. *Getting Ready for Court*. Kenosha, Wis.: Kid's Kourt Publications, 1995.

Drescher, Joan. *My Mother's Getting Married*. New York: Dial Book for Young Readers, 1986.

Field, Mary, and Hennie Shore. *My Life Turned Upside Down, but I Turned It Rightside Up*. King of Prussia, Pa.: The Center for Applied Psychology, 1994.

Gardner, Richard. *The Boys and Girls Book About Divorce*. New York: Bantam, 1970.

Girard, Linda Walvoord. *At Daddy's on Saturdays*. Morton Grove, Ill.: Albert Whitman & Co., 1987.

Jessie. *Please Tell! A Child's Story about Sexual Abuse*. Center City, Minn.: Hazelden Educational Materials, 1991.

Johnson, Laura, and Georglyn Rosenfeld. *Divorced Kids*. New York: Fawcett Crest, 1990.

Joselow, Beth, and Thea Joselow. *When Divorce Hits Home*. New York: Avon, 1996.

Krementz, Jill. *How It Feels When Parents Divorce*. New York: Knopf, 1994.

Lindsay, Warren Jeanne. *Do I Have a Daddy? A Story About a Single Parent Child*. Buena Park: Morning Glory Press, 1991.

Namka, Lynne. *The Mad Family Gets Their Mads Out*. Tucson: Talk, Trust, and Feel Therapeutics, 1995.

Paris, Susan. *Mommy and Daddy Are Fighting*. Seattle: Seal Press, 1986.

Rofes, Eric, ed. *The Kids Book of Divorce*. New York: Vintage, 1982.

Rogers, Fred. *Let's Talk About Divorce*. New York: Putnam, 1996.

Schab, Lisa. *My Dad Is Getting Married Again*. King of Prussia, Pa.: The Center for Applied Technology, 1995.

Willhoite, Michael. *Daddy's Roommate*. Boston: Alyson Publications, 1990.

Glossary

affidavit: A sworn and written statement of facts.

alimony: Money payments made by one spouse to another for support to a dependent spouse after divorce.

alimony pendente lite: Money payments made by one spouse to another while the divorce proceeding is pending or while the parties are separated.

allegation: A claim by one party against another.

answer: A written response to a complaint or petition.

appeal: A request by a party to review the decision of a lower court.

assets: Everything owned by a husband and wife that has a monetary value, which can include real or personal property.

chambers: A room generally off the courtroom where judges interview the parties and sometimes the children.

COBRA—Consolidated Omnibus Budget Reconciliation Act of 1985: Applies to group health insurance plans maintained by companies with at least twenty employees; it allows continuation of medical benefits for up to thirty-six months after divorce.

community property: All property owned by a husband and wife that is acquired during the marriage, exclusive of gifts or an inheritance. The property upon dissolution is usually split equally.

complaint: A filed document that starts the legal process, sets out the basic facts, and requests specific relief.

confession of judgment: A form that states you admit a sum of money is owed and will not contest the amount in court.

contempt: The willful violation of a court order.

cross-examination: Questions asked of you or your witnesses by your husband's attorney in any fact-finding hearing.

custodial parent: The parent with whom the child is living.

defendant: The party against whom an action is filed; also called the respondent.

deposition: A formal question-and-answer session (like a minihearing) in which the witness is under oath, usually taken with a court reporter or stenographer present.

direct examination: Questions asked by a party's attorney in any fact-finding hearing.

discovery: Documents requesting information from the other party prior to the formal hearing.

emancipation: The age at which a child is no longer considered a minor.

equitable distribution: A method of dividing property so that each side receives a fair share, which is determined by a fact-finder.

evidence: Oral testimony, written affidavits, physical evidence, or documents such as medical reports or bank statements.

forensic accountant: An accountant trained to investigate and usually testify about the assets of the other party, including what he or she may be hiding.

garnishment: The process whereby a spouse's employer deducts money from a paycheck and sends it to the court, to be given to the party owed.

guardian ad litem: A court-appointed advocate for a child; may be a therapist or an attorney.

interrogatories: Written questions addressed to the other party, which must be answered under oath.

joint legal custody: Both parents share the right to make major decisions regarding the children's education, religious upbringing, and medical issues.

joint physical custody: A custody arrangement in which the child alternates between living with both of his parents, usually in two separate residences.

leading questions: Questions that suggest an answer.

liabilities: Debts owed by either party.

mediation: The process by which two people try to resolve issues with the help of a third party (a mediator), as an alternative to going to court for a judicial resolution.

motion: A written or verbal request to the court asking for some type of legal relief such as temporary custody, child support, or alimony pendente lite.

opening statement: A speech to a judge or a jury outlining the issues that will be presented in a case.

order: The court's ruling on any issue before it.

parental alienation: A psychological term used to describe a situation where one parent criticizes the other to a point where the child is turned against that parent.

parenting plan: A plan that implements the custody arrangement and states the decision-making and physical custody arrangement; it can include financial agreements, transportation, child care, and other child-related issues.

perjury: Lying under oath.

plaintiff: The party who files an action or initiates a legal proceeding, also referred to as the petitioner.

primary physical custody: The parent with whom the child lives most of the time has primary physical custody.

protection from abuse order: A court order to prevent one person from abusing another.

rebuttal testimony: Evidence introduced to respond to and refute evidence introduced by the other party.

rehabilitative alimony: Money one spouse gives the other for a specified period of time to help that person become financially independent; the spouse may be earning a degree or learning a vocational skill to enter or reenter the workforce.

retainer: An advance for legal fees.

retainer letter: A letter written by a lawyer to a client confirming the terms of representation.

service: The delivery of a legal document commencing a proceeding or requesting relief in the midst of a proceeding; court rules specify how such delivery must be made.

settlement conference: Where both parties' attorneys meet in a lawyer's office or judge's chambers to try to settle the case.

sole custody: A custody arrangement in which one parent makes all the major decisions affecting the children, such as education, religious upbringing, and medical issues, and is responsible for day-to-day decisions.

split custody: One parent has custody of one or more of the children and the other parent has custody of the other child or children.

spousal support: Money payments made by one spouse to another.

temporary custody agreement: An interim custody agreement after separation and before a permanent arrangement is reached.

temporary order: An interim custody order entered by the court addressing the issues in the case.

Resources

Chapter 3: Getting a Grip on Custody Arrangements

Joint Custody Association
10606 Wilkins Ave.
Los Angeles, CA 90024
310-475-5352

   (Assists joint custody parents and advocates for joint custody.)

Chapter 4: Better Watch It! Risk Factors for Women

Lambda Legal Defense and Education Fund
120 Wall Street, Suite 1500
New York, NY 10005-3904
212-809-8585
or
6030 Wilshire Boulevard, Suite 200
Los Angeles, CA 90036
213-937-2728
or
11 East Adams, Suite 1008
Chicago, IL 60603-6303
312-663-4413
or
1447 Peachtree Street NE, Suite 1004
Atlanta, GA 30309-3027
404-897-1880

(Lesbian and gay legal organization; offers resource referrals and explains legal rights.)

The National Center for Lesbian Rights
870 Market Street
San Francisco, CA 94102
415-392-6257
E-mail: nclrsf@aol.com
Internet: http://www.nclrights.org

(Provides free legal advice and counseling; publications on gay and lesbian parenting issues.)

Gay & Lesbian Advocates & Defenders
P.O. Box 218
Boston, MA 02112
617-426-1350

(Legal information hot line—Monday–Friday, 1:30–4:30 P.M.—and lawyer referral service.)

Gay and Lesbian Parents Coalition International
P.O. Box 50360
Washington, DC 20091
202-583-8029

(A coalition of gay and lesbian parenting groups; provides information, education, a quarterly newsletter for parents, material for children; has an annual conference; membership is $25/year or $250 for a lifetime membership.)

Chapter 5: Choosing a Lawyer

The American Bar Association
Family Law Section
750 North Lake Shore Drive
Chicago, IL 60611
312-988-5000
Internet: http://www.abanet.org

(Provides a list of lawyers nationwide.)

American Academy of Matrimonial Lawyers
150 North Michigan Avenue, Suite 2040
Chicago, IL 60601
312-263-6477
Internet: http://www.aaml.org

    (Will direct you to the state chapter, which has the names of family law specialists who belong to the organization.)

Legal Aid lawyers: You may qualify for free legal help if you can't afford a private attorney; look under "Legal Aid" or "Legal Services Corporation" in the Government Pages of the telephone book for a legal office near you.

NOW Legal Defense and Education Fund
99 Hudson Street
New York, NY 10013
212-925-6635
Internet: http://www.nowldef.org

    (Offers free brochure on how to find a lawyer.)

Chapter 6: Which Route to Take? Mediation versus a Courtroom Battle

The Academy of Family Mediators
5 Militia Drive
Lexington, MA 02173
617-674-2663
E-mail: afmoffice@mediators.org

    (Mediator referral service for the U.S. and abroad.)

Association of Family and Conciliation Courts
329 West Wilson
Madison, WI 53703-3612
608-251-4001
E-mail: afcc@afccnet.org

(Referral service for lawyers, mediators, mental health professionals, and custody evaluators in the United States and other countries; members from forty different countries who belong to the association.)

Conflict Resolution Center, Inc.
204 37th Street
Pittsburgh, PA 5201-1850
412-687-6210
E-mail: crcii@conflictnet.org

(International resource center for more than 1,000 mediators.)

Society of Professionals in Dispute Resolution
1621 Connecticut Avenue NW, 4th Floor
Washington, DC 20009
202-783-7277
Internet: http://www.spidr.org

(Offers mediator and lawyer referral service.)

American Arbitration Association
140 West 51st Street
New York, NY 10020-1203
212-484-4000
(Can direct you to branch near you.)

Chapter 9: Mothers and Money

The Consumer Credit Counseling Service of Massachusetts
8 Winter Street
Boston, MA 02108
800-388-2227 for Mass., will provide number for other states and areas

(Counsels consumers about debt and credit; $5 to $35 one-time fee for advice, but will waive fee if necessary; part of the National Foundation of

Consumer Credit Counseling Service; will refer to counselors in other parts of the country.)

The Tightwad Gazette, Amy Dacyczyn, Random House, 1977, $12.99.

The Cheapskate's Guide to Living Cheaper and Better, Les Hamilton, Carol Publishing, 1996, $9.95.

Association for Children for Enforcement of Support
2260 Upton Avenue
Toledo, OH 43606
800-537-7072

(Information on how to collect child support payments.)

NOW Legal Defense and Education Fund
99 Hudson Street
New York, NY 10013
212-925-6635
Internet: http://www.nowldef.org

(Free child support kit; child custody kit and divorce and separation kit: cost, $5; also packet on how to find a lawyer.)

Chapter 13: Domestic Violence

National Domestic Violence Hotline
800-799-SAFE (7233)

(Twenty-four-hour hot line in English and Spanish; provides information and referrals; advocates will help victims develop a safety plan.)

National Clearinghouse for the Defense of Battered Women
125 South 9th Street, Suite 302
Philadelphia, PA 19107
215-351-0010

(Works with battered women charged with crimes.)

Chapter 14: Special Considerations

Center Kids
Family Project, the Lesbian and Gay Community Services Center
208 West 13th Street
New York, NY 10011
212-620-7310
E-mail: lgcsc.nyc@aol.com
Internet: http://www.gaycenter.org

(Offers workshops, packets, support groups; advocates for lesbian and gay parents and their children.)

Lavender Family's Research Network (formerly Lesbian Mothers' National
    Defense Fund)
P.O. Box 21567
Seattle, WA 98111
206-325-2643

(Attorney referrals, lists of support groups, and emotional support.)

Chapter 15: Blended Families

The Stepfamily Association of America
650 J Street, Suite 205
Lincoln, NE 68508
800-735-0329
E-mail: stepfamfs@aol.com
Internet: http://www.stepfam.org

(Provides education and support; referrals for support groups; membership costs $35/year and entitles you to a quarterly newsletter and catalog of books on stepfamilies.)

Stepfamily Foundation
333 West End Avenue
New York, NY 10023
212-877-3244
E-mail: stepfamily@aol.com
Internet: http:/www.stepfamily.org

(Provides counseling in person and on the telephone and offers information on stepfamilies.)

Chapter 16: What If You Don't Have Custody?

Mothers Without Custody
P.O. Box 36
Woodstock, IL 60098
800-457-MWOC
E-mail: jisham@aol.com

(A $23 annual membership fee; newsletter; local chapters.)

Parents Without Partners
8807 Colesville Road
Silver Spring, MD 20910
800-637-7974

(For single mothers and fathers; more than 650 chapters.)

Chapter 17: The Parental Kidnapping Possibility

The National Center for Missing and Exploited Children
2101 Wilson Boulevard, Suite 550
Arlington, VA 22201-3052
800-THE-LOST (843-5678)

(A national clearinghouse on missing and exploited children; distributes photographs and descriptions of missing children; provides information and advice to parents; offers a twenty-four-hour hot line in English and Spanish; accepts reports and sightings of missing children.)

National Organization of Victim Assistance
1757 Park Road NW
Washington, DC 20010
202-232-6682
E-mail: nova@try-nova.org
Internet: www.access.digex.net/'nova

(Referral to state financial compensation programs for families of missing children.)

National Victim Center
2111 Wilson Boulevard, Suite 300
Arlington, VA 22201
703-276-2880
E-mail: webmaster@mail.nvc.org
Internet: http://www.nvc.org

    (Referrals for missing children's organizations.)

Military Worldwide Locator Services
(Helps locate abductors who work or have worked in the military.)

U.S. Army
Army Worldwide Locator Service
Fort Benjamin Harrison, IN 46249-5301
317-542-4211

U.S. Air Force Headquarters
Worldwide Locator Service
AFPC/MISMDL
Randolph, TX 78150-4752
210-652-6377
210-652-5774

U.S. Navy
Naval Personnel Command 036CC
Navy Locator Service
Washington, DC 20370
703-614-3155

U.S. Marine Corps
Commandant of the Marine Corps
Code MMRB-10
Attention: Worldwide Locator Service
Washington, DC 20380-0001
703-640-3942

U.S. *Coast Guard*
Commandant, U.S. Coast Guard
2100 2nd Street SW
Washington, DC 20593
202-267-1615 (for enlisted personnel)
202-267-1667 (for officers)

Office of Personnel Management
1900 E Street NW
Washington, DC 20415
202-602-2424

   (If retired from military or civil service and receives retirement check or is active member of civil service.)

U.S. *Department of State*
Washington, DC 20520
202-647-4000

Office of Children's Issues
U.S. *Department of State*
Bureau of Consular Affairs
202-736-7000
Automated fax: 202-647-3000
Internet: http://travel.state.gov

   (Information on international parental abductions.)

Immigration and Naturalization Services (INS)
425 I Street NW
Washington, DC 20536
202-514-2000

Interpol
U.S. *Justice Department*
Washington, DC 20530
202-272-8383

U.S. Department of Justice
Welfare and Whereabouts Check
202-736-7000

International Academy of Matrimonial Lawyers
617-542-3881

International Bar Association
Family Law Division
703-532-9300

International Legal Defense Counsel
215-977-9982

Chapter 18: Your Single Life with the Children

Families Welcome!
92 North Main Street
Ashland, OR 97520
800-326-0724
E-mail: europalet.e-net

   (A $50 booking fee.)

Vacation Exchange Club
P.O. Box 650
Key West, FL 33041
800-638-3841
E-mail: homelink@conch.net
Internet: http://www. swapnow.com

   ($88 for two-year membership.)

Home Exchange Network
P.O. Box 915253
Longwood, FL 32791
407-862-7211)
E-mail: linda@ihen.com
Internet: http://www.ihen.com

   ($29.95/year.)

Intervac
P.O. Box 590504
San Francisco, CA 94159
800-756-4663
E-mail: intervacus@aol.com

($78/year.)

Trading Homes International
P.O. Box 787
Hermosa Beach, CA 90254
800-877-8723;
outside U.S., 310-798-3864
E-mail: Info@trading-homes.com
Internet: http://www.trading-homes.com

($65/year for publication or Internet listing; $95/year for both.)

GrandTravel
6900 Wisconsin Ave.
Chevy Chase, MD 20815
800-247-7651
E-mail: grandtravl@aol.com
Internet: http://www.grandtrvl.com

(Trips for grandparents and grandchildren.)

Index

About the Authors

Gayle Rosenwald Smith is a Philadelphia lawyer concentrating her practice in family law. She is a member of the family law sections of the American Bar Association and the Philadelphia Bar Association. Her articles have appeared in such newspapers as the *Chicago Tribune* and the *Philadelphia Inquirer*.

Sally Abrahms is the author of *Children in the Crossfire* and has published articles on family law issues in the *New York Times*, the *Wall Street Journal*, the *Los Angeles Times*, *USA Today*, *Ladies' Home Journal*, *McCall's*, and *Redbook*, among others. She currently writes a weekly feature for the Sunday *Boston Globe*.